The Physical University

The great universities of the world are, to a large extent, defined in the public imagination by their physical form: when people think of a university, they usually think of a distinctive place, rather than about, say, the teaching or the research that might go on there. This is understandable, both because universities usually stay rooted to the same spot over the centuries and because their physical forms may send powerful messages about the kinds of places they are.

The physical form of the university, and how the spaces within it become transformed by their users into places that hold meanings for them, has become of increased interest recently from both academic and institutional management perspectives when trying to understand more about how universities work, and how they may be made more effective. Yet, despite its seemingly obvious importance, the available literature on space and place in higher education internationally is scant when compared to that dealing with, say, teaching and learning methods, or with evaluating quality or many other topics.

This book brings together a range of academic and professional perspectives on university spaces and places, and shows how technical matters of building design, maintenance and use interact with academic considerations on the goals of the university. Space issues are located at an intellectual crossroads, where widely differing conceptual and professional perspectives meet and need to be integrated, and this important book brings together perspectives from around the world to show design and use issues are changing higher education.

Globally, higher education is being required to do more – to teach more students, to be better at research, to engage more with business and communities and many other things. These pressures are leading universities to reconsider their management processes, as well as their academic structures: an often-quoted saying is that 'we make our buildings, and afterwards they make us'. At a time when universities and colleges are seeking competitive advantages, ideas and analysis about space design and use are much needed and will be well received.

Paul Temple is Reader in Higher Education Management at the Institute of Education, University of London, and Co-Director of its Centre for Higher Education Studies.

International Studies in Higher Education

Series Editors:
David Palfreyman, OxCHEPS
Ted Tapper, OxCHEPS
Scott Thomas, Claremont Graduate University

The central purpose of this series is to see how different national and regional systems of higher education are responding to widely shared pressures for change. The most significant of these are: rapid expansion; reducing public funding; the increasing influence of market and global forces; and the widespread political desire to integrate higher education more closely into the wider needs of society and, more especially, the demands of the economic structure. The series will commence with an international overview of structural change in systems of higher education. It will then proceed to examine, on a global front, the change process in terms of topics that are both traditional (for example, institutional management and system governance) and emerging (for example, the growing influence of international organizations and the blending of academic and professional roles). At its conclusion, the series will have presented, through an international perspective, both a composite overview of contemporary systems of higher education, along with the competing interpretations of the process of change.

Published titles:

Structuring Mass Higher Education
The role of elite institutions
Edited by David Palfreyman and Ted Tapper

International Perspectives on the Governance of Higher Education
Alternative frameworks for coordination
Edited by Jeroen Huisman

International Organizations and Higher Education Policy
Thinking globally, acting locally?
Edited by Roberta Malee Bassett and Alma Maldonado-Maldonado

Academic and Professional Identities in Higher Education
The challenges of a diversifying workforce
Edited by Celia Whitchurch and George Gordon

International Research Collaborations
Much to be gained, many ways to get in trouble
Melissa S. Anderson and Nicholas H. Steneck

Cross-Border Partnerships in Higher Education
Strategies and issues
Robin Sakamoto and David Chapman

Accountability in Higher Education
Global perspectives on trust and power
Bjorn Stensaker and Lee Harvey

The Engaged University
International perspectives on civic engagement
David Watson, Robert Hollister, Susan E. Stroud and Elizabeth Babcock

Universities and the Public Sphere
Knowledge creation and state building in the era of globalization
*Edited by Brian Pusser, Ken Kempner, Simon Marginson
and Imanol Ordorika*

The Future University
Ideas and possibilities
Edited by Ronald Barnett

Universities in the Knowledge Economy
Higher education organisation and global change
Edited by Paul Temple

Tribes and Territories in the 21st Century
Rethinking the significance of disciplines in higher education
Edited by Paul Trowler, Murray Saunders and Veronica Bamber

Universities and Regional Development
A critical assessment of tensions and contradictions
Edited by Rómulo Pinheiro, Paul Benneworth and Glen A. Jones

The Global Student Experience
An international and comparative analysis
Edited by Camille B. Kandiko and Mark Weyers

Enhancing Quality in Higher Education
International perspectives
Edited by Ray Land and George Gordon

Student Financing of Higher Education
A comparative perspective
Edited by Donald Heller and Claire Callender

The Physical University
Contours of space and place in higher education
Edited by Paul Temple

The Physical University

Contours of Space and Place in Higher Education

Edited by Paul Temple

 Routledge
Taylor & Francis Group

LONDON AND NEW YORK

First published 2014
by Routledge
2 Park Square, Milton Park, Abingdon, Oxon OX14 4RN

and by Routledge
711 Third Avenue, New York, NY 10017

Routledge is an imprint of the Taylor & Francis Group, an informa business

British Library Cataloguing in Publication Data
A catalogue record for this book is available from the British Library

Library of Congress Cataloging in Publication Data
The physical university: contours of space and place in higher education /
    edited by Paul Temple.
    pages cm
    1. College campuses. 2. College buildings. 3. Space (Architecture).
    4. School sites. I. Temple, Paul, 1949– editor of compilation.
    LB3223.P52 2014
    378.1'96—c23
    2013035563   10 0724616 9

ISBN: 978-0-415-66231-4 (hbk)
ISBN: 978-1-315-81377-6 (ebk)

Typeset in Minion
by Florence Production Ltd, Stoodleigh, Devon, UK

Printed and bound by CPI Group (UK) Ltd, Croydon, CR0 4YY

Contents

Figures and Tables

Contributors

Paul Benneworth is Senior Researcher at the Center for Higher Education Policy Studies at the University of Twente in the Netherlands, where his work focuses on relationships between universities and society. He has carried out a wide range of research, including for the European Science Foundation, the OECD, the Dutch 3TU Federation, and the UK's National Endowment for Science, Technology and the Arts. He is the editor of volumes on higher education and regional development, and on universities and community engagement. He has held research fellowships at the Radboud University Nijmegen and at Newcastle University in the UK.

Timon Beyes is Professor of Design, Innovation and Aesthetics in the Department of Management, Politics and Philosophy at Copenhagen Business School and a Visiting Professor at the Institute for the Culture and Aesthetics of Digital Media, Leuphana University Lüneburg in Germany. His research focuses on the spaces and aesthetics of organization, entrepreneurship and innovation in the fields of digital culture, art and cities. His work has been published in a range of monographs, edited collections and international journals.

Brett Bligh is Lecturer in Technology Enhanced Learning in the Department of Educational Research, Lancaster University. He conducts research into the connections between our material surroundings, the technologies that permeate them and the ways we act, think and learn. Until recently at the University of Nottingham, he is a co-author of *Decoding Learning* (2012, Nesta) and the *JELS* report on institutional evaluation of higher education learning spaces (2009, JISC). He was a member of the EU's *STELLAR* Network of Excellence for Technology Enhanced Learning and the HEFCE-funded *Visual Learning Lab*.

Lorna Hards recently completed her PhD research, consisting of a critical review of art in the public realm in Birmingham, UK, from 1985 to 2010. This study, conducted through a collaboration between Birmingham City University and Birmingham City Council, focused on the evolution of works produced and the ongoing evolution in their meanings. It investigated the motivations and mechanisms for the commissioning of public art, looking at what influenced the art created and what impact it had in Birmingham and beyond.

Alexi Marmot is Professor of Facility and Environment Management at the Bartlett School at University College London. She is also a Director of AMA Alexi Marmot Associates, founded in 1990, an independent, niche firm offering high-level advice to organizations with complex space and people issues. AMA specializes in occupancy research, space programming and design for new ways of working. The firm has particular expertise in educational and research facilities design. She is joint author (with Joanna Eley) of *Understanding Offices* (1995, Penguin Business).

Christoph Michels is an Assistant Professor of the research cluster Cultures, Institutions, Markets (CIM) at the University of St Gallen, Switzerland. He was trained as an architect at the Swiss Federal Institute of Technology in Zurich and graduated from the University of St Gallen with a doctorate in organization studies in 2009. His research addresses a range of issues relating to architecture and organizing, including participatory politics in the organization of public spaces and the production of atmospheres in the cultural and educational institutions.

Mike Neary has been the Dean of Teaching and Learning at the University of Lincoln, UK since 2007. Prior to this appointment, he taught political sociology at the University of Warwick. He has a particular interest in the design and development of teaching and learning spaces within broader questions associated with the meaning and purpose of higher education. Recent publications on this topic include *Learning Landscapes in Higher Education: The Struggle for the Idea of the University* (2010, Neary and Saunders), and *Teaching Politically: Policy, Pedagogy and the New European University* (2012, Journal for Critical Education Policy Studies). He is Joint Editor of *Teaching in Public: Making the Modern University* (2011, Continuum).

Anthony Ossa-Richardson is Leverhulme Early Career Fellow at Queen Mary, University of London. His primary field of research is early modern intellectual history, as represented by his first book, *The Devil's Tabernacle* (2013, Princeton University Press). However, he has been interested in modern campus architecture and planning since studying for an MA at the University of York.

Paul Temple is Reader in Higher Education Management at the Institute of Education, University of London, and Co-Director of its Centre for Higher Education Studies, where he co-directs its MBA programme in higher education management. He was formerly head of the federal University of London's planning division, and, before that, worked on college and polytechnic planning in London. He has published a number of studies about the interaction of space and institutional effectiveness in higher education. He edited *Universities in the Knowledge Economy* (2012, Routledge) in the present series, and is Editor of the *London Review of Education*.

Eugene P. Trani is President Emeritus of Virginia Commonwealth University, USA, having retired in 2009 after a 19-year term as president. A specialist in US foreign affairs, he has written extensively on the historic development of US relations with other countries. He is the co-author of *The Presidency of Warren G. Harding* (1977, The Regent Press of Kansas) and co-author of *The First Cold War: The Legacy of Woodrow Wilson in U.S.–Soviet Relations* (2002, University of Missouri Press) and *Distorted Mirrors: Americans and Their Relations with Russia and China in the Twentieth Century* (2009, University of Missouri Press). He has also collaborated with Robert Holsworth on *The Indispensable University: Higher Education, Economic Development and the Knowledge Economy* (2010, Rowman & Littlefield/American Council on Education). His most recent book, co-authored with Donald Davis, is *The Reporter Who Knew Too Much: Harrison Salisbury and The New York Times* (2012, Rowman & Littlefield).

Marcella Ucci is Lecturer in Environmental and Healthy Buildings at the Bartlett Faculty of the Built Environment, University College London, where she teaches on an MSc in environmental design and engineering. With a background in architecture and a PhD in indoor air quality and modelling, her research focuses on the interactions and tensions between sustainable building design/operation and the needs of occupants in terms of comfort, health and well-being. She is Chair of the UK Indoor Environments Group (UKIEG), a multidisciplinary group that provides a focus for activity concerned with indoor environments, health and well-being.

Sian Vaughan is an art historian whose research interests concern the interpretation and mediation of engagement with contemporary art. She has previously taught art and design history in further and higher education. She is currently Senior Research Fellow and Keeper of Archives with Birmingham Institute of Art and Design (BIAD). She has published widely on the subjects of public art, archives, collection management and cultural organizations.

Phillip Waite is an Associate Professor and Field Studio Director in the department of Landscape Architecture and Environmental Planning at Utah State University, USA. Prior to becoming an academic, he served for 14 years as Assistant Director of Capital Planning and Capital Budgets, Campus

Planner, and Campus Landscape Architect at the University of Idaho. While at Idaho, he created a formalized process for project planning and architectural programming to ensure coordination between programme needs and institutional strategic plans. As a faculty member, he teaches landscape architectural design, construction and graphic communication, and his current research is directed at the affective power of place and how the landscape of campus affects student recruitment, retention and learning performance. His book, *The Non-Architect's Guide to Major Capital Projects*, was published by SCUP in 2005.

James Williams is Senior Researcher in the Social Research and Evaluation Unit at Birmingham City University, UK. His main focus of interest is the student experience and the use of student feedback in higher education. He has published widely on the student experience, graduate employability, widening participation and the history of higher education. He is Associate Editor of the international journal *Quality in Higher Education*.

Zhongyuan Zhang is Lecturer in the School of Management at Zhejiang University, China. He teaches organizational behaviour and social psychology to undergraduate and graduate students. He graduated from Warwick Business School, UK, with a PhD in organizational studies in 2009. His thesis was based on an ethnographic study on the production of bureaucratic space. His current research interests include the spatial implications for workplace creativity, and the uncanny space and alternative organizational rationalities.

Series Editors' Introduction

International Studies in Higher Education

This series is constructed around the premise that higher education systems are experiencing common pressures for fundamental change, reinforced by differing national and regional circumstances that also impact upon established institutional structures and procedures. There are four major dynamics for change that are of international significance:

1 mass higher education is a universal phenomenon;
2 national systems find themselves located in an increasingly global marketplace that has particular significance for their more prestigious institutions;
3 higher education institutions have acquired (or been obliged to acquire) a wider range of obligations, often under pressure from governments prepared to use state power to secure their policy goals; and
4 the balance between the public and private financing of higher education has shifted – markedly, in some cases – in favour of the latter.

In response to such pressures, many higher education systems have demonstrated their ability to be highly innovative. There are three significant developments. First, the idea of higher education as a private, as well as a public, good is expressed concretely in the search for market funding, incorporating the rise of for-profit universities. Second, there has been a marked increase in trans-institutional cooperation, which includes the emergence of international ties; coupled with this has been the move by some universities to establish overseas campuses. Third, we see the rise of the MOOCs (massive open online courses), which represent the severest challenge to traditional pedagogies, including our very understanding of what it means to acquire the experience of higher education. The world of the universities is in a state of flux. Change, rather than stability, is the order of the day.

Each volume in the series examines how systems of higher education are responding to this new and demanding political and socio-economic environment. Although it is easy to overstate the uniqueness of the present situation, it is not an exaggeration to say that higher education is undergoing a fundamental shift in its character, and one that is truly international in scope. We are witnessing a major transition in the relationship of higher education to state and society. What makes the present circumstances particularly interesting is to see how different systems – a product of social, cultural, economic and political contexts that have interacted and evolved over time – respond in their own peculiar ways to the changing environment. There is no assumption that the pressures for change have set in motion the trend towards a converging model of higher education, but we do believe that, in the present circumstances, no understanding of 'the idea of the university' remains sacrosanct.

Although this is a series with an international focus, it is not expected that each volume should cover every national system of higher education. This would be an impossible task. While aiming for a broad range of case studies, with each volume addressing a particular theme, the focus will be upon the most important and interesting examples of responses to the pressures for change. Most of the individual volumes will bring together a range of comparative quantitative and qualitative information, but the primary aim of each volume will be to present differing interpretations of critical developments in key aspects of the experience of higher education. The overarching objective is to explore the conflict of ideas and the political struggles that inevitably surround any significant policy development in higher education.

It can be expected that volume editors and their authors will adopt their own interpretations to explain the emerging patterns of development. There will be conflicting theoretical positions drawn from the increasingly multi-disciplinary field of higher education research. Thus, we can expect, in most volumes, to find an intermarriage of approaches drawn from sociology, economics, history, political science, cultural studies and the administrative sciences. However, while there will be different approaches to understanding the process of change in higher education, each volume editor will impose a framework upon the volume inasmuch as chapter authors will be required to address common issues and concerns.

This volume in the series, edited by Paul Temple, is, we believe, important in giving the idea of 'the physical university' a higher profile in the higher education literature. It brings together ideas and findings from several disciplines, notably architecture, planning, design, economics and sociology, and examines them in the specific context of higher education, thereby reaching some new conclusions – and, we suggest, further justifying the claim of higher education studies to be a distinctive field of research.

The built form of the university is too often taken for granted, simply being seen as a neutral backdrop against which the institution's teaching and research work happens. This book shows that it is much more than that: the built environment affects 'the feel' of the university and, moreover, its annual cost is invariably the next largest element within the overall budget after labour costs, and thus it needs to be managed efficiently and imaginatively, effectively and creatively. The understanding of the physical university helps us to appreciate better the total university as a central institution in contemporary society.

David Palfreyman
Director of OxCHEPS, New College, University of Oxford

Ted Tapper
OxCHEPS, New College, University of Oxford

Scott Thomas
Professor of Educational Studies,
Claremont Graduate University, California

Foreword

What they *do* tell you before you take up the top job in a university or college is how you need to prepare for financial responsibility. In UK universities, this involves being the 'accountable officer', as set out by the Higher Education Funding Council (HEFCE) *Financial Memorandum* (HEFCE 2010: 45–7). In other types of higher education, in the UK and around the world – public and private, statutory and chartered, charitable and commercial – similar strictures apply; if you mishandle the money, you will (proverbially) go to jail (in some circumstances, you may be able to take another institutional officer with you). You prepare for this, and you never forget it.

What they *do not* tell you is that just as instantly as you become the accountant of last resort, you become an estate agent. The physical resources of the institution, the buildings in which they are held, and the land on which they are built are just as critical to institutional success (and at least as risky) as the money in the bank (and elsewhere). And you learn fast. Here are some lessons about the physical university I have learned from being the head of two HEIs (one, a large, comprehensive university; the other, a small Oxford college).

First, it takes time. Diary exercises over a two-week period in both institutions, at intervals between 1994 and 2005, revealed that I spent between 11 and 17 per cent of my working week on estates and property matters (compared to between 12 and 25 per cent of time on financial affairs). This is (second lesson) partly because HEIs are very significantly property companies. Look at where the assets are recorded in the accounts and the securest record is in relation to buildings and land. In most cases, and especially if it has been recently reassessed, the value of the estate will cover the full liabilities of the operation. (This is, like much accounting, of course, an illusion; university accounts will rarely, and then only partially, include intellectual assets.)

It leads to a third lesson: follow the money. Commitments to property deals, to improvements and to major maintenance can, without careful consideration of affordability, certainty and flexibility, easily wreck your carefully laid plans for investment elsewhere. Many institutions have driven themselves into stasis as a result of the longer-term winding down and out of projects that felt like a good idea at the time. Simultaneously, your stewardship of the estate will secure (or damn) your role in the long history of the institution (did you leave it better than you found it?). This can be especially true if you have the joy and trial of historic buildings to contend with.

Next, it really does matter how the place looks and feels. In the UK, it was one of the triumphs of the newly liberated 'incorporated' institutions (post 1988 and 1992) that they were (in most cases) able to turn financial freedoms into environmental improvements (Price 1992; Watson and Bowden 2002). But with stewardship must go responsiveness. Ours is a constantly changing business. The heavy hand of PFI (the Private Finance Initiative) has fortunately lain less heavily on higher education than on, for example, the National Health Service. You cannot say exactly what you will need the estate to deliver in 30 years' time. In the compelling words of Jane Jacobs: 'Old ideas can sometimes use new buildings. New ideas must use old buildings' (Jacobs 1961: 188). This is especially true of communal buildings: just as the community will find its own rational folkways across your grass and avoid your carefully designed paths, so too will students (especially) and staff find their own ways to use (and misuse) your buildings.

The university is not an island. Every university (including the headquarters of the distance learning operation, such as the UK Open University's Walton Hall) has a neighbourhood. Planning is the litmus test of how good your community relations really are. Some proposals will test to the limit how universities can divide communities, including their own. Football stadiums are a case in point (Watson 2009: 86–8).

There are, finally, many bits of inherited social capital with which the university has to deal. One is the model of the residential university: the notion that living together is a prerequisite of learning together. It has entered university folklore that Lord James of Rusholme's biggest declared dilemma as first vice chancellor of the University of York was, 'where will the students sleep?'. This model has been swamped by the arrival of mass higher education, and, in particular, its part-time, mixed-mode, paid-employment-friendly and economically constricted variants: in other words, what Newman first called the 'virtual university' (Newman 1856: 14). The image of the ivy-clad quadrangle retains its hold, however. It is very hard to be recognized as 'world-class' in the beauty contests that pass as league tables without traditional infrastructure.

The wide-ranging essays in this valuable collection are about much more than easing the existential crises of university leaders, including in their guise as estate agents. They will serve to remind a much wider group of interested parties that while the modern university lives in the cloud, it has its feet (and its foundations) firmly on the ground.

Sir David Watson
Professor of Higher Education and Principal of
Green Templeton College, University of Oxford

References

HEFCE (2010) *Model Financial Memorandum between HEFCE and Institutions: Terms and Conditions for Payment of HEFCE Grants to Higher Education Institutions, 2010/19*, Bristol: HEFCE.

Jacobs, J. (1961) *The Death and Life of Great Cities*, New York: Random House.

Newman, J. (1856) *University Sketches*, London and Newcastle-upon-Tyne: Walter Scott Publishers.

Price, C. (1992) 'Elegant and democratic values: how will the new universities gel?', *Higher Education Quarterly*, 46(3), 243–51.

Watson, D. (2009) *The Question of Morale: Managing Happiness and Unhappiness in University Life*, Maidenhead: Open University Press.

Watson, D. and Bowden, R. (2002) *The New University Decade*, Brighton: University of Brighton.

Preface

By day, a lifted study-storehouse; night
Converts it to a flattened cube of light.
Whichever's shown, the symbol is the same:
Knowledge; a University; a name.

(Philip Larkin, 1983, on the University of
Hull's Brynmor Jones Library,
from *Collected Poems* (1988))

The purpose of this book is to show that the physical form of the university is both central to understanding the ways in which universities work and a worthwhile object of study in its own right. The buildings, the spaces within them, and the spaces round about them, which make up the physical university, are often taken for granted, seen as merely the blank canvas on which the organizational and intellectual life of the institution is painted – along with large parts of the personal lives of the staff and students who inhabit it. Thinking about the physical university systematically is usually left to the various, often separated, professional groups associated with the built environment – architects, planners, engineers, designers, facility managers – and several chapters in this book examine their various contributions (and, in their chapter here, Lorna Hards, Sian Vaughan and James Williams add 'artists' to this list). This book weaves discussions of these professional activities into a larger tapestry depicting the university's intellectual and social functions in a way that I believe has not previously been attempted.

Why have space and place not become more significant considerations in thinking about how universities work? The task seems, instead, to have been partly subcontracted to poets and novelists. A number of novels leave the reader with a powerful sense of the university places in which they are set: a Cambridge college in C. P. Snow's *The Masters*; an English 1960s university in Malcolm Bradbury's *The History Man*; an Ivy League university in Tom Wolfe's *I Am Charlotte Simmons* – the list could easily be extended, and the author of the foreword to this book, David Watson, is the authority here. It is noteworthy that novelists have recognized the importance for their literary aims of imparting a strong sense of place in their stories with university settings: they perhaps sense that, in universities, the interactions between people and the material world are more than usually significant. Would these writers have done the same if their novels had been set in, say, insurance companies?

In the UK, the design of schools has, at least from the London board schools of the 1870s onwards, had a model, usually quite explicit though subject to regular change, about how space could contribute to educational achievement – a debate that has been largely lacking in higher education (Temple 2007). Recent theoretical and empirical work, related to schools but surely with wider implications, has developed thinking about how 'designs for learning . . . the material and temporal conditions' in which learning occurs, are significant (Selander 2008), and how learning is linked to signs, signifying social relations, embodied in the built environment. This difference between the school and higher education sectors might be because of a sense that while school pedagogy needs the support of a sympathetic physical environment, containing built-in visual cues, the more cerebral demands of learning in higher education need no such help. One commentator suggests that a nineteenth-century view of American college life, that 'all that is really needed for education is a great teacher and a ready student', is still influential (Keohane 2006: 54). Only relatively recently has serious attention been given to the design of interior spaces in higher education to support pedagogic aims (for example, JISC 2006) as distinct from simply maximizing their use. Other writers who have argued for 'putting space back on the map of learning' (Edwards and Usher 2003) find themselves equally puzzled at its relative absence from educational debates.

Also, unlike schools, universities have tended to see themselves as international (or at least national) institutions, so not related to specific locales and their design traditions in the way that schools might be: the irony here being that, once established, universities hardly ever move – the ancient universities of Europe and the Americas remain on the exact spots where they were founded. It might, though, be argued that rather than responding to place, a university can often create it – as several chapters here will show. It has also been suggested that ideas of space and time have gained primacy in Western thought, no doubt in part because they appear to be readily measurable, leading to a subordination of ideas of place, with consequentially less interest in qualitative understandings of human/material interactions (Gruenewald 2003). In their chapter here, Christoph Michels and Timon Beyes propose that postmodern thinking has helped us to move towards a broader conception of these matters through sociology, architecture and human geography.

In this book, we want to argue, from a variety of perspectives, that, far from being a blank canvas, the physical, material form affects what takes place in the university in important ways, and thereby conditions the impact that the university has on the wider world. But there is more to it than that: there is a two-way process, with a constant, subtle interplay between space and the people in it. As Christoph Michels and Timon Beyes argue, space emerges from the interplay ('performance', as they put it) between material objects, people and their ordinary activities. Perhaps Philip Larkin – a university librarian, as well as a poet – gives a sense of this in his lines quoted above.

Philosophical and sociological accounts of space, asking questions about how power is exercised through space, and what ideas are encoded within it, are relatively modern approaches now associated with the field of critical geography. Henri Lefebvre is a key thinker here: his *The Production of Space* was first published in 1974, though the first English edition only appeared in 1991 Lefebvre was one of the first scholars to distinguish between physical, mental and social space, while also pointing out how they interacted with one another: space, he argues, is not so much built as produced. Other post-modernists, notably perhaps Derrida, Foucault and Harvey, have also provided conceptual accounts of space, focusing on individuals' relationships within spaces, and how the control of space is linked with control of social behaviour – an idea that Mike Neary develops in his chapter here.

Although many of these ideas about space, explored across the chapters here, are now generally accepted by specialist scholars, it is not obvious that they have gone on to influence wider discourses, let alone relevant policies and practices – as a visit to many modern university campuses around the world will quickly show. It should be a truism that university design needs to recognize that space has social dimensions, as well as the more obvious material ones; but, unfortunately, it is not. These social objectives, the meanings that spaces have for individuals, need to be recognized, as does the need to allow for uncertainty, spontaneity and an unknown future: an attempt to meet people's private needs within what must be an institutional structure. Here, Paul Benneworth and Anthony Ossa-Richardson, in their respective chapters, show how university designers have approached these challenges in different ways, to achieve what Paul Benneworth calls 'the spatial fix' that the campus represents. One aim of this book is to help in carrying specialist scholarship on these matters across to wider audiences.

The connection between these somewhat abstract ideas and (for once, literally) concrete policies and plans is traced in a number of chapters. Conceptualizing and problematizing ideas of space and place are prerequisites to developing coherent practical policies for them. Zhongyuan Zhang shows how Lefebvre's conceptualizations can enrich our understanding of how Chinese university students make sense of their campus – and how management decisions, made on apparently rational grounds, can have deleterious effects on the wider student experience. Phillip Waite shows how ideas from architectural theory can help in understanding how students and university staffs may experience aspects of the campus, and how their perceptions of its physical form may go on to affect their learning – and, indeed, their decisions on whether to join the institution at all. (It seems, by the way, that the first use of the word 'campus' in a university context in fact related to an idea of space, referring to the sense of openness found at the eighteenth-century College of New Jersey, later to become Princeton University; see Thelin 2004: xiv.)

Other chapters examine aspects of university campus design and operations that are usually considered to be the realms of specialist practitioners. Marcella Ucci asks some difficult questions about environmental sustainability and the typical university campus, which raise large issues about whether some aspects of the current university model may be sustainable in the longer term. Alexi Marmot examines how facilities management – usually found in too low a place in university management priorities – can be organized so as to make a positive contribution to student well-being.

Some striking resonances emerge from the chapters here, across time and geographies. Anthony Ossa-Richardson quotes Basil Spence, the architect of the 1960s University of Sussex, in England, as saying in 1966 of its design that 'There should be little areas of completeness, where students could go and realize that . . . this was their little world.' Zhongyuan Zhang's student inter- viewees at 'KK University' in contemporary China would certainly support this aim: in his account, many of its 45,000 students seem to be searching for 'their little worlds' in its two square-kilometre campus. One senses, too, that they would appreciate the design features described by Anthony Ossa-Richardson at the University of York, in England, such as 'a passage ambiguously surround- ing the walker now on both sides, now on one, first enclosed as a corridor and then opening out into a colonnaded path around a shallow, rectangular fountain'. This is the kind of rich, generous, complex campus environment that Phillip Waite argues for in his chapter, which can foster a sense of community and of engagement, which sends non-verbal messages and, as he says, 'speaks more about values and priorities than anything that may be said publicly' by the university's leaders. Universities often work hard to project a distinct 'brand': their built environment is one aspect of that which cannot be faked, but can be overlooked – and, as Alexi Marmot contends in her chapter, one or two iconic buildings by 'starchitects' are not a substitute for good design and maintenance right across the campus. Well-chosen public artworks can also contribute, as Lorna Hards, Sian Vaughan and James Williams suggest here, by giving the campus a sense of identity and coherence.

The interplay between universities' physical forms, at all levels, and social functions – in other words, how exactly space may be turned into place – is a theme running through many of the chapters. What several of them show (Paul Benneworth, Brett Bligh, Zhongyuan Zhang, myself and others) is that space, which is social, is often planned without 'social' inputs: the views of the 'common people', who then struggle with place-making, are easily overlooked. Space, as Christoph Michels and Timon Beyes put it, is not a container into which people can simply be placed. Mike Neary goes further, pursuing Lefebvre's thinking and seeing the democratic use of space or 'lived utopianism' as a potentially 'revolutionary project'.

The vast scale of Chinese university development chimes with the scale of science-based expansion in the United States – what Eugene Trani in his chapter calls the 'science wars', which, in their current manifestation, pour huge amounts of money into advanced science of all kinds, underpinning economic growth and leading to 'a capital construction frenzy in science and clinical facilities'. China is clearly heading in the same direction, with investment on a scale that probably only the US can match. There is surely a message here for Europe: small- or medium-sized countries, even ones that are rich on a per capita basis by global standards, are, acting alone, simply not going to be players in the twenty-first-century knowledge economy. This is not, of course, a zero-sum game: university expansion in China and the US is an opportunity for Europe, not necessarily a threat: but Europe's response to this opportunity needs to be framed in twenty-first-century terms, not those of the last century. Understanding the significance of university space and place, and undertaking university planning and design accordingly, should be part of this response.

Paul Temple
Centre for Higher Education Studies, Institute of
Education, University of London

References

Edwards, R. and Usher, R. (2003) 'Putting space back on the map of learning', in R. Edwards and R. Usher (eds), *Space, Curriculum and Learning*, Greenwich, CT: Information Age Publishing, p. 1.

Gruenewald, D. (2003) 'Foundations of place: a multidisciplinary framework for place-conscious education', *American Educational Research Journal*, 40(3), 619–54.

JISC (2006) *Designing Spaces for Effective Learning: A Guide to 21st Century Learning Space Design*, Bristol: JISC Development Group.

Keohane, N. (2006) *Higher Ground: Ethics and Leadership in the Modern University*, Durham, NC: Duke University Press.

Larkin, P. (1988) *Collected Poems*, London: Faber & Faber.

Lefebvre, H. (1991) *The Production of Space*, Oxford: Blackwell.

Selander, S. (2008) 'Designs for learning: a theoretical perspective', *Designs for Learning*, 1(1), 10–22.

Temple, P. (2007) *Learning Spaces for the 21st Century: A Review of the Literature*, York: Higher Education Academy.

Thelin, J. (2004) *A History of American Higher Education*, Baltimore, MD: Johns Hopkins University Press.

Abbreviations

BREEAM	Building Research Establishment Environmental Assessment Method (UK)
CATS	European credit accumulation and transfer scheme
CLASP	a prefabricated building system
DEC	Display Energy Certificate
EAUC	Environmental Association for Universities and Colleges (UK)
EMS	Estate Management Statistics
EU	European Union
FEC	further education (vocational) college (UK)
FM	facility management
FTE	full-time equivalent
HCI	human-computer interaction
HEFCE	Higher Education Funding Council for England
HEI	higher education institution
ICT	information and computing technology
PST	pedagogy–space–technology framework
RGU	Robert Gordon University (UK)
SSC	Social Science Centre (Lincoln, UK)
TELL	technology-enhanced learning laboratory
UCSF	University of California San Francisco (US)
UEA	University of East Anglia (UK)
UGC	University Grants Commission (UK)
UT	University of Twente (Netherlands)
UUK	Universities UK
VCU	Virginia Commonwealth University (US)

Part I
Space at Work

1

Space, Place and University Effectiveness

PAUL TEMPLE

The University Space and Place

Universities are special places – intellectually, culturally, economically – with varied epistemic and organisational dimensions, most of which have material consequences. These material consequences may be of many kinds – some relatively temporary (furniture and interior design, say) and others permanent, effectively eternal (campus location, say). These have, in turn, continuing effects on the activities that go on within institutions: some of these effects may be intended; many, probably most, are not. But if these propositions are accepted, it remains difficult to move on to derive conclusions about higher education planning and design that can be said unambiguously to support, rather than undermine, institutional aims to do with teaching and research, the student experience, social inclusivity, community links, or other goals. Difficult, but not impossible – as many later chapters in this book will argue.

The difficulty is that it is hard to produce empirically verifiable propositions about how space affects outputs, let alone outcomes, in universities. One study of how academic collaboration and interaction in a university building was affected by spatial arrangements concluded that although 'space clearly shapes behaviours of an organisation', it nevertheless remains 'inherently difficult to disentangle which behaviours stem from which influence [because] both spatial and organisational influences appear to have shaped the structures and evolution of academic collaboration networks' being studied in this case (Sailer *et al.* 2012). But it is equally easy to present examples of spatial change where the ordinary participants – called by Bligh in his chapter here the 'denizens' – are very clear that physical change has had an impact: 'There was such a sense of community [in the building from which staff had moved] and I think that's what everybody misses' is a comment reported in one study of physical change in an American university – and, in this case, the much-lamented former building had many material defects: 'dank . . . black mould . . . asbestos' (Kuntz *et al.* 2012). It was the social character of the building, not its objective physical qualities, that were missed. Students, equally, are reported to have reacted to changed learning spaces. Most studies are of spaces that have been changed with the aim of improving learning (sadly, from a research point of view, there will be few cases where the aim is otherwise), and usually students faithfully report that this has indeed been achieved in the 'seriously cool' new facilities provided (for example, Dittoe 2006). It remains open to question, though, whether the reported benefits (when these can be demonstrated, rather than simply asserted) result from change itself – the 'Hawthorne effect' – or because the particular physical environment does actually affect learning. If the latter, we must ask about the mechanisms linking space with learning.

We have already moved from talking about spaces to places: what people do with the space they inhabit, noting that the interaction may be two-way. I have argued that this interaction is the largely unacknowledged independent variable in understanding how universities and colleges work (Temple 2009). Space in the university is what it is as a result of the decisions and actions of designers, users, those who manage it and tend it in various ways. But there is also a sense in which space and place help to determine what the university is: as Hillier and Hanson (1984: 2) argue, 'the ordering of space in buildings is really about the ordering of relations between people'. The creation of space is, then, a social and political project. Considering this complex set of space/life relationships, Lefebvre (1991: 26) suggests that space 'serves as a tool of thought and of action . . . it is also a means of control . . . of power; yet . . . it escapes in part from those who would make use of it'. Or as a writer on the theory of place has put it, 'the relations of architecture to social behaviour are complex and culturally embedded' (Dovey 2008: 2). Following these ideas, it seems necessary to ask if, once space is created, or recreated, for the university, is an institution with particular characteristics likely to emerge? And, if so, which elements of the built environment bring about these characteristics?

University space and place might, in principle, affect in a number of ways the teaching and learning, the research and the other interconnected activities that go on within institutions. One possible way, well represented in the literature, is what we may call 'message-sending': that particular building or campus designs give out signals about, say, the importance of scholarship. Edwards (2000: 150) is an exponent of this approach, arguing that university buildings should be 'silent teachers' and that we may detect 'the exacting agendas of intellectual inquiry, of scientific experiment, and refined taste . . . in the design of many university buildings'. A less provocative version of this approach is Chapman's (2006: xxiii) claim that 'the institutional story is told through the campus . . . The campus is an unalloyed account of what the institution is all about.'

I have suggested (Temple 2007) that claims such as these – in effect, that epistemologies or narratives are embodied in buildings – need to be treated with caution. It seems more plausible that people consider university buildings to be important because they happen to think that universities are important places – rather than the other way around. A research study arguing that 'more distinctive perceptions of university visual attributes ... resulted in a more favourable reputation of the university [among those surveyed in the study]' (Alessandri *et al.* 2006) can be read from the other direction: respondents may have been positive about the university's campus and buildings *because* they imagined that valuable academic work took place there. The chapter here by Hards, Vaughan and Williams somewhat similarly critiques the public art policies of universities, which seem to expect that displaying works by distinguished artists will add to the institution's academic reputation.

Other writers have similarly noted that 'it is not obvious ... [how the] values that are related to the non-physical qualities of the institution are exchanged into the building' (Gabrielsen and Saugstad 2007). As Chapman (2006) argues, though, some designers of university buildings do, of course, want their creations to 'say' something about what the university is, or does. But his 'unalloyed account' claim surely requires qualification: while the built form of an institution can certainly tell *a* story, alternative readings of the 'text' will, as with any historical account, be possible. Ossa-Richardson, in his chapter here, shows how changing architectural tastes have affected perceptions of what buildings 'mean': what may be a clear and positive message to one generation (the projection of imperial power, say) may be either unclear or negative to a later generation. Dober (1992: 5) offers a useful metaphor when he suggests that iconic university buildings 'are cultural currency ... charged with allegorical significance and perceptual connotations and meaning' – though perhaps each visitor will set their own exchange rate for this currency. Even so, the psychological charge of the building may become intertwined with its architecture, to such an extent that they cannot be separated.

The Physical Context of University Work

Culturally significant aspects of the university built environment have now often been incorporated into thinking about the university 'brand'. Some universities are almost defined, at least in the public mind, by their physical presence – Oxford, the Sorbonne or Stanford, for example. However, student satisfaction surveys, internationally, tend to attach relatively low importance to physical issues as contributors to the overall student experience (Temple 2007: 64), possibly a counter-intuitive finding, but one supported by a good deal of empirical evidence. There may be a threshold effect operating here: providing universities offer physical facilities that are perceived as broadly acceptable as a whole, then features more directly associated with the value of the degree and the organisation of academic work may assume greater importance in students' minds. When asked directly about how *particular* sorts of space could support their learning, a recent US study did find students expressing clear preferences (Bennett 2007).

These somewhat contradictory (superficially, at least) conclusions point to the central yet variable, hard-to-define role of space in the educational process: the question of what the 'design for learning' may achieve (Selander 2008). A deeper level of theoretical understanding seems to be needed. I want to argue here for an understanding of space and place in the university that goes beyond suggestions that certain ideas are embodied in buildings, or that buildings help to create the brand, and instead to propose how space becomes place, and how it affects the academic work of the institution. And space and place almost always have been central features in thinking about the university. Although it seems that the very earliest universities of medieval Europe had few physical attributes, consisting simply of groups of teachers and their students, they quickly acquired a physical identity and, arguably, a sense of place. By the late twelfth century, the University of Paris was located on the left bank of the Seine near the Ile de la Cité (Cobban 1975: 77; Leff 1968), where much of it yet remains.

How might the university's physical form be linked with academic effectiveness? One way may be through the contribution of space to the creation of a sense of community (several respondents in Kuntz *et al.*'s (2012) study make this point), and thus of *place* – in the sense of space that (in higher education settings) is intimately bound up with the ways in which we live and understand ourselves, about our ideas of what is valued and validated, as well as what we (think we) know and do (Batchelor 2006). Other writers have, somewhat similarly, suggested that a sense of place arises when 'spatial stories' can 'inhabit our dreams, and produce a kind of spatial unconsciousness, and … a continuing sense of social critique' (Amin and Thrift 2002: 48). Sennett writes of 'narrative space', space designed in ways that permit people to develop their own uses for it, so becoming 'personified places' (Sennett 1990: 190, 192). Massey (2007: 15), in a similar vein, goes on to observe that places, once created, can assume particular powers, which may be projected to affect the wider world, and there are certainly examples of how some university places have been able to set intellectual agendas, so projecting their power on to a global stage. What is hard to judge is the extent to which place, as such, rather than the people inhabiting it, is significant here.

It seems possible to make a connection between these personal ideas of place and wider understandings of institutional life and effectiveness by reference to the concept of social capital. There is theoretical and empirical work proposing that social capital effects can mean that a strong institutional community may lead to the improved effectiveness of that institution (Lesser 2000; Preston 2004; Saaranen and Tossavainen 2009). In this case, the physical form of the university may be linked to institutional effectiveness (and indeed efficiency) indirectly through its role in assisting in community formation. This physical support for community formation, and hence social capital creation, might be done in various ways. Designing a campus on a human scale is one approach, with attention to design details such as pleasant places to sit and talk, which encourage social interactions and connectivity (Chapman 2006: 180). An account of the design of Miami University, for example, tells us that, seeking this human scale, 'it was designed to feel small' (Kuh *et al.* 2005: 106), and student learning, it is argued, may be improved through the informal inter- actions that result. Waite, in his chapter here, offers further examples.

In a broadly similar way, it has been proposed that the original layouts of human settlements around the world can be interpreted as various attempts to manage encounters between locals and strangers safely and efficiently, and to provide appropriate amounts of public and private space (Hillier and Hanson 1984: 20). The form of many towns in medieval Europe was determined by the need to provide a workable marketplace – where townspeople and outsiders could come together – usually in the very centre of the town, with security apparently in mind (Schofield and Vince 1994: 33). University design poses some similar questions: how to manage insider/outsider interactions (between the 'resident' staff members and 'visiting' students) effectively and safely; how to maximise the possibility of beneficial encounters; how to locate facilities to make them easily accessible; and, perhaps, how to use design to convey particular messages about the kind of place that one is in – how to manage 'the semantic field' (Dovey 2008: 143).

We might think of these ideas as being about 'encounter management': using design features to bring people together in settings where mutually beneficial interactions may occur. Modern cities have rather similarly been theorised as places that support encounters between different social networks, providing complexity and the unexpected, and so enabling the city to become 'a potent generator of novelty' (Amin and Thrift 2002: 41): the medieval marketplace, updated. City regions, similarly, are the major centres of creativity, as measured in the US by Florida's (2004: 245) 'creativity index', because they 'can offer abundant options' for interactions. As Florida argues, 'places with diverse mixes of creative people are more likely to generate new combinations [of ideas]' (Florida 2004: 249). The comparison with the university space and place – interlinked networks of creative people with a shared sense of com- munity – is surely suggestive.

Yet the city and the university have both different functions and different cultural bases: town-and-gown tensions are part of the story of universities from as far back as records go. Other than in the handful of world cities such as New York or London, the university will have a different, more global perspective than its host, inevitably leading to tensions between the two (Bender 1988: 290), although the symbiotic relationship is usually highly beneficial. The twentieth-century rise of the knowledge economy has made the university, especially the research university, one of the most prized assets that a city can have.

Creating Place

In his chapter here, Ossa-Richardson gives a case study of the University of York (UK). In York's campus, we see an encounter management approach apparent in its early 1960s design. York is one of the campuses that Muthesius (2000: 6) describes as 'utopianist', in that its design had particular educational aims in view, which involved directing its inhabitants' behaviours. One of these aims was specifically the encouragement of informal interactions. An important way of achieving this was through a collegiate organisation, bringing together living, working and leisure activities for manageable numbers of people, which mixed staff and students from different disciplines. But the design of the campus was intended to do more than simply provide organisational units small enough for people to relate to:

> Meeting, both accidental and deliberate, must be provided for by the greatest possible number of intersections en route (without producing congestion) and it should ideally be impossible to go from one unit of accommodation to a similar one without coming into contact with at least one of completely different academic or social character on the way.
>
> (University of York 1962: 13)

This is surely a remarkable university planning statement: that a key design principle was to create complexity, to mix people up, regardless of what their own wishes might be. This was one step on the way to changing space into a particular kind of place. (There is surely a parallel here with shopping mall design: one aim of mall design is to ensure that visitors walk past as many of the shops in the mall as possible, regardless of their own wishes.) There is a striking contrast between York's planning and that of recent buildings of the University of Copenhagen, where a design aim was segregation, to ensure 'that students and visitors should be served without disturbing . . . the scientific personnel' (Gabrielsen and Saugstad 2007).

Importantly, York's sheltered pedestrian routes, running across the campus, penetrated each group of buildings (rather than simply leading up to them), and intersected inside in social spaces. As Ossa-Richardson has argued, this design feature operates more subtly than by simply bringing people together:

> The passage which leads between Langwith and Derwent colleges is especially striking, ambiguously surrounding the viewer now on both

sides, now on one; first enclosed in a corridor, and then opening out into a colonnaded path around a wide fountain. [There is a] curious 'half-inside, half-outside' feeling created by these walkways.

(Ossa-Richardson 2007)

There is a sense here of the complexity, the unexpectedness and the potential of urban spaces, where the design and management of circulation is also a key characteristic (Amin and Thrift 2002: 81). Some of the most admired English urban designs of the past – eighteenth-century London squares, or Bath's circuses and crescents – have been seen in terms of offering solutions to these problems (Sennett 1990: 95). As Ossa-Richardson puts it:

The [University's] inhabitants . . . are offered by the dislocated layout an opportunity to explore for themselves, to create their own relationships to the environment. One's sense of being part of a greater whole is enhanced by the deep integration of the buildings with the sculpted greenery. But the campus always retains a measure of mystery.

(Ossa-Richardson 2007)

My own interviews with today's staff and students at York have tended to support this view – there was a sense, sometimes, that students remained unaware of the extent of the campus and what happened in its remoter reaches. From another perspective, though, this ambiguity and mystery becomes (to one of my respondents) 'a warren . . . with confusing spaces . . . and no front doors'. But, either way, a strong sense of place emerges.

Inasmuch, then, 'that the spatial structure of each building embodies knowledge of social relations' (Hillier and Hanson 1984: 184), we may see in this designed dislocation, in this ambiguity, a way of trying to erase this embodied knowledge and to allow those living there to create their individual, original, sets of social relations: their own place. Although Muthesius's (2000: 135) account of York's early planning notes that 'we are told explicitly what should happen' in particular spaces – for example, here 'one can stop and talk, eat or drink . . .' – it is clear that these aims are to be set within a socially permissive context, with a minimum of the sort of rules then applying in most UK universities, and with considerable possibilities for self-expression. (And, really, would a student be likely to take notice of an architect's prescriptions?) For some, perhaps for people used to a strictly ordered existence, this might be a problematic experience: the mystery might become a threat.

Nor was the branding issue (as it would now be described) overlooked: as the project architect responsible for York's original design has said, the aim was to provide a 'quality of remarkability . . . to express the particular identity of place and experience' (Derbyshire 2005). But these senses of 'remarkability' and identity go beyond mere branding: they seem to contribute to community-building.

While design features of the kind noted here may relate positively to learning and research outcomes, it is extremely difficult to find convincing evidence of this linkage. Most of the work in this field comes from the schools sector: here, despite many attempts to show a link between building design or quality and learning, the evidence is, at best, inconclusive – and much of the empirical work is flawed (Temple 2007: 57). One of the methodologically strongest studies of the contributors to UK secondary school effectiveness is known as the 'fifteen thousand hours' study: it is unusual in making a direct link with achievement in external examinations, rather than simply reporting on changed student perceptions. It concluded that while the physical environment generally (school size and age of the buildings) had negligible effects on learning, a good standard of cleaning and day-to-day maintenance did appear to lead to improved results. This was almost certainly because of the standard-setting effects of being in cared-for premises, leading to more harmonious social relations, more cohesive social groupings, and so to better learning (Rutter *et al.* 1979: 195). Again, we see the suggestion that the link to better educational outcomes comes through complex interactions between space and people, rather than simply by providing people with a particular type of working or social environment.

Space and Place, and What They Do

In higher education, one writer has noted that the relationship between campus design and the quality of the student experience has not been adequately defined (Jamieson 2003). Ronald Barnett and I, in agreeing with this, noted that 'few conceptual frameworks exist for understanding the connections between the physical form of the institutions and their academic effectiveness – and perhaps their sense of place' (Temple and Barnett 2007). I want briefly to consider some factors related to space and place, which I have previously linked to ideas of social capital, and other forms of 'capital' (Temple 2009).

I have touched on some of the factors that may affect what we think of as the quality of higher education space: its setting, its unique design and historical features, its scale, internal spatial relationships, and how well it is maintained. These are all features that we may straightforwardly categorise as *physical capital* issues. (Perhaps, in particular settings, we may suggest that 'natural capital' – a hill, a river, a coastline – also has a part to play.) Once the users of these spaces are brought into the picture, some different considerations arise. I have suggested that the idea of encounter management sums up the process of managing the ways in which people come into informal contact: one study suggests that, for university students, such encounters can be 'socially catalytic' in developing relationships and supporting learning (Strange and Banning 2001: 146). The idea of *locational capital*, which comes mainly from economic studies of firms' and workers' locations (for example, Gould 2007), is useful here: that certain activities have added value when they occur in particular locations. The perhaps self-evident sense that many activities take place where they do because there are economic benefits arising (software development in Silicon Valley is a well-studied example) – or, conversely, that incomes are depressed when activities take place in suboptimal locations – is well attested empirically (Cohen and Fields 2000; Leichenko 2003). The creation of a particular university physical setting, which stimulates high-quality interactions among teachers and students, can similarly be thought of as creating locational capital.

These interactions, conditioned by the physical environment, give rise to the community that exists within the institution, and help to form its culture. (The notion of 'a' university culture is a contested one, but, for the present, let us say that, within organisations, people tend to have certain shared, tacit understandings about the way the organisation does, and should, work that condition their behaviour, and are often considered to amount to an organisational culture.) The creation of a community and its culture turns, I suggest, the university space into a *place*. As a result, locational capital becomes transformed, through the mediation of an institutional culture, into *social capital*. The debate about the scope and value of the concept of social capital is an extensive one that I will not attempt to rehearse here: Field (2003) offers a concise account. The concept has come to be used in many guises, some quite distant from the ideas that Bourdieu, generally regarded as one of its originators, developed (Bourdieu 1986; Bourdieu and Passeron 1977). Bourdieu's interest was mainly to do with 'cultural capital', as used by elites, which he considered as straightforward economic capital in disguised form, rather than the later sense in which social capital has been used, of networks and the resources embodied in them, which can operate at societal level (Field 2003: 40). Sennett, incidentally, has proposed a link between the two uses, suggesting that possessors of cultural capital need 'a network of connections . . . [to keep] members of the network afloat' (Sennett 2003: 31).

I am using the concept in the later sense, where it may be defined as social networks, the norms of reciprocity and trust that arise from them, and the application of these assets in achieving mutual objectives (Field *et al.* 2000; Putnam 2000: 19). These are the assets that underlie all effective organisations, especially knowledge-based ones that depend on the effective transfer of information: a distinctive characteristic of social capital, in the sense that I am using it, is that it is available for use by network members who have not 'paid' into it. Social capital adds value to the intellectual resources of the university by encouraging sharing and trust, characteristics of effective organisations, especially knowledge-intensive ones. Learning and research outcomes thus emerge from the university *place* – which, incidentally, can be seen as defining what is now thought of as the university brand.

Conclusions

University space and place together have a complex effect on the academic life of university institutions and their performance. It is a more complex picture than simply one of the university campus, or individual buildings, sending messages or telling a story, though these functions should not be dismissed. The connection between space and place, which I have suggested involves the creation of social capital, is consistent with the ideas of commitment, authenticity and reciprocity that Barnett (2007) suggests support student learning. However it happens, there is an interaction between space and the university community, during which both are, in certain senses, changed. Physical design features, large and small, seem to be important in ensuring that this interaction is educationally positive, although I do not suggest that these features are, on their own, transformative. I have suggested that considering the ways in which space becomes place, through the transformation of physical capital into locational capital, and the subsequent creation of social capital, is a potentially useful way of studying this relationship. We need, I suggest, to study these interconnections more thoroughly.

References

Alessandri, S., Yang, S. and Kinsey, D. (2006) 'An integrative approach to university visual identity and reputation', *Corporate Reputation Review*, 9(4), 258–70.

Amin, A. and Thrift, N. (2002) *Cities: Reimagining the Urban*, Cambridge: Polity Press.

Barnett, R. (2007) *A Will to Learn: Being a Student in an Age of Uncertainty*, Maidenhead: Open University Press/McGraw-Hill.

Batchelor, D. (2006) 'Becoming what you want to be', *London Review of Education*, 4(3), 225–38.

Bender, T. (1988) 'Afterword', in T. Bender (ed.), *The University and the City: From Medieval Origins to the Present*, New York: Oxford University Press.

Bennett, S. (2007) 'Designing for uncertainty: three approaches', *The Journal of Academic Librarianship*, 13 (2), 165–79.

Bourdieu, P. (1986) 'The forms of capital', in J. G. Richardson (ed.), *Handbook of Theory and Research for the Sociology of Education*, Westport, CT: Greenwood Press.

Bourdieu, P. and Passeron, J.-C. (1977) *Reproduction in Education, Society and Culture*, London: Sage Publications.

Chapman, M. (2006) *American Places: In Search of the Twenty-first Century Campus*, Westport, CT: American Council on Education/Praeger.

Cobban, A. (1975) *The Medieval Universities: Their Development and Organisation*, London: Methuen & Co.

Cohen, S. S. and Fields, G. (2000) 'Social capital and capital gains in Silicon Valley (reprinted from *California Management Review*, 41, 1999', in E. L. Lesser (ed.), *Knowledge and Social Capital: Foundations and Applications*, Boston, MA: Butterworth-Heinemann, pp. 179–200.

Derbyshire, A. (2005) *The University of York Campus: 40 Years of Growth and Change: What Next?*, text of lecture given at the University of York, 24 November 2005.

Dittoe, W. (2006) 'Seriously cool places: the future of learning-centered built environments', in D. Oblinger (ed.), *Learning Spaces*, Washington, DC: Educause.

Dober, R. (1992) *Campus Design*, New York: John Wiley.

Dovey, K. (2008) *Framing Places: Mediating Power in Built Form*, Abingdon: Routledge.

Edwards, B. (2000) *University Architecture*, London: Spon Press.

Field, J. (2003) *Social Capital*, London: Routledge.

Field, J., Schuller, T. and Baron, S. (2000) 'Social capital and human capital revisited', in S. Baron, J. Field and T. Schuller (eds), *Social Capital: Critical Perspectives*, Oxford: Oxford University Press, pp. 243–63.

Florida, R. (2004) *The Rise of the Creative Class: And How it's Transforming Work, Leisure, Community and Everyday Life*, New York: Basic Books.

Gabrielsen, M. and Saugstad, T. (2007) 'From identity to facility – the new buildings for the Faculty of Humanities at the University of Copenhagen', *Scandinavian Journal of Educational Research*, 51(5), 531–46.

Gould, E. (2007) 'Cities, workers, and wages: a structural analysis of the urban wage premium', *Review of Economic Studies*, 74(2), 477–506.

Hillier, B. and Hanson, J. (1984) *The Social Logic of Space*, Cambridge: Cambridge University Press.

Jamieson, P. (2003) 'Designing more effective on-campus teaching and learning spaces: a role for academic developers', *International Journal for Academic Development*, 8(1/2), 119–33.

Kuh, G., Kinzie, J., Schuh, J. and Whitt, E. (2005) *Student Success in College: Creating Conditions that Matter*, San Francisco, CA: Jossey-Bass.

Kuntz, A., Petrovic, J. and Ginocchio, L. (2012) 'A changing sense of place: a case study of academic culture and the built environment', *Higher Education Policy*, 25, 433–51.

Lefebvre, H. (1991) *The Production of Space*, Oxford: Blackwell.

Leff, G. (1968) *Paris and Oxford Universities in the Thirteenth and Fourteenth Centuries*, New York: John Wiley.

Leichenko, R. (2003) 'Does place still matter? Accounting for income variations across American Indian tribal areas', *Economic Geography*, 79(4), 365–86.

Lesser, E. L. (2000) 'Leveraging social capital in organisations', in E. L. Lesser (ed.), *Knowledge and Social Capital: Foundations and Applications*, Boston, MA: Butterworth-Heinemann, pp. 3–16

Massey, D. (2007) *World City*, Cambridge: Polity Press.

Muthesius, S. (2000) *The Postwar University: Utopianist Campus and College*, New Haven, CT: Yale University Press.

Ossa-Richardson, A. (2007) '"A difficult place to find one's way about in": York University campus and the problem of architectural identity', unpublished.

Preston, J. (2004) '"A continuous effort of sociability": learning and social capital in adult life', in T. Schuller, J. Preston, C. Hammond, A. Brassett-Grundy and J. Bynner (eds), *The Benefits of Learning: The Impact of Education on Health, Family Life and Social Capital*, London: RoutledgeFalmer, pp. 119–36.

Putnam, R. D. (2000) *Bowling Alone: The Collapse and Revival of American Community*, New York: Simon and Schuster.

Rutter, M., Maughan, B., Mortimore, P. and Ouston, J. (1979). *Fifteen Thousand Hours: Secondary Schools and their Effects on Children*, London: Open Books.

Saaranen, T. and Tossavainen, K. (2009) 'Empowerment orientation and social capital as a basis for occupational well-being in school communities', in G. Tripp and M. Payne (eds), *Social Capital*, New York: Nova Science Publishers, pp. 49–65.

Sailer, K., Marmot, A. and Penn, A. (2012) *Spatial Configuration, Organisational Change and Academic Networks*, paper presented at the Conference on Applied Social Network Analysis, 4–7 September 2012, Zürich, Switzerland.

Schofield, J. and Vince, A. (1994) *Medieval Towns*, London: Leicester University Press.

Selander, S. (2008) 'Designs for learning: a theoretical perspective', *Designs for Learning*, 1(1), 10–22.

Sennett, R. (1990) *The Conscience of the Eye: The Design and Social Life of Cities*, New York: Norton.

Sennett, R. (2003) *Respect: The Formation of Character in a World of Inequality*, London: Penguin Books.

Strange, C. and Banning, J. (2001) *Educating by Design: Creating Campus Learning Environments that Work*, San Francisco, CA: Jossey-Bass.

Temple, P. (2007) *Learning Spaces for the 21st Century: A Review of the Literature*, York: Higher Education Academy, available at: www.heacademy.ac.uk/ourwork/research/litreviews.

Temple, P. (2009) 'From space to place: university performance and its built environment', *Higher Education Policy*, 22, 209–23.

Temple, P. and Barnett, R. (2007) 'Higher education space: future directions', *Planning for Higher Education*, 36(1), 5–15.

University of York (1962) *University of York: Development Plan 1962–72*, York: York University Promotion Committee.

2

Performing University Space
Multiplicity, Relationality, Affect

TIMON BEYES AND CHRISTOPH MICHELS

Introduction: Mapping University Space

> The only time I realize that there is such a thing as the university [in our city], is when there are limousines driving people from the Hotel Einstein to the university and back.

The introductory quote is taken from a student paper written for a graduate-level seminar on 'Cities and Creativity', co-taught by the authors of this chapter and a colleague at the University of St Gallen, Switzerland, in 2006.[1] The quote presents how an inhabitant of the city perceives the university, which is markedly different from the experiences we have and reproduce in our daily routines as scholars and teachers. While we might believe to know our university and its spaces inside out, the quote tells of a different space that is interwoven with a different reality and a different spatial experience. It hints at how the space of the university is entangled with the sociopolitical and affective performance of the city. The quote thus offers and produces a particular version of the university's spatial formation, a reality more or less invisible and impalpable to those who work and study on campus.

In his paper, the author, Gregor Hasler, presents further stories and drawings, 'mental maps',[2] of the spaces of our university and its relation to the city of St Gallen. They are collected from people who know the university in different ways and thus present a variety of different imaginations of its spaces. The quote above stems from a citizen who neither works nor studies at the university. Apart from the attendance of a number of public lectures, she knows the university mainly from the perspective of a local resident. Although, from the city centre, the campus can be reached through a short uphill walk, it feels distant to her. In an interview with the author, she explains that this distance is not explicable in terms of geographical indicators, but rather as a *felt* distance. She expresses this in her first drawing, in which the university is detached from the rest of the city (Figure 2.1). Indeed, she would rather use the hospital canteen than to have lunch at the university. Furthermore, on her mental map of the university campus (Figure 2.2), the main buildings do not appear; instead, there is a blank space, whereas the surrounding area is represented in more detail.

Figure 2.1 Mental map of university campus in relation to the city

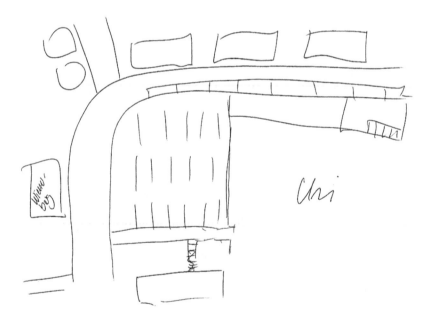

Figure 2.2 Mental map of university campus

Another interviewee, an architect who also is not affiliated with the university, refuses to draw a map of the campus. However, the story he tells about the place and its architecture differs strongly from the perception of the previous interviewee. For him, the university is a space of exemplary architecture, representing one of the two greatest buildings of the city of St Gallen. He tells us that during his architecture studies, he used to visit the campus on a regular basis, being thrilled by its construction process. In his description, the space of the university is placed firmly in a landscape of architectural history and stands for a representation of a specific, modernist architectural style, which he characterizes as being particularly honest.

A third interviewee describes the university in yet another way. He is a former student of the university and now works for one of its institutes. He does not perceive this institution of higher education as being isolated from the city, but thinks that the architecture does not blend in well with its environment. In general, he does not share the appreciation the architect had shown and describes the buildings as dull, uncomfortable and boring. His drawings reflect his experience of the campus. One of them presents the university as integrated in the urban environment (Figure 2.3), whereas

Figure 2.3 Mental map of university campus in relation to the city

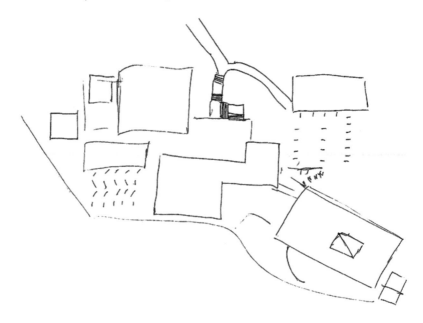

Figure 2.4 Mental map of university campus

the second drawing represents a functional, map-like view of the campus itself (Figure 2.4).

The author continues to present and analyse more stories and drawings of the university campus and its links to the city. (His overall assessment reflects rather unfavourably on the socio-spatial relations explored in his empirical work, culminating in the image of the university as a fortress and thus as a kind of gated community without visible gates.[3]) Here, we offer these representations as examples of how we may think of university spaces as not being constructed from brick and mortar alone. Instead, the empirical drawings and narratives suggest an approach to space as invariably performed through multiple spatial trajectories. From this perspective, the spatiality of organizations cannot be separated from, but is an effect of, the multiple and everyday performances of their socio-material relations. In our example, the campus is enacted in various ways, which rely on narratives, daily routines, affects and perceptions, imaginations and, last but not least, the mapping processes themselves. In the process of drawing (or refusing to draw) the maps, of narrating and reading the stories and of affectively experiencing a place, the 'physical university' is set into relation with various other elements and thus takes on its meanings.

In the following, we explore how what we suggest calling a performative understanding of space differs from understanding space as metaphor, or container, or a priori subjective perception. This has implications for the way we can apprehend, research and, perhaps, participate in shaping the socio-spatial formations of our universities. It calls for going beyond an understanding according to which space is a linguistic construction, on the one hand, or equal to its materiality, on the other. Space is invariably 'physical', but the force of its sheer materiality is not the only component in the formation of social spatialities. Such an approach relies on a processual understanding of the socio-material world and suggests that space emerges in the performance of various kinds of relations between material things, humans, words, narratives, technologies, everyday practices, moods or feelings, and a wealth of other material and immaterial elements. Telling a story about the university and its buildings is as much a performance of space as the routines performed in the everyday life on campus or in the city. These performances enact relations between our bodies, imaginations and sensations, and the environment in which we work and study.

According to a performative notion, then, there is no such thing as 'space as such'; there are multiple ways of *spacing*, of enacting socio-spatial relations. We call these processes multiple instead of plural because they are not independent of each other. They hang together as they affect the participating components in various ways, potentially setting them into tension. 'To space' (or to be in space) thus means to become part of the everyday performances of making space, co-producing specific socio-spatial relations. To explore the multiplicity of spatial performances, as, for example, Gregor Hasler sets out to do in his project, thus opens up a promising avenue of researching the spaces of universities. Moreover, it offers a reflexive stance with respect to the potential of becoming part of different spaces of research, education and administration; spaces that form the place we might then think of as a 'meshwork' (De Landa 1997) or a 'multiversity'.[4]

The remainder of this chapter is structured as follows. In the next section, we adumbrate the far-reaching transformations of spatial thinking, which are commonly referred to as the 'spatial turn', and unfold our understanding of it as a turn towards a relational, processual and performative notion of spatial multiplicity. Here, we acknowledge the pivotal work of Henri Lefebvre on the production of space; from there, we sketch a further radicalization of theorizing the complexity and performativity of space in the work of human geographers such as Doreen Massey and Nigel Thrift, or what is called 'non-representational theory', as well as in the philosopher Peter Sloterdijk's *Spheres* trilogy. This is followed by a more systematic discussion of the implications of these conceptual developments to exploring the spaces of the university, which we undertake by relating our introductory vignette to the notions of multiplicity, relationality and affect. In the concluding section, we reflect on the challenges the performative understanding of spatial multiplicity pose for apprehending and experimenting with university spaces – in other words, for undertaking research and teaching. We argue that such a 'take' on university spaces not only allows for the affirmation of their heterogeneity, but also for teaching experiments that help keep the university alive as a place of learning and reflexivity.

Towards a Performative Notion of Space (Or Spacing)

> Space is the everywhere of modern thought. It is the flesh that flatters the bones of theory. It is an all-purpose nostrum to be applied whenever things look sticky. It is an invocation which suggests that the writer is right on without her having to give too much away. It is flexibility as explanation: a term ready and waiting in the wings to perform that song-and-dance act one more time.
>
> (Crang and Thrift 2000: 1)

Here, we take a closer look at the 'the enormous, subterranean revolution in the art of spatial science' (Doel 1999: 2), which underpins our choice and intro-ductory discussion of the vignette and offers a promising perspective on apprehending and, perhaps, experimenting with the spaces of the university. To stick with slightly hyperbolic terms for the moment, we thus delve into the 'spatial turn'. To all appearances, the term 'spatial turn' saw the light of day in Soja's highly influential book *Postmodern Geographies*, published almost 25 years ago. Soja (1989: 16, 39) coined this term somewhat in passing in order to describe the event of an increasing attention to questions of space and geography, instead of time and history, in 'critical theory' of the late 1960s.[5]

Indeed, a relative neglect of 'space' as analytical category until the end of the twentieth century has been diagnosed in disciplines such as sociology (Löw 2001), but also in the more straightforwardly spatial fields of architectural thinking (Madanipour 1996; Wigley 1995) and human geography (Soja 1989). The attention that *Postmodern Geographies* received can thus be read as a symp-tom of a more sweeping undercurrent and a turn away from what Crang and Thrift (2000: 1) call the 'tyrannies of historicism and developmentalism'. This development can be epitomized in Foucault's often-quoted concern of how space could have come to be treated as 'the dead, the fixed, the undialectical, the immobile', while time would be seen as 'richness, fecundity, life, dialectic' (Foucault 1980/1976: 70).

By now, Foucault's concern has been met with a proliferation of texts across disciplines that seek to unfix, mobilize and enliven our understanding of the spatiality of human life, constituting a renaissance of 'space' as a conceptual and analytical category (Döring and Thielmann 2008; Thrift 2006). Tellingly,

Soja himself took a turn with regard to the spatial turn: having invented the term as an explorative intervention into Marxist and post-Marxist debates, having used it again only in passing in the book that followed *Postmodern Geographies*, called *Thirdspace* (Soja 1996), the human geographer has recently been compelled to announce the spatial as the master turn, so to speak. Emphatically, Soja (2008: 242 *et seq.*) now conceives of it as the new trans-disciplinary paradigm, a far-reaching reconfiguration and transformation of the research landscape that would show more profound effects than the fashions of 'small turns' (such as the performative, iconic, translational turns).

In this sense, perhaps space indeed has become 'the everywhere of modern thought', as the above-quoted Crang and Thrift have noted. Importantly, all the talk of spatial turns does not denote a monolithic and agreed-upon perspective on the spatiality of human life. Rather, there is a multifaceted land-scape of spatial thought extending across disciplines (Döring and Thielmann 2008); it is itself made up of multiple trajectories of inquiry into 'the wildness of space' (Wigley 1995: 217). Space, as with so many other 'grand terms' in the sciences of the human, designates a quite dizzying spectrum of partly differ-ent and partly contradictory things; it 'is contested in almost every sense' (Madanipour 1996: 332). Broadly put, the talk of a(nother) 'turn' indicates no more (and no less) than a heightened level of academic awareness of aspects that are regarded to have been more or less overlooked or simply taken for granted previously – in this case, the spatiality of human life.

For the purpose of this chapter, we suggest to see the 'spatial turn' as a profound opening towards a processual, relational and performative under-standing of spatial multiplicity. For a start, it perhaps helps to underscore what, from this perspective, space is not. It is *not* a metaphor, nor does it denote a 'container' waiting to be filled, nor does it designate a transcendental a priori of subjective perception (Thrift 2008: 16). Henri Lefebvre's (1991/1974: 27 *et seq.*) critique of what he calls the 'illusion of transparency' and 'the realistic illusion' has been particularly influential here. The first implies that space would be 'luminous', 'intelligible'; it thus corresponds to a perception of space as 'innocent' and 'free of traps or secret places', leading to the illusion of a broad coincidence between the mental space of thoughts/discourse and social space (a perspective that is usually traced back to a Kantian 'subjectivism–idealism'). Knowledge of space as an outcome of the mind's spatial workings does not imply a neglect of material appearances. However, knowing physical space becomes an exercise of thought, the spatial image or representation becomes the 'real' spatial order.

While this line of reasoning conceives of reality as confined to an internal world of imaginations (*res cogitans*), to 'thought things' that are projected on to the material world by the use of language, the second line locates reality in an external world of material things (*res extensa*) that can be represented by language. Therefore, the illusion of opacity befalls a naturalistic materialism or empiricism: here, space is objectively given in order to be measured and described accurately, as if objects would be placed in a kind of vacuum (thus, the 'container' notion of space would fall under this conception) (Lefebvre 1991/1974: 27 et seq.). For example, the city – its networks, nodes, flows, patterns, correlations, movements – is often read as an empirical text, either 'indigeneously' through careful descriptions of physical appearances or 'exogeneously' through social, psychological and biophysical explanations.[6]

As Schmid (2005: 204 et seq.) points out, Lefebvre's radical break with conventional spatial thinking consists of doing away with any notion of space as a universal category that would precede praxis – be it the Kantian a priori of perception or the notion of container space:

> The outcome is a vast moment in terms of which space can no longer be looked upon as an 'essence', as an object distinct from the point of view of (or as compared with) 'subjects', as answering to a logic of its own.
> (Lefebvre 1991/1974: 410 et seq.)

Instead, Lefebvre offers a threefold ontology of space, analytically distinguishing between physical, mental and social space, which need to be grasped in their simultaneous interrelations (Lefebvre 1991/1974: 11 et seq.). This spatial multiplicity constitutes an active force; it is both produced and producing. Central to Lefebvre's notion of space, thus, is the idea of processuality – at once produced and producing, a consequence and a generative force of socio-material relations, space is always 'becoming'.

While Lefebvre's seminal The Production of Space – which 'encompasses a great deal of what, 25 years later, has become stock-in-trade in the social sciences' (Löw 2008: 29) – is littered with cautions against tendencies to reify space, it is a matter of some debate whether there is an essentialist residue at work in his theory of space (Collinge 2008) or whether he enacts a 'dialectical mopping-up operation' (Doel 1999: 118) that might compel the (spatial) scholar to see everything in terms of an unfolding of contradictions between rather clearly demarcated types of spaces (see Beyes and Steyaert 2012). The qualifications of space as multiple, relational, processual and performative, already to be found in Lefebvre's work, can be coaxed out further by recourse to Doreen Massey's (2005) For Space. Apart from countering the illusions of transparency and opacity as outlined by Lefebvre, Massey's 'space of loose ends and missing links' (Massey 2005: 12) more clearly allows us to emphasize the 'contemporaneous heterogeneities of space' (Massey 2005: 5) that resist the folding of space into linear, narrative time[7] and into clearly demarcated analytical categories. First, space – and no matter of what scale – is conceived as 'the sphere of heterogeneity' (Massey 2005: 99). Second, space therefore becomes an effect of interrelations and interactions and simultaneously the 'sphere of relations, negotiations, practices of engagement, power in all its forms'. In this sense, the question of space cannot be untied from 'the question of the social, and thus of the political', precisely because it is 'produced *through* the social and the political' (Massey 2005: 99, original emphasis). Third, any researcher trying to write about space has to take into account several phenomena at the same time, a simultaneous co-presence of difference and plurality. The production of space follows neither teleology nor linear logic (Schlögel 2003); it is thus 'the sphere of the possibility of the existence of multiplicity in the sense of contemporaneous plurality . . . Without space, no multiplicity; without multiplicity, no space' (Massey 2005: 9). It follows that, *fourth*, space is always under construction, a continuous, unfinished process of deconstruction and reconstruction, 'a simultaneity of stories-so-far', as Massey (2005: 9) beautifully puts it.

Our stories-so-far have brought us to a notion of space, or rather 'spacing' (Beyes and Steyaert 2012), that enables us to think and apprehend the spaces of universities as made up of multiple, heterogenous and interrelated spatial trajectories, as processually produced and thus as performative. To conclude the sketch of Doel's above-quoted 'revolution in the art of spatial science' (Doel 1999: 2), we briefly refer to recent conceptual developments that do not alter this understanding of space but stress or add the important factors of affect, embodiment and materiality, as well as the question of how to research and write such spacings. For one, there is the loosely coupled body of work mainly in human geography that has been labeled 'non-representational theory' (Anderson and Harrison 2010; Thrift 2008). While constituting a fairly broad church, these writings can be said to be resolutely materialist in that spatial practices are not reduced to human agents but seen as material-relational bundles in which 'physical stuff . . . is a lively participant' (Latham *et al.* 2009: 62). It follows that human bodies are not seen as preformed entities, but as an outcome of, and the setting for, a play of connections and forces, a 'volatile combination of flesh, fluids, organs, skeletal structure and dreams, desires, ideas, social conventions and habits' (Latham *et al.* 2009: 108). (And it is here where the difference to Lefebvre's spatial theory and its idea of the 'proper' body as yardstick of space becomes most apparent.) In addition, in non-representational theory, these connections and forces are often discussed as affective intensities that sweep through and take hold of human bodies. Affects thus denote impersonal forces that take hold of and condition what human bodies can do (Massumi 2002). Trying to think and apprehend these pre-subjective forces, 'which prefigure encounters, which set up encounters, and which have to be worked on in these encounters' (Thrift 2000: 219), necessarily implies that 'space is therefore constitutive in the strongest possible sense and it is not a misuse of a term to call it performative' (Thrift 2003: 2023).

Finally, bearing some resemblances to non-representational theory, Peter Sloterdijk's *Spheres* trilogy offers an ambitious and idiosyncratic exploration of coming to terms with and learning to apprehend the spatio-material embeddedness of the social and of human becoming. Again, space is presented as an excessive composition of multiple forces, which include the mediating power of things or inhuman traffic and its material-technological relations, as well as the affective surges that sweep through the human body, which then have to be worked upon by human beings. As a sprawling meditation – even 'a hyperbolic novel' (Sloterdijk 2004: 16) – on being-in-the-world as a fundamentally spatial being-with or being-together in spheres, the philosopher's project is dedicated to the 'soft anthropospheres' of self-animated and immunological, thus fragile and protective, spaces we are born into, that we shape and that shape us.

Importantly, Sloterdijk radically experiments with a strange philosophico-literary language, a spatial poetics of affects, intensities, flows, floating, magnetisms, resonances and other spacings that seeks to apprehend these spatial concatenations, which are usually lost in the representational techniques of the social sciences. The *Spheres* trilogy thus constitutes one of the most far-reaching scholarly performances of 'writing space'. Indeed, the question of how the work of scholarship responds to a performative notion of space or spacing as we have tried to outline here is a thorny and challenging one, and one we will return to. After all, researching and writing on the spaces of the universities implies being in the middle of them and partaking in their multiple, heterogeneous and interrelated spatial trajectories.

Exploring the University's Complex Spatialities

On the basis of our wayfinding through the rich and fascinating landscape of contemporary spatial thinking, we now turn to implications of the performative notion of space (or spacing) for thinking and researching universities. Indeed, there is need for a 'better understanding of the role of space in the dynamics of creating more productive higher education communities and its connections with learning and research' (Temple 2008: 238). We thus need to ask what kind of effects a performative approach to university space may bring about. To do so, we identify and discuss three broad and interrelated themes, which seem to offer the biggest 'traction' in the context of this book: multiplicity, relationality and affect. Subsequently, and in conclusion, we point to the important and intriguing question of our co-performances as scholars and educators, briefly reflecting on the implications for research and education, and the potential of teaching experiments as performances of spatial multiplicity and 'other spaces' of learning.

Multiplicity

In his famous radio lecture on 'Les utopies réelles ou "lieux et autres lieux"' – later translated into English under the title 'Of other spaces' – Foucault (1986/ 1966) developed the outlines of a science of heterotopology. It would entail the study of heterotopic sites, where several real and imaginary spaces intersect and are thus all related to their surroundings and produce a difference, taking different spatio-temporal forms. Foucault's eclectic list of examples includes, among other things, festivals, brothels, prisons, colonies and cemeteries. In a talk on the state of universities, Sloterdijk (2008: 24, original emphasis) has added to Foucault's list the '*locus academicus*' as an 'other space' *par excellence* – an important reservoir of the imagination, which, he worries, is under threat due to the managerialization of higher education and the logic of the market and consumption that would have detrimental effects on the university's capacity to foster imagination and new thinking.

Supplementing the view of universities as heterotopic spaces in their relation to society – and therefore as driving forces of spatial multiplicity – we suggest apprehending university spaces as multiple in themselves: as perpetual results of the coming together of a variety of spatial trajectories. Consider our introductory example: the space of the University of St Gallen might not only be conceived as heterotopic in relation to its urban surroundings – it is produced through heterogeneous spatial performances in the first place. Picking up Lefebvre's spatial ontology, we can easily discern *the interplay of* physical space of its architecture, mental space of planning and imagination, and social space of everyday urban and university practices. Together, these spacings form the places where we research and teach. While the materiality of buildings, rooms and technical apparatuses certainly affects the labour of research and teaching, of studying and administering, we need to grasp space through its simultaneous imaginary, narrative, affective and embodied constitution, too. The spaces of the university can then be thought of as being multiple. They are not containers in which students, educators and administrators are placed, mere 'receivers' of architectural and internal design, which influences or steers the way academic work is done. Nor can built space solely be grasped as a function of social structure, as Hillier and Hanson (1984) suggest. While we share their concerns about a paradigm that 'conceptualises spaces as being without social content and society without spatial content' (Hillier and Hanson 1984: x), the notion of space outlined here entails yet goes beyond the assumption that built space is 'a function of the forms of social solidarity, and these are in turn a product of the structure of society' (Hillier and Hanson 1984: 22). We suggest seeing the spaces of universities as far messier spatial constellations or assemblages of a heterogeneity of generative spatial forces, which need to be taken into account. While the effects of managerial decisions on the design of university spaces (on students and staff) is certainly in need of further investigation (Temple 2008), the notion of space espoused here calls for expanding our approach to include the multiple and (in this sense) non-managerial processes of participating (or intervening) in the production of the sites of education and research.

Relationality

Expanding the conceptual and empirical sensibility for the 'contemporaneous heterogeneities of space' (Massey 2005: 5) entails a decidedly relational perspective, according to which space is an effect of the 'meeting' of different spatial trajectories. Again, consider the introductory vignette and how narratives, practices, affects and imaginations mingle with the built environment to produce the space(s) of a university. Physical designs therefore participate in the everyday production of space. University buildings are not understood as isolated factors, which cause certain social or pedagogical effects or reproduce a specific social logic, but as participants in the socio-material performances of the university. Of course, their specific qualities do play a role in how university life unfolds. However, this role is conceptualized in terms of the play of relationalities; it is one of co-constitution, of distributed agency. The question of design then shifts from the question 'What effects does a specific building produce on its users?', towards asking what one can do with a specific building or what potential performances a building may become part of. This may seem like a small shift in perspective, but we think it has significant reverberations for how we conceive of the relation between university life and its built environment. In addition to describing spaces of higher education as an effect of planning and building processes – of what Lefebvre (1991/1974) would call conceived and perceived space – the emphasis shifts towards (the potential for) everyday co-performances of spaces. It opens the study of university space for the interrelations of the various elements that participate in its production.

More provocatively put, a performative understanding would at least pose the question whether it is not more likely that reflexive and alternative 'uses' of space will emerge from everyday practices and their irritations, rather than from the planning of new buildings and infrastructures. Indeed, while the latter usually involves large amounts of money and reproduces the predominant styles of enacting the university, it is through the former – which is, of course, entangled with the physical designs and manifestations – that other imaginations, narratives and practices develop. The idea of turning universities into reflexive institutions of learning is thus predicated on the acknowledgement of the relational constitution of their spaces. In this sense, we think that the notion of performative space can help decentring the production of university space, away from planners, architects, investors and managers, towards a logic of (re)distributed agency that includes a wider constituency of university life.

Affect

Reframing the question of university space as one of relational performances of spatial multiplicity calls for a processual vocabulary of intensities, capacities, movements and forces. It asks us to comprehend spatial configurations as the taking place of encounters of things and bodies, from which sensible experiences emerge. Contemporary spatial thought of the kind that is presented here often works with the notion of affect in order to express the prefiguration, set-up and effects of these encounters.

That university space can be conceived as produced out of 'a spatial swirl of affects' (Thrift 2006: 143) is already hinted at in our introductory example. The distance the first interviewee feels, the excitement of the architect and the boredom of the employee, and the resulting imaginations of the spatial relations of the university, its campus and the city, indicate the affective 'swirl' that both produces and emanates from spatial configurations of researching and teaching. This is not a frivolous and negligible background noise to the proper work of designing or understanding space. These differing atmospheric assessments, expressed through words and drawings, allude to the generative effects of sensual and embodied perceptions, which are implicated in the production of university space.

Moreover, while related to the physical environment and its affective force, the sensations cannot be reduced to it. Indeed, a good part of the difficulty of exploring and discussing affects has to do with the fact that they can neither be subjectivized as stable individual emotions nor objectified as being wholly represented by, in this case, the physical spaces of the university. Instead, affects can be thought of as 'impersonal movements that constitute what a body can do' (Anderson and Holden 2008: 145). They constitute intensities across bodies, which are 'captured' and expressed through perceptions and emotions, that is, bodies that are affected (Massumi 2002). That is why the stories and maps of our example seem to point to multiple registers of sensing and expression, prone to change and variation, that are realized when encounters or collisions of things and bodies take place. It follows that:

> architecture consists not only in the uses and meanings of buildings and spaces. In architectural spaces, bodies have 'affective somatic responses' ... and these responses arise out of the 'assemblage' (mind/brain/body/building) that is the time and space of a building's inhabitation. Our experiences of a building arise not only out of our cognitive interpretations

of the building's allusions to historical or aesthetic meanings but also out of the corporality of the body's time/space as it exists in relation to the building.

(Ellsworth 2005: 4)

The amorphousness and fleetingness of such affective experiences seems incompatible with the concreteness of spatial reality typically 'read' by the distanced scholarly observer. Thrift (2004: 57–8) diagnoses a 'residual cultural Cartesianism' that would treat affect as 'a kind of frivolous or distracting background to the real work of deciding our way through the city'. In any case, affect theory poses difficult questions to the study of university space, at least if one, like the authors of this paper, has a background in architecture and organization studies.

In Conclusion: Spatial Performances of Research and Education

In advocating a performative notion of space, then, one is confronted with the problem of how to research such spacings. Moreover, the case for scholarly enactments of the university as a spatial performance extends to the practice of teaching: how it can open up to the potential of spatial multiplicity. In conclusion, we offer some preliminary remarks on these two issues.

First, the notions of multiplicity (the co-presence of difference), relationality (the interconnectedness of spatial trajectories) and affect (pre-subjective forces that collide with human bodies, provoking sensations) imply that there, invariably, is an excess of space that exceeds the scholarly gaze and discourse. Space is unrepresentable in a mimetic sense (Massey 2005: 28); it cannot be 'tamed' by representational moves: 'There is too much that lies beneath the surface, unknown and perhaps unknowable, for a complete story to be told' (Soja 2000: 12). What is called for, then, is a more modest 'cultivation of a mode of perception that dwells in the midst of things' (McCormack 2007: 369), as well as 'experimental kinds of response' (Lorimer 2008: 556) with regard to form, style and method of research and writing. A mode of perception that dwells in the midst of things implies embodied apprehensions of the everyday performing of space. It goes beyond theoretical diagnostics of the kind enacted here and attempts forms of living space inquiry (Steyaert 2009). Experimental kinds of response can, for instance, take the form of a montage of mental maps and empirical narratives, as in the case of our student, or – more daunting still – that of a spatial poetics of affects, intensities, flows, floating, magnetisms, resonances and other spacings, as in the case of Sloterdijk's *Spheres* project. There is no shared heuristics to enact a performative spatial analysis, but there is a growing body of different forms of research creation and presentation that seeks to apprehend the affectively charged concatenations of space (see Beyes and Steyaert 2012; Lorimer 2008).

Second, if universities potentially constitute heterotopias *par excellence*, and thus potential reservoirs of imagination, then a performative understanding of university space implies the need for an experimental way of relating to it. To be playful in the performance of the university spaces allows for exploring other ways of assembling them and to thus reflect on possible alternatives of enacting them. This relates to teaching, of course, and the way we bring 'space in the making' into educational practices. How can one acknowledge and experiment with spatial multiplicity, and the contradictions and tensions this entails? To address this question, we would like to add a few notes on our own practices and modest interventions within and on the spaces of a business university. These are no more than exemplary indicators of what might be done, under the perhaps particularly ambivalent conditions, moreover, of an institution of higher learning dedicated to conveying and instilling a managerial and entrepreneurial mindset.

On the basis of our experience and that of colleagues, then, we end with three tentative axioms or slogans. First, *enable self-reflexive engagements with the spaces of the university*. Consider one more time Gregor Hasler's explorative study, with which we began this chapter and which was conducted in our course on 'Cities and Creativity'. For us, the student's work presents an example of a problematization of 'inside' perceptions of university spaces. By applying fairly inventive methods to apprehend spatial multiplicity, the project demonstrates how the physical spaces of the university are entangled with different spatial stories, routines, affects and experiences, and how they are thus enacted in complex and contradictory ways.

Second, *undo everyday spatial routines of the university*. In a rather large-scale experimental teaching project that took place in 2005, we worked with 850 newly enrolled students, as well as artists and architects, to conceive of and visualize a city of the future within five days (Beyes and Michels 2011). One of the most striking characteristics of the event was the way the spatial practices of regular university life were both reproduced and (temporally) reconfigured. With regard to the latter, it seemed to be the aesthetic repertoires and techniques of learning, further provoked by the presence of architects and artists, that messed with usual business university routines, leading to struggles around the production of educational space and the emergence of imaginative, 'lived' spaces through the students' work.

Third, *leave the spaces of the university for urban life*. As both cases indicate, we are very fond of thematizing the city and thus the multiplicity of urban space in our teaching activities on the ordering and disordering of space. Leaving classrooms and campus, we ask students to conduct mini- or quasi-ethnographies of urban spaces and their everyday meshworks of buildings, streets, sidewalks and objects, narratives, images and imaginations, as well as affective 'swirls'. Students-as-researchers are thus confronted with, or rather involved in, the processuality of the urban; they learn (or so we hope) 'by being affected by the intensities, connections and blockages in everyday interactions and practices of urban living' (Steyaert 2009).

After all, the critical and creative task of research and education guided by the performative notion of spacing is thus: to embed ourselves in, face, help resonate and add to the relational multiplicity and openness of space.

Notes

1   We turned the papers into a little book on St Gallen (Beyes *et al.* 2006).
2   The technique of mental mapping is an experimental method of cartography, through which memory, orientation and major architectural features, as well as images of spatial appropriations, are combined. Imprecise and distorted as they often appear, such maps present aesthetical, imagined and ideological expressions, and often symbolic interpretations of perceptions and experiences of spaces. Their analysis thus helps to show how space influences urban dwellers and how spaces are co-produced through their use, adaptation and imagination (Wildner and Schäfer 2009).
3   To speak as teachers: it was a very good paper indeed.
4   'Multiversity' is a term we borrow from a movement for a decolonized educational system in India, Asia, Africa and the two Americas (Alvares 2004). This movement aims at living the multiversity as a place that cultivates multiple ways of knowing the world. This understanding not only makes space for a reflexive way of knowledge (re)production, but also allows for relating and tending to local ways of knowing. We find 'multiversity' an inspiring notion for thinking of places of research and learning (also in the Western world) in terms of their spatial multiplicity and relationality.
5   However, as the anthology compiled by Dünne and Günzel (2006) demonstrates, what Soja (1989: 34) admits to be a 'broad and sweeping depiction of modernization and modernism', and of the corresponding erasure of a spatial imagination, seems hard to be upheld as a general claim. One could think here of the writings of 'Weimar critics' such as Simmel and Benjamin. Another area where a spatial imagination played an important role is, of course, art. For instance, the symbolic dimension of the city is unveiled by Hugo, its paradigmatic dimension by Baudelaire and the many other flaneur poets. As Kristin Ross (2008/1988: 35) writes in her magnificent study on 'Rimbaud and the Paris Commune', aptly titled *The Emergence of Social Space*: 'Instead of the abstract visual constructions proper to the stasis of a geographic notion of space, the poem [Rimbaud's 'Rêvé pour l'hiver', an erotic poem from 1870] creates a "nonpassive" spatiality – space as a specific form of operations and interactions'. This poetics of exploration poses an invitation 'to conceive of space not as a static reality but as active, generative, to experience space as created by interaction, as something that our bodies reactivate, and that through this reactivation, in turn modifies and transforms us'.
6   Somewhat differently to Lefebvre's approach, the history of spatial thinking is often discussed alongside a broad 'cut', namely the dichotomy of absolute and relational space (Löw 2001). Within the former notion, often referred to as 'container space',

space is either designated as having an own reality independent of human beings or conceptualized as Euclid's three-dimensional space assumed to be an inevitable prerequisite for each constitution of space. According to Löw (2001), this includes Kant's conceptualization of space. Although the latter denies the possibility of representing objects and things 'out there', it assumes the Euclidian principles as a priori concept 'steering' the subjective constitution of the mind. The notion of relational space, on the other hand, is traced back to Leibnitz and his concept of space-in-relations, of space as being manifest in relations between events or aspects of events that would render the idea of a space that exists independently of its relations unnecessary.

7   A topic beyond this paper's scope is the conceptualization of the relation between space and time. Following Massey's (2005: 55) propositions, it can be argued that 'neither time nor space is reducible to the other; they are distinct. They are, however, co-implicated. On the side of space, there is the integral temporality of a dynamic simultaneity. On the side of time, there is the necessary production of change through practices of interrelation'.

References

Alvares, C. (ed.) (2004) *Multiversity: Freeing Children from the Tyranny of Schooling, Bringing Colour Back into Academic Studies*, Mapusa: Other India Press.

Anderson, B. and Harrison, P. (2010) *Taking-Place: Non-Representational Theories and Geography*, Farnham: Ashgate Publishing.

Anderson, B. and Holden, A. (2008) 'Affective urbanism and the event of hope', *Space and Culture*, 11(2), 142–59.

Beyes, T. and Michels, C. (2011) 'The production of educational space: heterotopia and the business university', *Management Learning*, 42(5), 523–38.

Beyes, T. and Steyaert, C. (2012) 'Spacing organization: non-representational theorizing and the spatial turn in organizational research', *Organization*, 19(1), 45–61.

Beyes, T., Steyaert, C. and Michels, C. (eds) (2006) *St Gallen A–Z: What Can You Do in a City?*, St Gallen: University of St Gallen.

Collinge, C. (2008) 'Positions without negations? Dialectical reason and the contingencies of space', *Environment and Planning A*, 40(11), 2613–22.

Crang, M. and Thrift, N. (2000) 'Introduction', in M. Crang and N. Thrift (eds), *Thinking Space*, London: Routledge, pp. 1–30.

De Landa, M. (1997) *A Thousand Years of Nonlinear History*, New York: Zone Books.

Doel, M. A. (1999) *Poststructuralist Geographies: The Diabolical Art of Spatial Science*, Edinburgh: Edinburgh University Press.

Döring, J. and Thielmann, T. (2008) ‚Einleitung: was lesen wir im Raume? Der *Spatial Turn* und das geheime Wissen der Geographen', in J. Döring and T. Thielmann (eds), *Spatial Turn: Das Raumparadigma in den Kultur- und Sozialwissenschaften*, Bielefeld: Transcript, pp. 7–45.

Dünne, J. and Günzel, S. (eds) (2006) *Raumtheorie: Grundlagentexte aus Philosophie und Kulturwissenschaften*, Frankfurt: Suhrkamp.

Ellsworth, E. (2005) *Places of Learning: Media, Architecture, Pedagogy*, London: Routledge.

Foucault, M. (1980/1976) 'Questions on geography', in M. Foucault, *Power/Knowledge: Selected Interviews and Other Writings, 1972–1977*, New York: Pantheon Books, pp. 63–77.

Foucault, M. (1986/1966) 'Of other spaces', *Diacritics*, 16, 22–7.

Hillier, B. and Hanson, J. (1984) *The Social Logic of Space*, Cambridge: Cambridge University Press.

Latham, A., McCormack, D. P., McNamara, K. and McNeill, D. (2009) *Key Concepts in Urban Geography*, London: Sage.

Lefebvre, H. (1991/1974) *The Production of Space*, Oxford: Blackwell.

Lorimer, H. (2008) 'Cultural geography: non-representational conditions and concerns', *Progress in Human Geography*, 32(4), 551–9.

Löw, M. (2001) *Raumsoziologie*, Frankfurt: Suhrkamp.

Löw, M. (2008) 'The constitution of space: the structuration of spaces through the simultaneity of effect and perception', *European Journal of Social Theory*, 11(1), 24–49.

Madanipour, A. (1996) 'Urban design and dilemmas of space', *Environment and Planning D: Society and Space*, 14(3), 331–55.

Massey, D. (2005) *For Space*, London: Sage.

Massumi, B. (2002) *Parables for the Virtual: Movement, Affect, Sensation*, Durham, NC: Duke University Press.

McCormack, D. P. (2007) 'Molecular affects in human geographies', *Environment and Planning A*, 39(2), 359–77.

Ross, K. (2008/1988) *The Emergence of Social Space: Rimbaud and the Paris Commune*, London: Verso.

Schlögel, K. (2003) *Im Raume lesen wir die Zeit. Über Zivilisationsgeschichte und Geopolitik*, Munich: Carl Hanser.

Schmid, C. (2005) *Stadt, Raum und Gesellschaft: Henri Lefebvre und die Theorie der Produktion des Raumes*, Munich: Franz Steiner.

Sloterdijk, P. (2004) *Sphären III: Schäume. Plurale Sphärologie*, Frankfurt: Suhrkamp.

Sloterdijk, P. (2008) 'Die Akademie als Heterotopie', in M. Jongen (ed.), *Philosophie des Raumes: Standortbestimmungen ästhetischer und politischer Theorie*, Munich: Wilhelm Fink, pp. 23–32.

Soja, E. W. (1989) *Postmodern Geographies: The Reassertion of Space in Critical Social Theory*, London: Verso.

Soja, E. (1996) *Thirdspace: Journeys to Los Angels and Other Real-and-Imagined Places*, Oxford: Blackwell.

Soja, E. W. (2000) *Postmetropolis: Critical Studies of Cities and Regions*, Oxford: Blackwell.

Soja, E. W. (2008) 'Vom "Zeitgeist" zum "Raumgeist": new twists on the *Spatial Turn*', in J. Döring and T. Thielmann (eds), *Spatial Turn: Das Raumparadigma in den Kultur- und Sozialwissenschaften*, Bielefeld: Transcript, pp. 241–62.

Steyaert, C. (2009) 'Enacting urban ethnographies of artistic interventions in the entrepreneurial city', in T. Beyes, S.-T. Krempl and A. Deuflhard (eds), *Parcitypate: Art and Urban Space*, Sulgen and Zurich: Niggli.

Temple, P. (2008) 'Learning spaces in higher education: an under-researched topic', *London Review of Education*, 6(3), 229–41.

Thrift, N. (2000) 'Afterwords', *Environment and Planning D: Society and Space*, 18(2), 213–55.

Thrift, N. (2003) 'Performance and . . .', *Environment and Planning A*, 35(11), 2019–24.

Thrift, N. (2004) 'Intensities of feeling: towards a spatial politics of affect', *Geografiska Annaler*, 86B(1), 57–78.

Thrift, N. (2006) 'Space', *Theory, Culture and Society*, 23(2/3), 139–46.

Thrift, N. (2008) *Non-Representational Theory: Space, Politics, Affect*, Abingdon: Routledge.

Wigley, M. (1995) *The Architecture of Deconstruction: Derrida's Haunt*, Cambridge, MA: MIT Press.

Wildner, K. and Schäfer, C. (2009) 'Planned gentrification or temporary art zone? An associative tour of the Grosse Bergstrasse with Christoph Schäfer', in T. Beyes, S.-T. Krempl and A. Deuflhard (eds), *Parcitypate: Art and Urban Space*, Sulgen and Zurich: Niggli.

3
Examining New Processes for Learning Space Design

BRETT BLIGH

Overview

The emergent literature on learning spaces in higher education articulates a desire to better engage academics and other stakeholders in the conceptualisation, design and development of university spaces.

New processes that aim to support more participation in design are proposed. This chapter reviews a range of these processes using an activity-theoretical concept of *distributed agency*. Much of the examined literature proposes to intervene in estates life cycles within particular, bounded activities. It is argued that forming long-term relations between university stakeholders, based on decentralised negotiation and peer review, would further expand the possibility of socially producing university learning spaces.

Introduction

Perhaps one of the most elementary characteristics of the nascent learning spaces literature is the argument that the material environment is, or rather should be, a core pedagogical concern (Jamieson *et al.* 2000; Temple 2008). Taken seriously, this general perspective invites a host of more particular questions. How to theorise the relationships between learning and space? How to design spaces so that they support a range of pedagogical objectives?

One particular query is driven by the notion that many individuals with an interest in pedagogical issues have little input into institutional space. This question, which is the focus of this chapter, might be phrased as follows: how can people whose main interest is in pedagogy gain access to institutional discussions of space and effectively make their voice heard? Questions such as this are prominent within the literature, though straightforward solutions remain elusive (Boys 2011: 101).

When considering the range of questions related to learning spaces, we must immediately acknowledge that many of the underpinning issues are linked. The absence of clear theoretical perspectives on learning space relations, for example, serves to constrain the manner in which university spaces are designed and evaluated (Bligh and Pearshouse 2011). The present author has previously written about how a range of different pedagogical and learning sciences perspectives can provide insight into relationships between learning and space, while acknowledging that these perspectives are in disagreement on a range of key issues (Bligh and Crook in press). This chapter proceeds from the view that space should be seen as *socially constitutive*, created as a social product and manifest through institutional and societal forms that act on our consciousness. Boys (2011) adopts a broadly compatible viewpoint, though with an idiosyncratic emphasis on the 'communities of practice' literature that I will not maintain here. Boys also provides a useful overview of relevant developments in architectural theory.

The issue of broadening access to institutional space design processes has sparked much discussion within the literature. To interrogate such work, and to frame my later arguments about the potential for denizens' more extensive engagement with space production, I use several concepts developed by Engeström (1987, 2008). These concepts, such as *distributed agency*, originate in an analysis of workplace teams underpinned by activity theory. This work is sufficiently extensive that a large degree of abbreviation is required, and I endeavour to explain terms as they arise. Nonetheless, it is essential to set out from the beginning that Engeström's (1987) influential formulation of activity systems forms the backdrop to the present analysis.

Engeström describes collective activity as relating subjects, objects and communities within interlocking processes of production, distribution, exchange and consumption (terms that Engeström adopts from Marx's *Grundrisse*). These interlocking processes are *mediated* by a complex structure of tools, rules and the division of labour. Systemic contradictions within and between activities act as a motor of change because human beings, with varying degrees of success, attempt to overcome contradictions and, in doing so, reshape their activity systems.

Typically, the learning spaces literature suggests that space management processes ought to become more inclusive towards academics and staff developers, students, and technical and administrative support staff. These stakeholders are not themselves a homogeneous group. Yet, I will often use the term *denizens* to highlight some aspects that they do have in common. First, a denizen is an *inhabitant*; in most cases, their opinion of institutional space is sought because they inhabit those spaces and are thought capable of providing insight into how learning happens there that would otherwise remain inaccessible to estates managers (and their commissioned architects). Second, a denizen is only *partly enfranchised*; existing space management procedures and norms restrict the extent to which their opinions about space are institutionally heeded, relative to other actors such as estates managers, architects and, perhaps, timetabling officers (the analogous term for whom would be *citizens*). Third, the expertise of these new contributors with regard to spatial concepts and design will be limited; concerns about the material environment will hitherto have fallen largely outside their professional remit. So, it seems necessary that they receive appropriate support when contributing their ideas. This chapter critically reviews a number of approaches that seek to provide such support.

To examine these issues, I consider a selection of proposed mechanisms that aim to support denizens' wider participation in learning spaces design processes. The mechanisms examined take the form of activities where the object appears to be, in turn: *consensus and ownership* (vis-à-vis innovative spaces), the *local experiences of space users*, *institutional processes* (and their spatial implications), the development of *design briefs*, and *academic value* in institutional identity. Many of these mechanisms appear to be relatively contained activities with defined boundaries, as yet undertaken only at relatively small scale. This is partly a function of their novelty, and their typical reportage as case studies, yet it is a limitation when the mechanisms are contemplated within the context of established estates management processes. I conclude by considering what it would mean for denizens to engage more extensively in the social production of the spaces they inhabit.

Distributed Agency

In this chapter, I consider a range of specific examples of work that involve denizens within processes of learning space design in novel ways. I focus on these examples of new processes at the expense of the (much larger) body of work that proposes 'design principles' for spaces based on pedagogic insight. In each case, I aim to emphasise and critique the nature of the *distributed agency* that is attained. I borrow from Engeström in order to provide content for this phrase:

> I argue that employees' collective capacity to create organizational transformations and innovations is becoming a crucially important asset that gives a new, dynamic content to notions of collaborative work and social capital. In philosophy, sociology, anthropology, and cognitive science, such capacity is conceptualized as distributed agency or collective intentionality.
>
> (Engeström 2008: 199)

As this quotation illustrates, issues of distributed agency are recognised as important for their capacity to produce innovation within institutional and organisational contexts. What, then, can we say about the 'dynamic content' generated by the kinds of collaborative work envisaged within the learning spaces literature?

Engeström (2008: 217) suggests that a number of prerequisites must be addressed if distributed agency is to have any meaning: distributed agency must be 'purposefully cultivated', the attendant collaboration facilitated, and the agency *manifest* 'in situations of collaborative decision making and problem solving'. Engeström (2008: 207) investigates manifestations of distributed agency in several concrete cases, such as inter-agency working in a Finnish health care setting, and concludes that 'five principles of cultural-historical activity theory seem relevant for the study of collective intentionality and distributed agency'. Since I will rely on these five principles in the remainder of this chapter to examine how distributed agency is manifest within new processes of learning space design, it is necessary to begin by providing a brief summary:

1   *Object-orientation.* This principle 'calls attention to the object of the activities under scrutiny' (Engeström 2008: 213). We need to ask questions such as 'What actually is the object here? What are these people talking about and trying to accomplish?' (Engeström 2008: 222). Objects give purpose and meaning to collective activity, yet they can be frustratingly difficult to construct (Engeström 2008: 204). Moreover, forming a *shared* object must be regarded as a major collaborative, analytical achievement (Engeström 2008: 163).
2   *Mediation by tools and signs.* This principle asks us to look at the artefacts that mediate the activity. More specifically, Engeström suggests that we examine 'the potentials of artifacts as means of eliciting or triggering voluntary action' (Engeström 2008: 223).
3   *Mutual constitution of actions and activity.* This principle focuses attention on the links between the situated, contingent and concrete *decisions* that are made within the activity and more 'future-oriented visions' (Engeström 2008: 214).
4   *Contradictions and deviations as source of change.* This principle requires that we examine the *systemic* tensions within the activity (Engeström 2008: 215). As outlined in the introduction, activity theory suggests that contradictions are a driving force of systemic change and innovation, as people attempt to overcome the contradictions that confront them.
5   *Historicity.* This principle directs us to 'explore the successive and intersecting developmental layers, including the emergent new ones, in the activities under scrutiny' (Engeström 2008: 215).

It should not be imagined that each of these principles will feature equally throughout my subsequent analysis. Some principles may feature more prominently than others within discussion of particular approaches, while the nature of how work is documented in the literature will serve to restrict the reach of my analysis. In particular, my examination of *historicity* will be repeatedly rendered problematic by the case study format of most source materials – wherein authors are keen to demonstrate how their approach confronts historical problems and might lead to the future design of better spaces, but devote rather less attention to discussing how their own methods might be *further* developed in light of experience.

In what follows, I organise work from within the learning spaces literature into clusters according to the *object-orientation* of attendant reports. While my method of exposition will necessarily vary by context, as a default I will start by examining the relationship between the object and the *history* of the work (the existing problems that the authors suggest they are addressing), before subsequently examining, in turn, the nature of mediation by tools and signs, the relationship between actions and activity, and the systemic contradictions.

Consensus and Ownership

The argument that participatory design enables the integration of partici-pants' perspectives, and fosters a feeling of ownership with regard to the resulting spaces, is prominent within the learning spaces design literature (see Boys 2011: 101–4). Here, I focus on two (related) examples of work, both from Australia, where these issues are explicitly made into the object of activity: the *pedagogy–space–technology* (PST) framework of Radcliffe (2008), and the *pedagogy–space–people–technology design model* (PaSsPorT) of Reushle (2012). Both of these examples focus on issues of consensus and ownership within a particular institution, though Radcliffe (2008: 14) *also* discusses how the lessons learnt might be consolidated across the nascent (Australian) learning spaces community.

Both Radcliffe (2008) and Reushle (2012) start out by railing against the power disparities between professions evident in the procedural norms of estates management. Reushle (2012: 89) sets out her desire to move towards more input for 'users' (by which is meant teachers and students) and away from procedural domination by technological, architectural and operational con-siderations. Radcliffe (2008: 11), additionally, suggests that new pressures – such as 'social patterns, generational change, a changing funding environment, new and emerging technology and the shift to a more learner-centred pedagogy' – are placing pressure on these norms and 'driving innovation and experi-mentation in the design of learning spaces'.

The reason that consensus and ownership is set as the *object* of the activity in these cases is because the authors desire to create new, *experimental* learning spaces within an institutional setting, and wish to ameliorate some of the attendant risk. Radcliffe (2008: 12), for example, is mainly concerned to support the development of what he calls 'next generation libraries', 'collaborative learning centres' and 'advanced concept teaching spaces'. Reushle (2012: 88–9) specifically documents the development of the technology-enhanced learning laboratory (TELL) at Queensland, a 'facility for staff and students to investigate technology-enhanced learning innovations' intended as an 'enabler of change' rather than a 'fixed design'. In both cases, it seems crucial that local stakeholders 'buy in' to the new spaces. Reushle (2012: 96), for example, suggests that the iterative, design-evaluation cycle she describes creates a 'shared vision' across stakeholders so as to 'promote the TELL across the university'. More explicitly, Radcliffe (2008: 11) states: 'In the early years of occupation all the people involved to this stage [conceptual design] should be the promoters of the initiative.' The object here is not merely about consultation, of a type already evident in the procedural norms of many institutions. Instead, the aim is to *change people* so that they become political allies within the institution, *supportive* of the (unorthodox) spaces that are designed.

The *mediating tools* of PST and PaSsPorT are similar, since Reushle (2012) cites PST as a major influence on the development of PaSsPorT. Two tools are emphasised in each case: a *flow diagram* and a *tabulated set of trigger questions*. Each is intended to be used by stakeholders to reflect on ideas and outcomes 'at every stage in the life cycle of a learning space' (Reushle 2012: 92). The flow diagram is constant and the structure of the table similar in both frameworks, while the range of particular questions differs. The flow diagram provides a graphic illustration of suggested relationships between pedagogy, space and technology: it is suggested that pedagogy is *enabled* by space and *enlarged* by technology; that space *encourages* pedagogy and *embeds* technology; and that technology *enhances* pedagogy and *extends* space (Reushle 2012: 92).

The trigger questions presented in the table are deliberately intended to be 'generic'; justification for this is sought on the grounds that by 'using a set of generic trigger questions all stakeholders potentially have equal access to the design conversation' (Radcliffe 2008: 14). Within the PST framework, trigger questions are divided across two columns – *conception and design*, and *implementation and operation* – and suggested questions are provided that focus on pedagogy, space, technology and 'overall' (Radcliffe 2008: 15). Within PaSsPorT, an additional row is provided for questions about people. The range of questions formulated in each case seek collective specification regarding a wide range of 'who', 'what', 'which' and 'how' issues. Importantly, the completed table provides a *persistent* record of the design discussions: '[PST] is inherently self-documenting and aides [*sic*] the elicitation of lessons learned for future projects' (Radcliffe 2008: 14).

What is noticeable about many of the questions in both frameworks under examination is the predominance of questions related to future-oriented visions as opposed to those seeking concrete, contingent decisions. For example, of the 26 clusters of questions in the PST framework, only one, relating to the conception and design of space, asks for detailed decision-making. Even this question is somewhat open-ended, being set out as follows: 'What aspects of the design of the space and provisioning of furniture and fittings will foster these modes of learning (and teaching)?' (Radcliffe 2008: 15).

The underlying systemic *contradiction* driving the kind of change proposed by both PST and PaSsPorT seems to be that between producing *innovative* space and the attendant risks of doing so. The need to produce innovative space is driven by perception of broad market forces and by aims to support different forms of learning. For example, Radcliffe (2008: 11) posits a need to challenge those students of the current generation who are bored, as evidenced by their 'net-surfing, instant messaging, and text-messaging during scheduled meetings'. Yet, the attendant risk is that students and staff might view the new spaces negatively. As Jamieson (2008, quoted in Boys 2011: 103) argues elsewhere: 'Understandably, students may not favour situations of change where they perceive that the adoption of new teaching practices may jeopardise their own learning experiences and/or grades.'

Both Radcliffe (2008) and Reushle (2012) seek to resolve this contradiction by explicitly taking risks within particular spaces set up to provide a *capacity to experiment* (Reushle 2012: 96). These experimental spaces will require political support across all stages of their life cycle, including design, and these processes aim to develop an appropriate network to provide such support. Such a diplomatic initiative inevitably involves a desire to work, where possible, *within* existing infrastructures – in particular, to cooperate, wherever possible, with the established institutional norms of estates management. As Radcliffe (2008: 14) states regarding PST, 'if a particular institution has a prescribed set of project stages with decision points (stage gates), then the basic PST framework questions can be re-written to suit the declared delivery steps or stages for the institution'.

Local Experiences of Space Users

A number of examples of research can be found in the literature that examine the local experiences of space users. Such work investigates the relationships between spatial, material and sensory qualities and social and cultural factors, as these are manifest within particular (institutional) settings. For example, Melhuish (2011) uses ethnographic methods to investigate student and staff perceptions of spaces used for creative design education. In particular, Melhuish highlights perceptual relationships of symbolism (such as visibility, exclusivity and interface) and functionality (including flexibility, regulation and interactivity). Crook and Mitchell (2012), on the other hand, used structured observations, on-the-spot interviews and focus groups to examine students' experiences when using an area of a university library designed to support collaborative learning. Crook and Mitchell draw attention to the nuanced experience of 'sociality' that space users found valuable in the space – a variety of intermittent exchanges, serendipitous encounters and apparently solitary study occurring within an *ambiently sociable* setting, as well as the episodes of intense collaboration that the space had been explicitly designed to support.

Yet, few such examples of work in universities focus on the attendant opportunities for design. Thus, in this section, I examine work drawn from the museum sector, where links to space design are discussed explicitly. Ciolfi and Bannon (2005) document work undertaken in the Hunt Museum, which houses a collection of fine art and antiquities in Limerick, Ireland. The object of activity is that of 'articulating the concept of *place* for design' (Ciolfi and Bannon 2005: 223, added emphasis), based on an underlying motive to design new 'technologically-enhanced physical spaces' within the museum (Ciolfi and Bannon 2005: 221).

To examine *historicity* in this case, we must appreciate that Ciolfi and Bannon's (2005) work is located in the tradition of *interaction design* (i.e. designing user experiences by applying the principles of human-computer interaction (HCI)). The process aims to build on work within HCI concerned with 'the relationship between physical spaces and their inhabitants, on the connections between the properties of an environment and the patterns of action and behaviour occurring within them' (Ciolfi and Bannon 2005: 219). One strand of this endeavour has involved augmenting the physical environment, using technology to introduce overlapping *layers* of information (Ciolfi and Bannon 2005: 218). Ciolfi and Bannon aim to gain better insight into designing augmented spaces by incorporating an understanding of *place*, derived from work in humanistic geography and its antecedents. The authors provide a potted history of work within this tradition and urge that we refrain from viewing space as merely a physical container (Ciolfi and Bannon 2005: 221–3). Instead, Ciolfi and Bannon wish to focus attention on the *design potential* accorded when material space is conceived as providing 'raw materials' underpinning *place*, a localised experience that can be articulated with appropriate support. It should be emphasised that the range of learning theories that implicate space do *not* universally concur about the centrality of the concept of place, and that this concept is not central to work such as that by Melhuish (2011) or Crook and Mitchell (2012). Ciolfi and Bannon's particular discussion of the topic does, however, take what Bligh and Crook (in press) call an *associative* view of space and learning, where humans are assumed to engage in a cognitive process of place construction that relies, to some extent, on material resources.

Ciolfi and Bannon's (2005) suggested process involves researchers observing the actions of visitors to the museum. A particular framework is used to guide interpretation and opportunities are taken to elicit visitors' own verbal reactions. Two kinds of tools are important here. First, artefacts from the museum's collections are used to mediate the experiences of the visitors being observed. The artefacts are selected (generally, those chosen are not prominently featured in existing museum exhibitions) and sited within the museum space so as to provoke reactions. Second, the researchers themselves use a conceptual, dia-grammatic representation of place, understood as constituted by *layers* of cultural, social, personal and physical dimensions (Ciolfi and Bannon 2005: 224). The tool, which is based explicitly on the work of (humanistic geographer) Yi-Fu Tuan, is intended to provide 'a visual articulation of the concept of place that highlights the different dimensions as interconnected aspects of the individual's experience' (Ciolfi and Bannon 2005: 224). The tool thereby functions as a *why artefact* (i.e. one used for the diagnosis and explanation of objects) (Engeström 2008: 129).

The source of *contradiction* in Ciolfi and Bannon's (2005) work arises from the fact that place is a particularly troublesome object for design activity. The experience of place, while influenced by social factors, is understood as being unique to the individual. Ciolfi and Bannon (2005: 225) themselves recognise this when they state that place cannot be designed, but only *designed for*. While part of the benefit of the approach is to help users articulate their local experience of place, it is the role of a researcher to aggregate these experiences and combine them with analysis of secondary materials such as institutional policies (Ciolfi and Bannon 2005: 226). The task of compiling together a package of source material amenable for interaction designers is thus professionalised.

The *mutual constitution of actions and activity* here should also be understood in relation to the researchers, as opposed to the museum visitors. While Ciolfi and Bannon (2005: 227-9) go on to describe their designs for two new spaces within the Hunt Museum – the 'Study Room' and the 'Room of Opinions' – these seem to be provided as mere illustrations of principle. The design work itself is seen as producing a '*site-specific intervention* [whose] rationale is deeply grounded in the fabric of the museum' (Ciolfi and Bannon 2005: 226, original emphasis). Such an attitude stands in contrast to other examples, such as the work of Radcliffe (2008), discussed above, where it is suggested that the broader learning spaces community might reach consensus around particular designs. In examples of work that examine the local experiences of users, it seems that it is the tools and procedures that might be improved through experience, perhaps in tandem with the craft knowledge of the designer.

Institutional Processes and Spatial Implications

The work that I consider in this section involves instigating a structured investigation of *processes* (or 'activities') within an institution. Subsequent stages involve deciding for which processes the need for specific institutional support is compelling, and constructing appropriate representations of those processes to aid in planning decisions. Two outcomes are hoped for. First, that participants come to realize that not all processes need to be supported through the design of space (or even within the institution). Second, that those processes where material, institutional provision *is* required will benefit from better provision due to the insight afforded by the process specifications that are developed.

To illustrate these issues, I consider two examples of work whose scholarly motivations are quite different. The first example is provided by Boys (2011), who describes an activity where the object is to focus on *improving* the processes through which the university operates. The second example is taken from Quintana (2012), who discusses the use of HCI methods to represent the intended *activity*, *context* and *audiences* within a proposed space.

The *historicity* of these works is ostensibly quite different. Boys (2011) suggests that she wants to *challenge* two increasingly common assumptions: first, that spatial designs in educational institutions 'represent' the learning that occurs within them and, second, that better space design requires wider participation (i.e. the premise underpinning much work reviewed in this chapter). Boys's concern is that relying on metaphorical representations of space invites those who are inexperienced in design matters (such as denizens) to make 'common-sense' design choices. Such choices often fail to take into account the 'non-congruence and partial translation between intentions, representation in form, and lived experiences' (Boys 2011: 101). Instead, Boys suggests that participants might more appropriately focus on what she calls *the space of the teaching and learning relationship*. By this is meant those activities occurring within institutional boundaries and the relationships between them, as well as 'the sets of connections and disconnections that any participant has with all the activities of that institution' (Boys 2011: 113).

Quintana (2012) establishes his historical point of departure from a more personal perspective. Quintana was an experienced HCI researcher and technology designer, yet with little background in architecture, who became involved in space design due to his senior faculty position. Tasked with contributing locally to the creation of a new building and recognising his own inexperience, Quintana opted to draw on his professional expertise in *learner-centred design* (Quintana 2012: 1). Like Boys, Quintana's decision seems taken so as to avoid the misconceptions of 'common-sense'. Quintana documents his experiences using a *process space analysis* approach, where the key task is to 'understand and describe activity, along with the context in which that activity is situated and the audiences engaging in that activity' (Quintana 2012: 2).[1]

Quintana's (2012) approach involves researchers working to create those *tools* that will later mediate discussions with denizens. First, the researchers construct 'educational activity descriptions' that try to articulate 'the full set of roles, activities, artifacts, information objects and services' being envisioned for the new building (Quintana 2012: 2). Second, the researchers work up some of these activity descriptions into prose form as *current scenarios*, detailing how users might currently engage in a particular activity, including 'the problems, complexities, and successes that arose for students in the current spaces' (Quintana 2012: 2). Third, a separate set of *future scenarios* is constructed. These describe 'how students *might* engage in the same kind of activity in the new spaces we were designing, which forced us to think about how we could create the new spaces to address the problems' (Quintana 2012: 2, original emphasis). These current and future scenarios are then used to 'tell a set of stories about the emerging Brandon Centre vision to the other stakeholders in the building' (Quintana 2012: 2). Denizens can engage with these stories, and revise or add to them before they are turned over to the professional design team.

Boys (2011) describes the use of simpler tools. Determined that 'shared consensus' should not be required in order to proceed, Boys describes work that begins by examining the official *institutional description* of particular processes. In the example that Boys discusses, this documentation concerns student enrolment (Boys 2011: 114). Participants subsequently use simple artefacts to examine these processes:

> one activity involved passing round a piece of paper to act out what a student needed to do in order to enrol at the university. At one stage, the paper went backwards and forwards between two participants, due to uncertainty about what should be the next stage in the process . . . which powerfully showed the process's underlying problems.
>
> (Boys 2011: 115)

Both of these process-focused approaches quite directly involve the *mutual constitution of actions and activity*. Boys (2011: 114–15) discusses how analysis can serve to redefine the boundaries of processes while also providing direct insight into spatial implications:

> Such an approach was able to re-think social and spatial practices simultaneously so that, for example, a one-stop shop (literally like a shop-front, centrally located and easily accessible on the university campus) was

introduced to handle new student enquiries as well as related recruitment aspects.

(Boys 2011: 116)

Quintana (2012: 3) describes how discussion involved linking the particular scenario narratives with 'budgets and timelines that had to be met, and the prioritisation decisions that come with such a project', describing this as a 'learning experience' for participants.

Two main contradictions are evident here. The first closely mirrors that discussed previously in relation to consensus approaches (i.e. that certain spatial repertoires have become established for good reasons and that innovation, while desirable, carries a degree of risk). Quintana (2012: 2) notes that considering *future scenarios* 'forced us to think about how we could create the new spaces to address the problems and issues in the existing scenarios without losing some of the favorable aspects'. Boys (2011: 115) argues that a main aim of the method she describes is to 'reveal gaps in, and unintended consequences of, existing social and spatial practices'.

The second attendant contradiction is discussed at more length in both examples. The tension is that technological developments are serving to render obsolete a range of services hitherto provided by institutions on their campuses. Their replacement by institutional Web services may be appropriate, but, in other cases, the institution may divest altogether. Boys (2011: 116–17) cites an illustrative example of work concerning university library services. Here, the process re-engineering approach examined *appropriate scales* of services and distinguished between those at institutional and sub-institutional scales. For example, some provision for information searching was deemed obsolete due to developments in online search engines such as Google, while other services, such as catalogue databases, could be placed online but still required institutional support. Rare book collections, on the other hand, were seen as presenting particular space requirements, as well as requiring skilled institutional curation. Quintana (2012: 3) discusses similar issues in relation to a library video database.

Design Briefs

The approaches described thus far have only implicitly addressed the issue of constructing *design briefs*. It has been assumed that writing briefs will remain a professionalised activity, thereby perpetuating a separation between 'creative' consultation and more 'concrete' decision-making undertaken later within the auspices of estates management processes. This assumption is, perhaps, understandable – as a response to denizens' typical lack of experience in spatial design (or comprehension of spatial theories). Yet, as I will elaborate more fully in the conclusion, separating participants from concrete, consequential decision-making is a significant problem from the vantage point of activity theory. As a consequence, I want to focus on a particular example of work by Sherringham and Stewart (2011) that does involve denizens constructing briefs, notwithstanding that such work is rather rare in the literature. Within the school-design literature, Woolner (2010) also provides a description of how young pupils can contribute to briefs by 'diamond ranking' designs, or by developing their own through drawing. I do not consider Woolner's account in great detail, however, because her extensive accounting for primary-age cognitive abilities renders much of her discussion tangential to current purposes.

The activity described by Sherringham and Stewart (2011) is straight-forwardly oriented towards the brief:

> A design brief is a crucial document, crystalizing and communicating stakeholder desires for the outcome of a building program. [Thus, the] aim of the research project was to design tools, models and other supports for enabling a collaborative and participatory brief development process.
>
> (Sherringham and Stewart 2011: 106)

Sherringham and Stewart suggest that one of their underlying motives is to move away from replicating familiar spatial models towards producing more *'innovative and appropriate* design briefs' (Sherringham and Stewart 2011: 111–12, added emphasis).

The particular *historicity* of Sherringham and Stewart's (2011: 108–9) work arises from a scathing assessment of the Enlightenment concept of *bildung*; this concept, they suggest, remains manifest in how university spaces typically seek to draw attention *away* from the physical environment. Thereby, such spaces 'support a focussed, disembodied attention to the information being imparted by the teacher [allowing] the mind to be engaged and the body to be neutralised' (Sherringham and Stewart 2011: 109).

Sherringham and Stewart use practice theory (that of Bourdieu) to establish that neutralising the body in this way means not supporting 'authentic learning' (Sherringham and Stewart 2011: 106). It is noted that students can identify incongruities between educational space provision and their own practice, yet it is observed that unaided conversations can become overly focused on function. In other words, the underlying *contradiction* is that interviewees can identify what does not work, but are unable to articulate *how* institutional spaces fail to evoke the proper disposition or mood for their practice.

To overcome this problem, Sherringham and Stewart (2011) suggest the concept of *activity-scapes* as a focus for discussion, an abstraction comparable to Boys' (2011) *space of the teaching and learning relationship* above. An activity-scape is defined as 'the supportive experiential, spatial, equipmental and service environment immediate to the performance of a particular activity' (Sherringham and Stewart 2011: 113).

Sherringham and Stewart (2011: 112–14) suggest that a number of *tools* might 'scaffold' attendant discussion. First, the concept of activity-scape itself is used to guide and direct the discussion; participants are asked to explore five 'dimensions' of the activity-scape (relating to orientations, aids, tools, support and boundary conditions). Second, a set of visual tools serve as 'triggers or conversation pieces [providing] a non-linguistic way of developing generative narratives and interpretable artefacts' (Sherringham and Stewart 2011: 112).

These visual tools are used in participatory and *playful* engagements, intended to 'defuse' power relations between players, and help participants access tacit knowledge within a risk-free atmosphere. Sherringham and Stewart (2011) describe their workshops as divided into two phases. Phase 1 involves working collaboratively to formulate an appropriate learning activity-scape, constructing a representation from an array of cards that provide 'multiple options for identifying various needs, supports or conditions for learning' in a range of representational forms, from 'fairly abstract visual prompts to explicit words and cues' (Sherringham and Stewart 2011: 114). Phase 2 involves testing and iteratively developing this activity-scape:

> A set of 'what if?' cards introduces possible shifts in the context for learning, including broader changes to the physical, technological, social, political and economic environment of the educational institution. The activity-scape is also tested against both present and future institutional identity and industry expectations. In this way, the workshops are modelled to create a form of reciprocal learning, within which stakeholders and designers engage in playfully framed exchanges.
>
> (Sherringham and Stewart 2011: 114–15)

Sherringham and Stewart's work contains a strong sense of the *mutual constitution of actions and activity*. This arises from the relationship between the testing and reciprocal learning, described above, and the overarching focus on 'authentic learning'. This authentic learning is understood to occur 'when the learning scenario experienced by the student reflects contexts for action typical of those for which the student is being prepared' (Sherringham and Stewart 2011: 106). Thus, participants are being asked to think about the relationships between the envisaged spaces and the ways in which the student will eventually interact with the world after leaving the education system. What Sherringham and Stewart discuss insufficiently, in my view, is whether these 'contexts for action' are to be conceptualised as relating to students' later ability to participate within a democratic society, or whether the focus is on narrower concerns of vocational preparedness.

Academic Value in Institutional Identity

In this section, I consider two related examples of work whose object is the re-shaping of institutional identity, so as to support the construction of universities that reflect academic values. The first is the 'Learning Landscapes' work of Neary *et al.* (2010), while the second is the subsequent 'E4V Model' presented by Duggan (2011). Each example aims to harness a 'silent revolution' apparently already in progress within higher education, whereby the landscape is being altered by a combination of technological and societal factors that are manifest within institutions via the demands of staff and students (Neary *et al.* 2010: 10). The common aim is to harness this revolution, empowering academics and others to engage with and influence institutional vision.

Neary *et al.* (2010) take as their *historical* starting point the three-year research programme of the UK Higher Education Space Management Group (SMG) that began in 2006. Initially motivated by concern about space utilisation rates in higher education, the SMG's work expanded to include investigations of space management and innovative practice (Neary *et al.* 2010: 8). Within this context, Neary *et al.* (2010) identify a 'need to develop a better under-standing of the relationship between academics and estates in the leadership, governance and management of space in universities' – in particular, a better understanding that takes into account those good practices associated with innovative spaces. The concept of *learning landscapes* is used to describe holistic, multidimensional thinking about *campuses* as learning spaces (Neary *et al.* 2010: 10). Duggan (2011: 147) starts from the more particular observation that (institutional) conversations about space are 'increasingly dominated by spreadsheet generated data', a problem exacerbated when space is perceived as in short supply. She suggests that 'the answer lies with key stakeholder groups who are empowered to collectively explore how the space of their university, college or other educational provision is described, designed, allocated, managed and evaluated'.

Neary *et al.* (2010) examine institutional identity, stating a desire to increase the influence of academic values over that identity. In part, it is suggested that academics should use discussion of learning spaces as a mechanism for reasserting academic values over the institution. Those academic values need to be underpinned, it is argued, by a *research* attitude to campus space, recourse to insight from academic *disciplines* when engaging in design, and an emphasis on the academic tradition when engaging in inter-professional collaboration. Duggan (2011: 148–9) emphasises the different values that stakeholders will bring to discussions concerning space. It is Duggan's hope that:

through an ongoing process of sharing perspectives, agreeing values and moving towards collective *sense-making*, conversations about physical space can become increasingly open and hopeful, no longer so focused on the limitations of scarce space, but rather on ways in which its full potential can be realised.

(Duggan 2011: 147, original emphasis)

Both examples of work document tools intended to support this sharing of perspectives; indeed, Neary *et al.* (2010) proffer five such tools. Four of these five are research-derived frameworks, provided in the form of brief documents used to support stakeholders' thinking and collaborative discussions. *Teaching with space in mind*, for example, aims to stimulate the spatial imagination of academics with regard to their own pedagogy, so as to support the specification of *educational briefs* for learning space projects (Neary *et al.* 2010: 35). Similarly, *pragmatics of place* provides a guide for estates professionals when they communicate about learning spaces with academics (Neary *et al.* 2010: 36), *talking our futures into being* supports inter-professional exploration of the university's role as a *client* when commissioning spaces (Neary *et al.* 2010: 37), and *the idea of the university* supports 'a fundamental discussion about the nature and role of the university' (Neary *et al.* 2010: 38) based on a summary of historical ideal-types.

The fifth of the tools set out by Neary *et al.* (2010: 33–4) is the *campus mapping profile*. This is a visual template whose content is 'filled in' during *in situ* analysis of institutional campus provision. It is envisaged that the completed tool provides a visual overview of how the campus estate fulfils institutional vision, and helps to establish where there are 'gaps' in provision. To do so, a matrix of criteria is provided. These criteria are divided into three categories, which are suggested to comprise fundamental qualities of good design: *expression*, *efficiency* and *effectiveness* (Neary *et al.* 2010: 18–19).

The later E4V model proposed by Duggan (2011) elaborates these three categories along with a fourth. The E4V model is constructed to support discussion of the *efficient*, *effective*, *expressive* and *enduring* qualities of space (Duggan 2011: 149). Aided by a representation of these four qualities, inter-professional groups are asked to articulate what value they ascribe for each of these elements. Thus, suggests Duggan, 'as the priorities of each stakeholder group become clearer, a collective set of priorities starts to emerge. This . . . enriches the range of issues included when discussing space needs' (Duggan 2011: 150).

In different ways, these tools mutually constitute *actions* and *activity* by locating particular, spatially focussed discussions within their institutional context and then opening up that context to the possibility of critique. Neary *et al.*'s (2010) *campus mapping profile*, for example, suggests that participants focus their attention on those aspects of spatial provision whose current provision most fails to realise the stated institutional vision; then *the idea of the university* examines the institution itself, inviting academic engagement with that vision.

Duggan's (2011) exposition of the E4V model deals more explicitly with the issue of how such mutual constitution might occur within particular discussions. Deploying an argument that parallels work on consensus-building as the object of the activity, above, Duggan (2011: 150) suggests that discussants are most likely to agree about conceptions of future-oriented visions, such as long-term views of education. For Duggan, by establishing early common ground regarding these general perspectives, it is hoped to buttress later discussions when more granular, divisive issues arise. It is suggested, for example, that particular discussants might be prepared to move from their original negotiating positions once they understand what others *need* in order to achieve those wider objectives that served as vehicles for earlier consensus.

This issue of consensus is a source of *contradiction*. While it is trivially obvious that attaining such consensus may be difficult in practice, it is also dubious whether this is a desirable outcome in principle. Duggan (2011: 148) suggests that systemic tensions between different views of institutional space are exacerbated when such space is seen as scarce. Yet, quite correctly, elements of the E4V model serve to draw attention *towards* this scarcity, such as when highlighting the concept of *efficiency* in space design. Neary *et al.* (2010: 35) explicitly recognise the need to recognise what they term 'Diversity, Difference and Dissensus'. It seems implied that striving for consensus is likely to produce either groupthink, insincere acquiescence or to be simply fruitless. I suggest that participating denizens might usefully spend time clarifying the nature of their dissensus; the work discussed in this section suggests useful mechanisms for locating the attendant expressions of opinion in their institutional context, and for better understanding and reshaping this institutional context as a product of academic traditions and activity.

Concluding Comments

The learning spaces literature commonly incites academics, students and others to become more involved in designing and creating spaces within universities. This chapter has conceptualised these people as *denizens*, a term intended to convey that their insight derives from their experiences *inhabiting* particular spaces rather than from theoretical or procedural expertise, and to call attention to their *partial* enfranchisement *vis-à-vis* institutional estates processes. Subsequently, a range of new methods from the learning spaces literature have been examined using the concept of *distributed agency*. Table 3.1 provides a summary of the issues that were uncovered by these analyses. Established institutional norms serve to constrain the ways in which denizens can contribute to the design of university spaces. Indeed, the opportunity for denizens to participate *at all* is frequently determined, strategically, by high-level committees. Leighton and Weber (1999), for example, provide an overview of the set of committees usually involved in the US, while Lewis (2010) discusses the strategic partnerships involved within a high-profile UK project. Furthermore, those denizens that do take up the opportunity to participate in 'faculty committees', 'design teams' or 'strategic partnerships' seem *set-up* to express parochial concerns, notwithstanding their own actual priorities, by the remit they are given and by the limited period of their involvement. In this chapter, I have drawn attention to examples of work that seek to ameliorate this situation.

Nonetheless, I suggest that one common (though not universal) limitation of attempts in the learning spaces literature to incubate *distributed agency* is that what are proposed are bounded activities that draw in denizens only in relation to particular projects. In other contexts, such as the design and production of new technologies, or in leisure industries, new kinds of collective agency are being enabled by forms of social production that transcend the limitations of more conventional institutional hierarchies and internal markets. It will not be possible here to sketch out detailed plans for such social production of spaces within particular institutions. Indeed, I suggest that this should become a focus of subsequent research. But I do wish to conclude the chapter by pointing out some elements of social production that are currently lacking.

Engeström (2008:196) uses the term *knotworking* to frame social production. The term describes a longitudinal process without a particular endpoint where the object of activity is repeatedly co-configured, and a variety of relationships (knots) are negotiated, formed and dissolved. Knotworking needs to be distinguished clearly from *networks* (i.e. webs of links between organisational units that become stable over time) (Engeström 2008: 208). Crucially, networks support the *co-ordination* of work and emphasise the designated *roles* of particular people, while knotworking involves *cooperation* centred upon *tasks*, and *self-reflective communication* (Engeström 2008: 197). Engeström identifies a range of features associated with knotworking and social production, and here I examine the most obvious gaps that exist between these features and how learning spaces are currently created within institutions.

Social production, suggests Engeström (2008), involves peer review and negotiation as a coordinating mechanism, in place of a central 'broker'. Furthermore, knotworking involves critiquing and negating existing wisdom

Table 3.1 Distributed agency found in new processes of learning space design.

Object-orientation	Historicity	Tool mediation	Mutual constitution of actions and activity	Contradictions
Consensus and ownership. Desired outcome: attaining stakeholder buy-in for unorthodox, flagship spaces.	Desire for greater user input into design processes seen as dominated by architectural and operational considerations. Stakeholder 'buy-in': to gain acceptance of unorthodox spaces and to incubate new ideas within the institution.	Trigger questions and flow diagram. Invite discourse about a space's life cycle stages and what relationships between space, technology and learning are proposed. Tools *broaden access* to design conversations and create *persistent documentation*.	Focus on developing a vision and then communicating it to those developing the design brief. Think critically about who is to develop the brief.	Institutions are driven to produce innovative spaces by market forces and a desire to adapt to new forms of learning; yet, unorthodox spaces are at risk of being perceived negatively (and provoking complaint). Desire to build a capacity to experiment.
Local experiences of space users. Desired outcome: articulating local experience to inform local design.	Environment seen as 'raw materials' for human experience; need to investigate relations between environment and inhabitants. Desire to maximise *design potential* through subtle insight.	Diagrammatic representation of a space model to guide interpretations of field observers. Actual spaces and *in situ* artefacts used to mediate the experience of the users who are observed.	Focus on understanding *localised* experiences and developing *site-specific* interventions. Gain experience for designers and iterate the methods themselves.	Experiences are unique to the individual and thus problematic for designers. 'Place' cannot be designed, but only *designed for*.
Institutional processes and spatial implications.	Desire to map out institutional processes in detail to understand their	Embodied mapping of processes (e.g. moving physical artefacts to	Analyse processes and examine their current boundaries.	Changing processes in response to demand or technology will reshape

Desired outcome: improving processes and mapping changing space requirements.	changing spatial implications. Perceived need to side-step the limitations of participants' 'common-sense' understanding of spatiality.	represent the 'flow' of a process). Producing written scenarios (both current and future) to stimulate discussion around processual change.	Link stories with timelines, decisions about priorities, and different scales of services provided within or outside the institution.	spatial provision. There is a tension between being responsive to process users while positioning some provision online or outside institutional provision.
Design briefs. Desired outcome: directly embedding experience of authentic learning into design.	Reaction against perceived historical separation of mind and body in space design. Desire to draw attention to the body in space, not distract from it.	Visual tools (e.g. conceptual 'what if' cards, images of learning spaces) to support playful engagement. Constructing representations of learning scenarios (e.g. 'activity-scapes').	Consider the relations of spaces to practices of authentic learning and so trigger wider speculation about how the practices learnt prepare students for their subsequent life.	Denizens can identify what does not work (i.e. instances where current spaces fail to support authentic practice) but are frequently unable to articulate alternatives for design.
Academic value in institutional identity. Desired outcome: critiquing the dialectical relationship between space provision, academic value and institutional identity.	Position spatial provision as realising institutional identity, rather than as (quantitatively) fulfilling user demands. Empower stakeholders to exert agency over the institution, including institutional identity and space management.	Research-derived frameworks designed to support inter-professional dialogue and reflection by particular stakeholders (e.g. academics). Tools for *in situ* analysis of campus provision and for synthesis of disparate data.	Locate spatial analysis within wider institutional vision statements. Critique the identity of the institution itself and open up the possibility of reimagining how it is realised through campus provision.	Consensus around high-level visions of institutional mission may not lead to agreement about spatial provision. Informed dissensus is valuable and should be documented.

and authority. There are no explicit membership criteria, but instead members can be 'identified by their activism' (Engeström 2008: 229). Institutional space production, on the other hand, typically involves a hierarchy of committees that each act as brokers for those at lower levels (Leighton and Weber 1999). The extent and form of denizens' participation is carefully managed. Notwithstanding that the insight of denizens is relevant because they inhabit particular spaces, their professional roles often determine what interest they are assumed to have in ongoing processes. For example, Bickford's (2002) discussion of estates 'design teams' assumes that stakeholders will have little inclination to participate beyond articulating their existing professional concerns. Estates departments act as particular brokers because of their ongoing responsibilities and expertise. For peer review and negotiation to regulate learning space creation, I suggest that more direct relationships will be required between the various denizens, between denizens and architects, and across the boundaries of estates departments. Rather than each participant focusing on their own fragment of the object, knotworking involves constant negotiation and rapid integration of expertise. It involves the construction of a *negotiated order* that allows different participants to pursue their intersecting activities. The range of different plans, including specific *pedagogical briefs* (Neuman 2003), being recommended in both the estates management and the learning spaces literature, seem to provide one platform for less inhibited, intersecting avenues of development to be pursued.

Importantly for social production, a range of particular, bounded activity systems operate within a wider 'substrate' that develops over a lengthy period of time. Engeström (2008: 228) uses the term *mycorrhizae* to describe this substrate, by analogy with fungal biology. The point is that a fungus is essentially an underground organism, potentially *very* large, that forms long-term symbiotic associations with other plants; the mushrooms that are visible above ground are merely reproductive structures activated under particular conditions (Engeström 2008: 228). Similarly, knotworking involves an element of 'latent organisation', an expanding bundle of developing connections within a durable structure that may nonetheless remain apparently dormant for periods of time until being activated.

By this analogy, the particular activities that I examine in this chapter would serve as mushrooms (i.e. definite structures pertinent to particular conditions). Such activities can serve as 'bridgeheads' for the underlying substrate; if they do not come to be formed, then it will eventually wither and die. But if such structures are not themselves supported by an underlying, latent organisation, then their very compartmentalisation is a significant obstacle.

I suggest that this mycorrhiza-like structure is lacking in relation to the topic of learning spaces in an overwhelming majority of institutions. Such a situation stands in contrast to those substrates that have developed to support other areas of common inquiry, such as the use of technology to support learning, where significant work often occurs across numerous sub-communities. A mycorrhiza structure for learning spaces would *generate* particular activities as appropriate – perhaps related to institutional values, the support of processes, the creation of design briefs and the understanding of user experiences. It might also perhaps undertake collective political lobbying in favour of particular projects. Within the structure, it would not be necessary for *everyone* to collaborate with *everyone else*; instead, different hubs of activity would emerge for periods of time, connected to other hubs and particular people by ongoing, negotiated relationships (Engeström 2008: 212).

It should be clear from this description that social production would involve people changing and developing through their involvement. Existing procedural norms assume that this is unlikely, and thus focus on constrained participation based on existing, professionalised interests; for a list of such assumed 'interests', see Bickford (2002: 47). I suggest that such an assumption needs to be challenged and the associated structures overcome in practice. Furthermore, social production would involve change not merely of people, but also of the object of collective activity. In social production, as ongoing developments in the mycorrhiza create tools and organisations that generate unintended consequences, so it becomes necessary for the object to be iteratively renegotiated. The result is a *runaway object* of activity (Engeström 2008: 202). At present, particular infrastructures of planning are constructed in particular project *programming* phases (Lauber 2003); here, again, social production poses a distinct challenge to the *status quo*.

Moving to a social production model would also challenge the boundaries that underpin existing infrastructures. I have already mentioned the desirability of enabling new relationships across particular boundaries, such as those of estates departments, but it needs to be understood that social production invites trajectories of working that pass across the boundaries of institutions themselves. This would involve cooperation and self-reflective communication between individuals in different institutions. Such a situation would invite significant and useful contributions from the nascent academic community investigating the issue of learning spaces, of which this book serves as one particular outlet.

Note

1   To avoid confusion with the use of terms elsewhere in this chapter, it should be emphasised that Quintana (2012) defines a number of concepts within *process space analysis* (such as *activity*, *artifacts* and *objects*) in ways that are not synonymous with how the same terms are understood within activity theory. Indeed, Quintana explicitly acknowledges that he is not adhering to activity theory definitions (p. 2).

56 · Brett Bligh

References

Bickford, D. (2002) 'Navigating the white waters of collaborative work in shaping learning environments', *New Directions for Teaching and Learning*, 92, 43–52.

Bligh, B. and Crook, C. (in press) 'Learning spaces: departure points for a spatial turn in technology enhanced learning', in E. Duval, M. Sharples and R. Sutherland (eds), *A Reader in Technology-Enhanced Learning*, Berlin: Springer.

Bligh, B. and Pearshouse, I. (2011) 'Doing learning space evaluations', in A. Boddington and J. Boys (eds), *Re-shaping Learning: A Critical Reader – the Future of Learning Spaces in Post-Compulsory Education*, Rotterdam: Sense Publishers, pp. 3–18.

Boys, J. (2011) *Towards Creative Learning Spaces: Re-thinking the Architecture of Post-Compulsory Education*, London and New York: Routledge.

Ciolfi, L. and Bannon, L. (2005) 'Space, place and the design of technologically-enhanced physical environments', in P. Turner and E. Davenport (eds), *Spaces, Spatiality and Technology*, Dordrecht: Springer, pp. 217–32.

Crook, C. and Mitchell, G. (2012) 'Ambience in social learning: student engagement with new designs for learning spaces', *Cambridge Journal of Education*, 42(2), 121–39.

Duggan, F. (2011) 'Some models for re-shaping learning spaces', in A. Boddington and J. Boys (eds), *Re-shaping Learning: A Critical Reader – the Future of Learning Spaces in Post-Compulsory Education*, Rotterdam: Sense Publishers, pp. 147–54.

Engeström, Y. (1987) *Learning by Expanding: An Activity-Theoretical Approach to Developmental Research*, Helsinki: Orienta-Konsultit Oy.

Engeström, Y. (2008) *From Teams to Knots: Activity-Theoretical Studies of Collaboration and Learning at Work*, Cambridge and New York: Cambridge University Press.

Jamieson, P., Taylor, P., Fisher, K., Trevitt, A. and Gilding, T. (2000) 'Place and space in the design of new learning environments', *Higher Education Research and Development*, 19(2), 221–36.

Lauber, M. (2003) 'Science teaching and research facilities', in D. Neuman (ed.), *Building Type Basics for College and University Facilities*, Hoboken, NJ: John Wiley & Sons, pp. 121–60.

Leighton, P. and Weber, D. (1999) *Planning Academic and Research Library Buildings, Third Edition*, Chicago, IL and London: American Library Association.

Lewis, M. (2010) 'The University of Sheffield library information commons: a case study', *Journal of Library Administration*, 50(2), 161–78.

Melhuish, C. (2011) 'Methods for understanding the relationships between learning and space', in A. Boddington and J. Boys (eds), *Re-shaping Learning: A Critical Reader – the Future of Learning Spaces in Post-Compulsory Education*, Rotterdam: Sense Publishers, pp. 19–32.

Neary, M., Harrison, A., Crellin, G., Parekh, N., Saunders, G., Duggan, F., Williams, S. and Austin, S. (2010) *Learning Landscapes in Higher Education*, Lincoln: Centre for Educational Research and Development.

Neuman, D. (2003) 'Campus planning', in D. Neuman (ed.), *Building Type Basics for College and University Facilities*, Hoboken, NJ: John Wiley & Sons, pp. 1–44.

Quintana, C. (2012) 'Reflections on the use of HCI methods for the design of learning spaces', *Ar-CHI-tecture: Architecture and Interaction Workshop, ACM SIGCHI Conference on Human Factors in Computing Systems*, Austin, Texas, 5–10 May.

Radcliffe, D. (2008) 'A pedagogy-space-technology (PST) framework for designing and evaluating learning places', in D. Radcliffe, H. Wilson, D. Powell and B. Tibbetts (eds), *Learning Spaces in Higher Education: Positive Outcomes by Design*, St. Lucia: University of Queensland, pp. 9–16.

Reushle, S. (2012) 'Designing and evaluating learning spaces: PaSsPorT and design-based research', in M. Keppell, K. Souter and M. Riddle (eds), *Physical and Virtual Learning Spaces in Higher Education: Concepts for the Modern Learning Environment*, Hershey, PA: IGI Global, pp. 87–101.

Sherringham, S. and Stewart, S. (2011) 'Fragile constructions: processes for reshaping learning spaces', in A. Boddington and J. Boys (eds), *Re-shaping Learning: A Critical Reader – the Future of Learning Spaces in Post-Compulsory Education*, Rotterdam: Sense Publishers, pp. 105–18.

Temple, P. (2008) 'Learning spaces in higher education: an under-researched topic', *London Review of Education*, 6(3), 229–41.

Woolner, P. (2010) *The Design of Learning Spaces*, London and New York: Continuum International Publishing Group.

4

Managing the Campus

Facility Management and Design, the Student Experience and University Effectiveness

ALEXI MARMOT

Context: Higher Education Estates, Space and Architecture

For almost 1,000 years, universities have existed as physical entities. The oldest universities – Bologna (founded in 1088), Paris, Oxford and other ancient foundations – still thrive today, arguably part of the most persistent global growth industry ever known. By the beginning of the twentieth century, universities taught about half a million students worldwide, a figure that had multiplied 200 times by the year 2000, though the global population had only quadrupled within the same period. Within the next decade, student numbers grew by half again to 150 million students (Kamenetz 2010: vii). The poorest nations in Africa now have a participation rate equal to that enjoyed by the UK in the 1960s, around 5 per cent of the typical university student age group (IFS 2010).

The endurance of the impressive physical estate of the oldest universities, still preserved and used daily, is now being questioned. Lawrence Summers, former president of the first North American university, Harvard, founded in 1636, states: 'The solid classical buildings of great universities may look permanent but the storms of change threaten them' (Barber *et al.* 2013: 1). The arguments put forward by Barber and colleagues for rethinking universities include the continuing need for spreading mass education, the cost challenge, increasing penetration of teaching technologies that can foster remote learning, and the globalisation of universities.

This chapter focuses on the endurance of place-based learning as an important component of global higher education. Focusing mainly on the UK, it examines the size, scale and spatial qualities of educational estates, and their management. It discusses the role of the university estate in enhancing or lowering the student experience, the staff experience and effective learning, and puts forward the case for more evidence-based and consultative approaches to the creation, management and operation of university estates.

Higher education establishments, located in many cities around the world, comprise a vast estate. In the UK alone, university buildings, excluding student residential accommodation, account for 27 million square metres (280 million square feet) gross internal area, are valued at £61 billion (US$90 billion) and account for an average annual operating budget of 9–11 per cent of university income (HEFCE 2011: 46, 48). UK university space is becoming relatively less generous per person as the pace of its estate expansion has lagged behind growth in student numbers. In practice, this means that the median space per person (students and staff FTE) has dropped from 9.6 to 8.8 square metres (103 to 95 square feet) net internal area per person FTE (HEFCE 2011: 14). Space norms, the suggested amount of space per student in different disciplines, have reduced considerably over the past few decades in response to more efficient space use and different delivery of academic activities, although it is noted that the space per person in academic offices has stayed constant or possibly increased (HEFCE 2006: 3, 12; HEFCE 2011: 15). Financial pressures drive university managers to seek efficiencies in the cost of their estates, which, in turn, often results in pressure to work space harder – 'sweat the asset' – and a reduction in space quantum per person. Effective means of achieving this are described later in this chapter.

The 'edifice complex' is demonstrated in many universities. This commonly takes two forms. The first is investment in iconic new buildings intended to transform some aspect of the student experience or research frontiers, while acting as a marketing image. Iconic new buildings can be found on most campuses, often designed by world-renowned architects – 'starchitects' – drawing attention to themselves and to the university by their audacious shapes, structure, colour and materials (Borden 2008). UK examples include Daniel Leibeskind's London Metropolitan University's Graduate Centre of sloping forms defying normal horizontality; Will Alsop's Blizard Building at St Mary's University, whose brilliantly coloured sculptural meeting hubs arise from a vast sea of laboratory benches; Schmidt Hammer Lassen's Library at Aberdeen University, towering like a grand, striped cathedral dwarfing the city below; and Lord Foster's Law Faculty building at Cambridge University, belittling James Stirling's adjacent History Faculty building that was an architectural sensation three decades earlier. Further afield are Frank Gehry's chaotically modulated, 'highly reticulated' Stata Centre at MIT (Mitchell 2007: 75) and 'scrunched up brown bags' Business School at the University of Technology, Sydney; Will Alsop's 'flying tabletop' in Toronto, otherwise known as the Centre for Design at the Ontario College of Art and Design University; and Sanaa's Rolex library in the Ecole Polytechnique Fédérale de Lausanne, whose rolling white form draws attention not only to the university, but to the patron. In nations where the university sector is expanding, starchitect-studded campuses may be found, for example, in the Masdar Institute in Abu Dhabi,

United Arab Emirates, where Foster and Partners' innovative designs respond to the climate. Regeneration of a whole conurbation or region is sometimes celebrated through the design of an iconic facility on a highly visible site, such as the proposed designs by Skidmore Owings and Merrill for Cornell-Technion on Roosevelt Island in New York harbour to develop New York City's innovation in computer science and engineering. London's Imperial College has similar ambitions in the proposed £1 billion investment in Imperial West at White City, as a research translation and commercialization hub (THE 2013).

The second form of edifice complex deploys buildings as a power base for their inhabitants. Naming a structure as the Biology or Chemistry or Engineering Building is an invitation for those within that discipline never to decamp, whether or not the subject has grown or shrunk, or evolved new spatial needs. Naming buildings after donors is another invitation for academics to remain there, immune to external change, citing the terms of the bequest.

The Effect Of Estates on the Student Experience and University Effectiveness

The physical infrastructure of universities can affect students and university effectiveness in several ways, both directly and indirectly. Adopting a view of the student experience across five stages – decision to study; transition to study; while studying; transition from studies; alumnus – it becomes apparent that the physical environment can mainly affect the first three stages; however, it should be noted that in the fifth stage, universities in the US may create large sports stadia to strengthen alumni allegiance to the university.

Starting with the first stage of selecting a university, evidence indicates that location is an important factor, whether it be choosing a university close to the student's home to eliminate the need to find and fund residential accommodation, or pay out-of-state or international fees, or choosing a university in a city deemed attractive to students, especially for its social and night life. The quality of the university buildings and environment shown on open days, in brochures and as virtual tours on websites appears to be of little significance to university choice, compared to other factors, notably subject choice, general reputation and ranking. This calls into question the oft-cited value of investing in iconic buildings in order to attract students.

During the second stage of preparing for and arrival at a new university, the most important spatial qualities are likely to be feeling welcome and 'at home' in student residences, and in the academic environment. A building that acts as a home base, access to a common room or social study space in which students within the same discipline can meet, work together and chat to staff, plus union facilities, coffee shops and cafeterias, help to create the social learning environment that is greatly appreciated by students. These same spatial solutions also improve the student experience while studying, when the impact of physical space is potentially highly significant in providing students with effective places in which to live, learn, and engage with staff and students.

How do facilities influence student evaluations of their educational experience? The National Student Survey, sent to all UK final-year undergraduates, seeks views on aspects of learning resources: 'The library resources and services are good enough for my needs'; 'I have been able to access general IT resources when I needed to'; 'I have been able to access specialised equipment, facilities, or rooms when I needed to'. In fact, UK undergraduates generally rate their learning resources highly, with 82 per cent definitely or mostly satisfied in 2012 (HEFCE 2012a). Interestingly, it is staff rather than students who are generally more critical of university physical space (CABE 2005). Perhaps this is not surprising, given that staff generally spend more time on university premises than do students – more hours per week, more weeks per year, across many more years.

To reflect on the impact of built space on university effectiveness requires a framework for conceptualising effectiveness. Inputs and outputs are a useful structure. Inputs are typically described by metrics such as the quantity and cost of space, its resource use, allocation and utilisation. University administrators and estates departments are usually concerned to reduce space and its associated cost as far as possible, while supporting the core business of teaching, research and real-world impact, together with financial sustainability. Research excellence is measured in different ways around the world through metrics such as the percentage of high-quality publications by academic staff, prizes and impact of their work. The core business of teaching and learning can, in turn, be measured by diverse metrics, including the ratio of applicants to students accepted on each course, prerequisite grades for acceptance of applicants, student attendance, progression and pass rates, employment and income after studies, and the students' own evaluation of their studies. In the UK, these concepts have been developed into Key Information Sets that are made available widely to prospective students to aid their selection of subject and university (HEFCE 2012b).

However, research that finds a clear connection between the physical estate and university effectiveness on these metrics is rare, given the complexity of factors bearing on learning outcomes. Staff themselves, their own modes of pedagogy, their means of communicating with students and encouraging and evaluating student work, are probably the most important factor. However, they may be affected, in part, by the physical environment in which they work and teach. The 'affordances' of space, that is, the modes of acting that are encouraged or inhibited by spatial and infrastructure provision, are important

(Gibson 1977). An academic staff member who wishes to introduce group work into a teaching session that includes online references can do so only if the arrangement of rooms, furniture and data infrastructure permits or 'affords' that possibility. Similarly, a prospective new academic staff member requiring specialised research and teaching laboratories will only accept a job if those facilities are also offered.

Achieving Effective Design and Management

Whatever the link between built facilities, student experience and university effectiveness, it is imperative that built environment professions operating within the university sector know how to design buildings well, deliver them efficiently and manage them through the lifetime of the facility. The following sections draw largely on the author's observations as an academic, and from many years directing an evidence-based architectural consultancy whose clients number scores of universities seeking more effective organisation and management of their space assets.

The professions involved are numerous. They include surveyors, estate managers, architects, planners, interior designers, facility managers, and project and construction managers. Guidance on the design, management and efficiency of new learning spaces suggests the importance of linking learning space design to different forms of pedagogy, using a variety of technologies, and incorporating flexibility, among other attributes (AMA 2006; HEFCE 2006; JISC 2006). Post-occupancy studies have documented common problems in school, college and university buildings, such as poor air quality and limited control over the internal environment; bland colours; narrow corridors; limited external landscape and structures; inadequate space and storage; inflexible, small assembly halls; poor management and cleanliness of toilets; and carbon emissions at least twice the predicted level. Positive features include involving users in briefing; wide corridors; durable finishes and comfortable furniture; accessible staff rooms; good security systems; flexible dining areas; external landscaping and structures; and privacy in changing rooms and toilets (Gupta and Chandiwala 2007; Mumovic et al. 2008; PWC 2010).

Laudable processes have been established in the UK in order to ensure lessons are learnt at several key stages in the building performance cycle to inform other building projects. University buildings are recommended to deploy the HEDQF (Higher Education Design Quality Forum) tool or the AUDE (Association of University Directors of Estates) post-occupancy toolkit to encourage the creation of buildings that meet or exceed user expectations, contribute to the immediate surroundings, promote a sense of community and social interaction, are economic to maintain and run, future-proofed, environmentally appropriate, provide value for money, and are constructed on time and within budget (AUDE 2006; HEDQF n.d.). All educational buildings are encouraged to use the BREEAM Education tool to ensure they are environmentally sound, or BREEAM In-Use or BREEAM Refurbishment. Yet, practice reveals that prediction of energy efficiency and carbon emissions can bear little resemblance to actual results of building performance. CarbonBuzz data, as noted in Ucci's chapter here, demonstrates that university educational buildings, on average, emit almost three times more carbon than predicted (28.1 predicted compared to 80.0 actual kg $CO_2/m^2/year$; CarbonBuzz 2013).

A serious challenge in running an effective physical estate is the achievement of joined-up design and delivery. Many parties are involved in creating and managing effective facilities and resources. Strategic decisions on estate and infrastructure growth and change normally involve the highest level of board or governing body, university chief executive, senior administrators (especially those involved in finance) and academic staff. Ongoing allocation and management of space involves deans and academics requesting space, and a common perception is that the right space, with the right equipment and technical underpinnings, is either not available at all or is not allocated to them. Meanwhile, estate professionals and facility managers often perceive academic staff as *prima donnas* demanding unreasonable or unavailable resources. Coordination of the different parties responsible for design and delivery of space – room bookings, information technology, audiovisual and media departments, e-learning technologists, estates and facilities professionals – is frequently not achieved. This results in the underperformance of rooms, negatively affecting learning. For example, room allocations are often made before enrolments are known, so some are too small for the students who eventually show up. Light fittings may be placed so that they wash out data projected on to screens – the result of lack of coordination between academics, designers, electricians and audiovisual teams. While new academic staff are required to undergo formal training on teaching and learning, educational theory and techniques, such training usually omits conscious attention to the way in which physical space, furniture and spatial layouts, technology, lighting, and atmosphere may affect the overall educational ambience and communication between teachers and students.

Upon entering a teaching space that has just been vacated by another group, academic staff are usually under time pressure to set up the space spatially and technically to deliver the session they have planned. Unsurprisingly, they experience stress on finding that IT consoles that control computer feeds, data projectors, loudspeakers – and sometimes also blinds, lights and air conditioning – vary across the campus and have non-intuitive controls. Some teaching rooms have devices such as personal voter response systems or lecture recording facilities already installed, while others require portable systems to be brought in by the teacher, yet room booking systems do not always record the latest technology installed in the rooms, or describe the possible flexibility of room layouts and the ensuing seat capacity. While these problems are most acute at the start of a term, in fact they are indicative of the need for careful integration of different systems in order to provide effective classroom experiences for both students and staff.

Facility management teams within universities are responsible for the operational underpinnings of the physical institution. Along with information technology teams, their work is fundamental in ensuring that staff and students are able to do what they need to throughout the day. When facilities fail to work, for example when there is a power cut, or a flood, or lifts fail to function, the university may be unable to operate at all. Positively run facilities are rarely noticed, but complaints accumulate as soon as anything fails. In the past, a typical way of saving costs in universities was to cut the frequency and thoroughness of cleaning and decorations; however, it is now understood that such savings reduce the staff and student experience of the university.

Facility management (FM) is commonly one activity within estates departments. New building projects or major refurbishments, which take several months or years in preparation and construction, are delivered to the facility management team for ongoing operations. The FM team's remit typically covers room bookings and allocation, security, cleaning, recycling, catering, moves, portering, repairs, maintenance and minor works, and may also include landscape maintenance, vehicle parking, green travel plans, engineering services such as power supply, heating and cooling, and environmental sustainability. Resilience planning for business continuity, for example in laboratories for which continuous power is imperative, is usually an activity for which the facility team is responsible, along with laboratory managers. The precise locus of, and responsibility for, services such as information technology, data networks, telephony, audiovisual and videoconference equipment varies in different universities between IT departments, library services, FM and estates.

Facility management in universities follows global industrial trends and is today increasingly outsourced to companies responsible for delivering either a unique service such as move management, or several services such as catering, security and cleaning. Pressure is now on for more customer-focused FM operations for universities in the future.

Design and Management of Key Spatial Types

Radical change to place-based universities at a time of demographic, financial and technological change manifests itself in essential changes to the main functional spaces of universities.

The library is often conceived as the intellectual heart of the university, where knowledge and information are held. Historically, both university chapel and library were the buildings on which most design attention was lavished. From the nineteenth century, the library has dominated, and is often in the spatial centre, or is the most prominent edifice, within the university complex. The rise of digital media over the past two decades has altered dramatically the role of university libraries from hard copy depository and reference point, to internet-flooded gateways for digital and physical information. Virtual users of the university collection now typically dominate the volume of users who are present in body. In the process, silent solo spaces in which to work, where food and drink were prohibited, have now been supplanted by social learning spaces where food and drink are permitted, where students can undertake individual or group work. Floorspace now freed of rarely accessed books and journals that have been relegated to remote storage has been converted to a wide variety of study environments accommodating more students working in different ways, using their own or university PCs, reading or listening to music, watching videos, or creating multimedia content. A typical vision for change is described, for example, in Southampton University's library project (Brown and Wake 2009: 104). Research on student percep-tions of university buildings regularly reveals that the most appreciated spaces are the library, ranked far above the rest of the teaching and learning spaces and above many social spaces. As the public library has been conceived as the 'urban living room', so the university library can be reimagined as the 'university living room'. In some instances, it is also part exhibition space, a showcase for student work and university artefacts and gifts, displayed for students and the general public.

Generic teaching/learning rooms include lecture theatres and classrooms in which students are gathered to learn from the 'sage on the stage'. Traditionally, these spaces have followed the ecclesiastical format of rows of seats all pointed to the front where the teacher stands using different devices, from voice alone, to white or blackboard, data projection, film and sound recording or conducting scientific experimentation at the front bench. The standard traditional session relied on delivery of material followed by a short period of questions and answers. While this approach to teaching has many strengths, it is increasingly being adapted from a reflective mode to more active learning. Lecturers who are 'flipping the classroom' expect students to have reviewed their 'lecture' online in advance, and to have arrived primed with questions and ready to test and debate the new material. This demands a changed layout: instead of all eyes to the front focused on the lecturer, it requires everyone to be potentially seen and heard by all other students, as well as the lecturer. The lecturer becomes the 'guide by the side', wandering around the room ready to interact with students who themselves work alone or in groups on the material already absorbed. The business school case study form of pedagogy similarly demands all to see all, resulting in curved, horseshoe layouts. Another variant is the bimodal session in which the learning mode shifts between sage-on-the-stage to active group work by students, aided by the roving lecturer. Furniture solutions require seats that can face forward or to the group, with suitable tables. Raked floors in large lecture theatres pose a challenge in creating the two modes. The technical infrastructure in these generic lecture and teaching rooms increasingly needs to support wireless internet access, power supply to recharge multiple devices simultaneously, and the ability for any screen to be shown to part or all of the learning group.

Specialised teaching/learning rooms for active learning include spaces such as teaching laboratories, immersive environments, studios and workshops, whose designs constantly chase the latest technical developments in the discipline. Digital technologies and automation are common changes that affect the necessary equipment and layout. Engineering and architectural workshops, for example, have increasingly seen structural, fire, thermal, lighting and wind testing laboratories give way to computerised digital simulation models, while chemical laboratories have automated testing machines to detect different compounds. Messy wood, metal and plastic workshops in art and design disciplines are becoming less popular compared to pristine workshops of 3D printers and laser cutters, while darkrooms become redundant as silver photography is eclipsed by digital. In some disciplines, though, little has changed. Music students still need practice and performance rooms for traditional instruments and voice, in parallel with the rise of digital instruments and composition. Fashion and textile students still need to weave and knit, sew and steam, while drama and dance students still deploy their bodies and fine motor skills to develop their creativity.

Research and innovation laboratories for scientific, medical and applied disciplines, such as engineering, are usually the most technically complex and expensive facilities within universities. Normally requiring a high standard of controlled indoor conditions such as no vibrations, external noise, or light, or a small variation in external temperature, they are expensive to build and expensive to operate as they often need to be in peak operational condition 24 hours a day, year-round, and may demand generators for backup power. Yet, without such investments, scientific and technical research cannot progress, and new academic talent cannot be attracted – indeed, negotiations on new staff appointments may be conditional on investment in research laboratories. The relationship between laboratories and write-up spaces for researchers is critical, with the desire for proximity to the bench needing to be balanced by the need for separation for safety reasons. As universities increasingly seek strong links to industry, new incubator and innovation laboratories shared between the parties are being shaped, particularly in biotechnology, nano-technology, computer science and pharmaceutical fields.

Staff workplaces, together with spaces for *meetings and tutorials* are on the tipping point of significant change. For several decades, office workspaces throughout the economy have become denser and more open-plan in response to economic pressure, the desire for more collaborative work, and the underuse of office workspaces as an increasingly mobile and flexible workforce deploys technology for 'anywhere, anytime' working. While these same pressures affect working practices within universities, the tradition of the academic thinker working alone in (usually) his or her book-lined solo office still survives in many institutions. Despite administrative pressure for space efficiency, with cost and carbon savings, many academics believe that they are unable to concentrate on their work, meet colleagues or hold student tutorials without their own four walls. They fear that information will be lost if storage space for books and hard-copy papers is reduced, even though most is now 'born digital'. They fear that a move towards shared offices or open-plan working will negatively affect their own output, limit the possibility of attracting high-quality new staff, and create barriers to meeting students informally as meeting spaces would need to be found.

Solutions to the fear of change include the concept of 'activity-based working', in which staff see students and colleagues by moving from their desk in a shared or open-plan room to a meeting room, tutorial room, or to a coffee/social zone. To help with this, staff need to take reference materials with them easily, either on a laptop or tablet, or by logging on to a monitor.

Social spaces, including coffee areas, cafeterias, student unions and atria, have undergone a recent revolution in their specification and use. Once used only for food and recreation, they have become a form of social learning space, almost indistinguishable from libraries and common rooms. Even sports facilities usually have a coffee/work/social learning area, while wide corridors in any building are made to multitask as internet access points and social learning places through the provision of wireless broadband, computer terminals, benches and seating. Coffee shops in the vicinity of a university are also used in this manner, where the price of a cup of coffee is expected to come with the right to do several hours of work alone or in a group, using free wireless broadband and free power to charge mobile devices. Special social events celebrating induction, end of term, end of exams or graduation are held in places that are specially adapted, decorated and lit for the occasion, making them stand out from their normal use.

Residential accommodation provided by universities is increasingly available for only a small proportion of students in the UK, usually limited to first-year undergraduates and international students. The rest find accommodation either by remaining in their family home or renting on the open market. The real estate industry perceives university residential accommodation as a safe investment yielding steady, long-term returns, hence attracting private investors who take responsibility for building and managing university accommodation, leaving universities to raise capital for investment in academic space. Standard new student accommodation normally includes an en suite shower and WC, and a compact study bedroom, within a cluster of about five to 15 student rooms sharing a communal kitchen. A building with several hundred students may provide some social living and learning space in addition, and have wardens on hand to arrange social events and help in case of difficulties.

Residential space is important to the student experience, acting as the locus for much of their time, including learning time. Studies reveal that students can spend almost as much waking time working in their study/bedrooms as being on location at the university.

Balance areas are additional to the spaces for specific uses described above. Universities have a considerable area devoted to essential infrastructure and operations, including computer servers, plant rooms, workshops, garages for vehicles, stores, kitchens, refuse areas, WCs, lifts, lobbies and corridors. Such spaces typically comprise around 40 per cent of the total built area of universities. Artful designers and estate managers seek to minimise the floor area necessary for such purposes and maximise the use made of such spaces.

Integrating Campus Design and Management with Future Learning

The challenge for higher education bodies in the coming decades, when the spatial-virtual educational choice and different modes of pedagogy are battling for supremacy, is to provide excellent campuses that support staff and students in place-based learning, while also acting as the hub for research, innovation and virtual learning, including resilient provision for server farms either on their own estates or in the cloud (Eyring 2011: 287). Universities that plan to grow their face-to-face student body need strategies to invest in extra accommodation by expansion on their existing land, acquisition of new sites and buildings, leasing space from other educational bodies, and regularly refurbishing the existing stock to adapt to new demands. An estate strategy of planning at once for growth, decline and change in an uncertain market is common within the commercial world, from which universities can learn many lessons.

Estate strategies that are particular to higher education are the need to integrate spatial planning, design and management with teaching and learning strategies, audiovisual and information technology, selection of equipment, furniture, and accessories and signage, especially with the academic aspirations of each faculty. All stakeholders discussed above need to be involved at some stage in suggesting the right environment and then be informed about how the campus infrastructure has actually been provided and how it can be used to meet their needs. Time and budget for change management and communication activities to inform the academic community of new provision need to be factored into investment in capital works, new IT and AV.

Estate departments need to keep track of their assets, with readily available data on the quantity and quality of each space, how well it is utilised across the day, week and year, its condition, and how energy, waste and water are managed. Room databases, computer-aided facility management systems and building information modelling tools (CAFM and BIM) can be helpful in this endeavour, as can regular surveys to match the use of space with its booked or theoretical capacity. Equipment inventories matched to location can also be tracked with these tools. Even campuses where staff perceive they have insufficient space are often found to contain significant amounts of empty or underused teaching, research, office and social learning space, even during the peak of academic terms or semesters. To aid fair space allocation between competing demands, estate and facility managers find that clear policies on space standards and estate decision-making processes are a bonus. To ensure that the right space is provided, and well-operated, essential tools are 'space data sheets', developed as a collaborative effort by estates and design teams, academics and students, to agree and record the intended range of functions within every spatial type. On that basis, carefully designed aesthetic and technical solutions can be found to ensure that the spaces deliver the appropriate environment to meet institutional expectations. Such space data sheets typically describe necessary features such as AV and IT equipment, power and data requirements, signage, furniture and accessories, the internal environmental conditions (air quality, temperature, lighting, acoustic levels, and their control), hours of opening, required security, plus any special requirements such as gas, water pressure, or other provision in laboratories. The best space data sheets also describe the atmosphere and quality of the spaces, the various manners in which they are likely to be used, and the desired flexibility of layout, furniture and technical infrastructure. For example, rooms used for formal 'talk and chalk' classes may also be required as group work spaces, interactive 'brainstorm' rooms, formal meeting rooms, or to house social events. Moveable furniture, adaptive lighting and pervasive wireless connectivity are some of the small-scale features that will enable or discourage such varied activities. Student classrooms may be rented out for conference activity at night, weekends or during term breaks – but that may demand a higher than normal standard of finish, management and cleanliness. Evidence points to the crucial importance of small-scale items in affecting user experiences within buildings. Colour, texture, views, light, acoustics, temperature and air quality, and a decent level of cleaning strongly influence satisfaction with different places. Ergonomic seating and tables, storage including lockers and a place to leave coats, equipment such as data screens displaying the range of events that are available, university news, and where library spaces are free convert higher education spaces into the places in which excellent student experiences can take place and university effectiveness can be enhanced.

References

AMA (Alexi Marmot Associates) (2006) *Spaces for Learning: A Review of Learning Spaces in Further and Higher Education*, Edinburgh: Scottish Funding Council (SFC).

AUDE (2006) *Guide to Post-Occupancy Evaluation*, Bristol: Higher Education Funding Council for England, available at: www.architecture.com/Files/RIBAHoldings/PolicyAndInternationalRelations/ClientForums/Higher/PostOccupancyReviewOfBuildings/brochure.pdf (accessed 10 July 2013).

Barber, M., Donnelly, K. and Rizvi, S. (2013) *An Avalanche is Coming*, London: IPPR.

Borden, I. (2008) 'Universities tempt students with radical architecture', available at: www.guardian.co.uk/education/2008/may/30/highereducation.uk (accessed 22 June 2013).

Brown, M. and Wake, R. (2009) 'Hartey Library, University of Southampton: from accretion to integration, 2002–2007', in M. Dewe (ed.), *Renewing our Libraries: Case Studies in Planning and Refurbishment*, Farnham: Ashgate.

CarbonBuzz (2013) 'CarbonBuzz', available at: www.carbonbuzz.org/index.jsp#performancegap (accessed 16 June 2013).

CABE (Commission for Architecture and the Built Environment) (2005) *Design with Distinction: The Value of Good Building Design in Higher Education*, London: CABE.

Eyring, H. (2011) *The Innovative University*, San Francisco, CA: Jossey-Bass.

Gibson, J. J. (1977) 'The theory of affordances', in R. Shaw and S. Bransford (eds), *Perceiving, Acting and Knowing*, New York: Wiley.

Gupta, R. and Chandiwala, A. (2007) *Case Study of an FE College: Merton College*, Oxford: Oxford Institute for Sustainable Development.

HEFCE (2006) *Space Management Group, Review of Space Norms*, Bristol: HEFCE.

HEFCE (2011) *Performance in Higher Education Estates*, EMS Annual Report 2010, Bristol: HEFCE.

HEFCE (2012a) 'Highest ever satisfaction rates in 2012 student survey', 27 September 2012, available at: www.hefce.ac.uk/news/newsarchive/2012/name,75522,en.html (accessed 16 June 2013).

HEFCE (2012b) 'Key information sets', available at: www.hefce.ac.uk/whatwedo/lt/publicinfo/kis/ (accessed 10 July 2013).

IFS (Institute for Fiscal Studies) (2010) *Widening Participation in Higher Education: Analyses Using Linked Administrative Data*, London: IFS.

JISC (Joint Infrastructure Committee Development Group) (2006) *Designing Spaces for Effective Learning: 21st Century Learning Space Design*, Bristol: JISC.

Kamenetz, A. (2010) *DIY U*, White River Junction, VT: Chelsea Green.

Mitchell, W. J. (2007) *Imagining MIT: Designing a Campus for the Twenty-First Century*, Cambridge, MA: MIT Press.

Mumovic, D. *et al.* (2008) 'Winter indoor air quality, thermal comfort and acoustic performance of newly built secondary schools in England', *Building and Environment*, 44(7), 1466–77.

PWC (PricewaterhouseCoopers) (2010) *Evaluation of Building Schools for the Future: 2nd and 3rd Annual Report*, London: PricewaterhouseCoopers for Department for Children, Schools and Families.

THE (Times Higher Education) (2013) 'Imperial College London's new £1bn campus', available at: www.timeshighereducation.co.uk/news/imperial-college-londons-new-1bn-campus/2002304.article (accessed 7 July 2013).

5

Reading Campus Landscapes

PHILLIP WAITE

> To each of us you reveal yourself differently:
> to the ship as coastline, to the shore as ship.
>
> (Rainer Maria Rilke)

This chapter will explore how the landscape of the university or college campus is perceived, read and used by students, faculty and staff. Campus landscapes are the connective tissue that holds together the disparate parts and spaces of a campus. Throughout this chapter, when using the term 'campus landscapes', 'campus environment' or just 'campus', I am referring to all of the physical space of campus outside the walls of its buildings. By these terms, I mean to include the physical appearance of the buildings without specifying their interiors. Thus, by these terms, I am including all of the interstitial connective spaces between buildings that include typical 'softscape' elements such as turf and plantings of trees, shrubs and ground covers, as well as 'hardscape' elements such as sidewalks, parking areas and other paved spaces such as patios and courtyards with their accompanying site fixtures. In his landmark essay 'On campus-making in America', Stefanos Polyzoides identifies five landscape spatial types that define the American campus. These are: patio, courtyard, quadrangle, lawn and field (Ojeda *et al.* 1997). Each includes varying degrees of softscape and hardscape, but all are outside of buildings. The full impact of the landscape is often realized in unconscious ways below the threshold of our awareness and is thus hard to quantify. But this interstitial space of the landscape plays a multifactorial role in the recruitment of students, faculty, and other staff, as well as crucial roles in student engagement, retention, and student learning.

The physical environment that is the university or college campus has many roles in the educational enterprise. First, we know the 'physical features of a campus can either hinder or promote learning' (Strange 2001: 31). We know from studies on other mammals that brain growth – the actual dynamics of neural growth and connections in the brain – is stimulated by enriched environments and hindered by dull environments (Howard 2006: 522). We know that there are two periods when dendritic bloom (i.e. the period when explosive brain growth and neural connections occurs both rapidly and extensively) is greatest in the human brain: the first time in a child between the ages of birth and about 6, and the second time in a teenager's brain between the ages of about 14 and 21 – some even place the point of brain maturity as late as the age of 25 (Howard 2006: 94). In the environments of younger children such as nurseries, daycares, and kindergarten rooms, there are always a lot of visual stimulation, colors, and shapes to stimulate brain growth. But do our college campus environments offer a comparable level of visual, aural, and tactile stimulation that a kindergarten room does? Too often in the environments of 17- to 22-year-olds, our campus environments can tend to be very dull and prosaic places.

Campus environments influence student retention through fostering social engagement. While we know that campus environments do not *cause* social interaction, their presence, design, arrangement, and flexibility *influence* whether or not social interactions can occur (Strange 2001: 145). It is an interesting relationship: the physical environment is not determinative except in the negative: the absence of appropriate spaces and affordances can have a negative effect on the occurrence of some behaviors. Jon Lang expresses it this way:

> Even though an environment affords a particular set of behaviors, this does not mean that the behaviors will take place, even though the people perceive the affordances and are competent to use them. On the other hand, if the affordances are not there, the behavior cannot take place.
>
> (Lang 1987: 103)

Spaces that encourage individuals to linger with others can be described as 'sociopetal' or 'socially catalytic'. In that they catalyze social behavior, they are key to fostering a sense of community and engagement. This sense of community and engagement is an essential aspect of student retention.

Lastly, the physical environment of campus plays a significant role in institutional marketing, as well as the recruitment and retention of not only students, but also of faculty and staff. The linkages are well established though often misunderstood and underappreciated. Ernest Boyer found that 62 per cent of high school seniors made their choice of institution on the basis of the appearance of the campus buildings and grounds. He states: 'The appearance of campus is, by far, the most influential characteristic during campus visits . . . when it comes to recruiting students, the director of buildings and grounds may be more important than the academic dean' (Boyer 1987: 16).

Further:

> Admissions directors have stated that prospective students form an opinion
> of a campus in the first ten minutes of their visit, and in the next thirty
> minutes they make a decision whether to rule the college out or to continue
> the application process.
>
> (Kenney *et al.* 2005: 76)

What have these prospective students seen in the first 10 to 30 minutes on a campus? Probably the entry sign, that portion of campus in which they were lost while they tried to find admissions, and the parking lot and walkway to the admissions office or new student services. First impressions are critical, and the campus that fails to address them makes a grave mistake.

Campus landscapes, like all environments made by humans, are artifacts of culture and, as such, are also a means of communication: they send messages. That is, the very physical arrangement of campus space and the elements within it transmit non-verbal messages. These messages are embodied in the physical landscape, its arrangements, and appurtenances. That is not to say that the messages are always clear and obvious – they are not. Peirce Lewis states, 'Most objects in the landscape – although they convey all kinds of "messages" – do not convey those messages in any obvious ways' (Meinig 1979: 26). But sometimes these messages are intentional and overt. Consider the monumental forms of some civic architecture or the self-aggrandizing mansions of the nouveau riche. At other times, these messages are unintentional such as the occasional failure of designers to include access for the disabled in their designs. Such an occurrence is a clear message of the designer's lack of sensitivity to the needs of a diverse and differently abled audience. Whether intentionally or unintentionally, designers 'encode' these non-verbal messages into the places and objects they design and users 'decode' the message (Strange 2001: 16; see Figure 5.1.)

Very broadly, there are two kinds of messages embodied in the landscape: functional messages and symbolic messages (Strange 2001: 15). The functional messages can be as simple as a bench that communicates the functional message of 'sit here'. A campus bike rack sends the functional message 'park your bicycle here'. A symbolic message, on the other hand, transmits a message about institutional values and priorities. For instance, if a campus bicycle rack is located behind a building and adjacent to the garbage bin, it transmits a different symbolic message than if the bicycle rack is placed on the front of the building and adjacent to the front entry. In both instances, the functional message is the same: 'park your bicycle here'. But in the case of the bike rack by the garbage bin, the message is 'neither you nor your bike are valued enough to place this rack at the front of the building'.

Figure 5.1 A built-in bench designed as part of a plinth base of the architecture. A later college administration decided that it did not want students resting here. The 'embedded' message is clear.

Several points are to be made with regard to the messages embodied in physical environments. First, non-verbal and symbolic messages are 'often seen as more truthful than verbal or written messages' (Strange 2001: 17). In the previous example of the campus bicycle rack, students would perceive the placement of the bike rack behind the building as a more truthful statement on the part of the institution about how much it values alternative transportation than any written statement in its public relations materials. What the institution actually does in the physical environment speaks more about values and priorities than anything that may be said publicly. For example, if an institution proclaims that it has a pedestrian campus, but they have no benches, no drinking fountains, no pedestrian amenities, or they allow campus staff to drive through the heart of campus with disregard to pedestrians, then what they are actually doing speaks more loudly than what they say in marketing materials (see Figures 5.2 and 5.3).

Next, while it is within the purview of designers (and their clients, the university administrators) to 'encode' non-verbal messages (intentionally or unintentionally) into the physical environment, it is within the purview of the users (students, faculty, staff, and visitors) to 'decode' those messages and derive meaning (Strange 2001: 16). Sometimes the messages are decoded accurately, but sometimes they are not. An architect (and his or her institutional client) may consciously (or unconsciously) encode in a design messages about

Figure 5.2 This bench was designed to prohibit skateboarders from 'grinding' on the edge. Unfortunately, the design also prohibited anyone from sitting comfortably. The message transmitted to users was that preventing skateboarding was more important than everyone else's comfort.

the institution's (or the designer's) prestige, status, and fame. But the message decoded (consciously or unconsciously) by a student (or visiting potential student) might be that the institution is outdated, narcissistic, more focused on courting donors than current students, and more concerned about the institutional endowment than students' well-being. All too often, campus environments:

> may be expressing a set of values and objectives different from and inconsistent with those held by the persons inhabiting the space, however congruent they may be with those held by that part of society responsible for creating these structures.
>
> (Becker 1977: 7)

This power disparity between those who fund and design campus spaces and those who use them is highlighted elsewhere in this chapter.

What institutions and designers must realize is that different user groups 'read' the campus landscape differently and thus interpret and decode embedded messages differently. In that effort, the first point to be made is that both

Figure 5.3 This bench acknowledged that user comfort should outweigh the need to prohibit skateboarders.

'consciously and unconsciously we interpret our physical environments in a variety of ways' (Becker 1977: 2). But it should be stressed that the unconscious 'reading' carries greater weight in the interpretation process. In point of fact, it is estimated that 95 per cent of thinking occurs 'in the shadows of the mind', below the threshold of conscious awareness – and that quantifying such thought processes is difficult at best (Zaltman 2003: 50). Not impossible, but challenging. The environments that surround us have significant influence on us, especially on our choices and decision-making, but that influence rarely rises to the level of conscious thought (Gigerenzer 2007; LeDoux 1996; Mlodinow 2012; Zaltman 2003).

As we think about the campus as a place, we must understand that different people have a different relationship to it. The intent of the rest of this chapter is to explore how the landscape of campus is perceived and used by students, faculty, staff, administrators, and visitors.

With indebtedness to D. W. Meinig for the concept, different users see (and, in essence, read) the landscape differently. Meinig's essay 'The beholding eye: ten versions of the same scene' explores how 10 different users might read the exact same scene in radically different ways (Meinig 1979). For our purposes, we can generally categorize users of a campus landscape into one of five categories. First, there is the university administration that is charged with the development and maintenance of the physical spaces of campus. Then there is a subset of the administration that is specifically tasked with the physical maintenance of the physical campus. Next are three different user groups: the faculty and staff, enrolled or matriculated students, and, lastly, visitors to campus (which includes potential students).

In order to understand how each different user group might read the campus landscape differently, one should consider questions that get at the reality of how they really think about the campus landscape. We might ask, first, what is the central working component or idea of what the campus is? Next, we might ask what is the *raison d'être* of the campus – what is it used for? Related to this, who values it and what is it valued for? What is the motivation for its use? Does the user have (or develop) a sense of ownership of the campus?

Perhaps a metaphor is best for examining how different user groups think about and read campus. Consider a condominium building: there is usually a developer or landlord that owns the whole building. The developer hires a custodian or building superintendent that acts in a maintenance and/or janitorial capacity. Then there are owners – many of the individual units within the condominium complex are privately owned. But other condominium units are rented out to tenants as apartments. Lastly, there are visitors or potential owners and potential tenants who tour the building and may decide to live there.

To parse this metaphor, the condominium complex is the environment of campus including the landscape and buildings. The 'developer' of the campus is the institutional administration. The developer's 'custodian' is that unit of the administration tasked with managing campus – sometimes the grounds superintendent or facilities operations and management. The individual condominium owners in this metaphor equate to the faculty and staff who work on the campus, some for decades. Because of long use and a tradition of shared governance, these individuals are vested with a sense of ownership, even though it is the administration that technically 'owns' and is responsible for campus. The tenants in our metaphor are like students in the environment of campus. They both are viewed and view themselves as temporary residents only there until they finish their degrees. They enjoy it; they take advantage of the various facilities, but always with a sense of it being temporary. Lastly are the visitors – those who do not live in the condominium complex yet, but are checking it out to see if it 'fits' their needs and desires. Each of these different groups reads campus differently.

Let us unpack this metaphor a little more closely, looking at how each group reads the campus. I have, for nearly 40 years, been in one or more of these roles: visitor, student, staff, faculty, and administrator. These conclusions, drawn from decades of experience, are admittedly generalizations. But that does not mean there is not truth in the broad brush.

Reading Campus as a Budget line

Beginning with the administration: the central working idea for the administration is that they tend to view the campus as a *budget line item* – it is a cost to be weighed against all other costs. In this sense, the campus landscape is seen as a budget item that *competes* against other budget line items such as academics, research, the arts, housing, and auxiliary services. It is not that they do not value the landscape – they do. But it is seen more as an investment and they are looking for a quantifiable ROI (return on investment). The campus landscape's utility is as a necessary frame and connective tissue that holds the parts and pieces of campus together. It may be used as a tool for recruitment and especially in branding, marketing, and establishing an 'image' for the institution. The administration is clearly the 'owner', responsible for the funding, design, development, and maintenance of the campus landscape. But the administration does not experience the campus in the same way as other user groups. It tends to be held at arm's length and evaluated with a dispassionate financial eye. Two recent reports published by APPA[1] bear witness to this critical and detached mindset: *Thought Leaders Report 2012: Campus Space . . . an Asset and a Burden* (APPA 2012a) and *Buildings . . . the Gifts that Keep on Taking* (APPA 2012b). This campus as a budget line item view is also reflected when a college or university's funding is reduced; one of the first items cut from the general budget is campus maintenance. This contributes to American campuses having an accumulated deferred maintenance in excess of $26 billion (Kaiser and Davis 1996).

Reading Campus as Employment

For the college and university staff that maintain the campus landscape (i.e. grounds maintenance, facilities maintenance, or physical plant operations), the central working idea of campus is that of *employment*. That is not to accuse them of mercenary intent, being a 'hireling', or to say that they do not care: many have extensive training and care deeply for what they do. But at the end of the day, it is still a job. The value and utility of the campus landscape is just that: it represents employment. Their motivation is an income. They do have a sense of both responsibility and ownership in the environment of campus because of their investment of labor. But because of their responsibilities to the campus environment, they do not always experience it as a place per se:

they cannot not see tasks and things that must be done. For example, a student may not even see a piece of litter on the ground; a faculty member may wonder why someone from facilities has not picked it up yet; but the grounds worker is the only one who will stoop and pick it up. They can only see their responsibility to the landscape and, consequently, fail to experience and read the landscape as more than a task.

Reading Campus as Home Ground

For the faculty and non-grounds staff who work on campus everyday (and often for years, if not decades), the central working idea of the campus is that it is habitat or *home ground*. Certainly, during the academic year, faculty and staff may spend more waking hours on campus than away from it. For those institutions with a long tradition of shared governance, many faculty and staff feel, like our metaphorical condominium owners, a vested interest in the environment of campus. The term 'habitat' is not used loosely: 'all the essentials for development and existence are present' (Marsh 1964: 157). To be sure, the campus is used for their circulation and passage from place to place, but it is more than that. It is also their experiential milieu – the *terroir*, if you will, that shapes much of their quotidian experience. Though some faculty might see investment in the landscape as a 'frivolity' (Van Yahres and Knight 1995: 21), many do not. In a 2008 survey of U.S. college employees, *The Chronicle of Higher Education* asked what they valued most about their jobs. Surprisingly, the number one element was that their physical space met their needs and that the campus had a pleasing appearance (Biemiller 2008). Many faculty and staff care deeply about the landscape, pay attention to it experientially, and mark their transit of the seasons by it. The proliferation of university committees dedicated only to 'tree preservation' testifies to the level of investment that many faculty and staff feel towards their campuses.

Reading Campus as Temporary Home

For most of the students, the central working idea when reading the campus is that it is *a temporary home*. The campus represents a transitory way stop on their life journey. For most, they will be on campus for four to six years, or however long it takes to finish their chosen degree paths. They use the campus for circulation, passage, socialization, play, and relationships, but do not usually exhibit the same sense of ownership that long-term faculty and staff do. Because they do not have the same level of attachment, their approach to campus is more 'contractual' – they are the paying tenants and if the administration does not provide sufficient amenity through the landscape, they may look elsewhere for a better fit. One of the values that the campus landscape environment provides is a connection (however vague and tenuous) with things *natural*. The campus is valued for its therapeutic role in stress relief and temporary escapism from the pressures of deadlines, exams, papers, and projects. College students performed better on attention-demanding tasks when their dorm rooms looked out on natural settings (Kaplan and Kaplan 1998: 68). For some (notably those in the design disciplines), campus also sometimes acts as 'classroom' – an outdoor learning environment and venue for application. To be sure, there are memorable moments when relationships are begun or ended, where insights are apprehended, traditions experienced, and events cemented in memory, and these all have a physical setting as context. For instance, at George Fox University in Oregon, there is a bench where it is so common for students to have a 'let's define our relationship' talk that it is known by all the students as the 'DTR (Define the Relationship) Bench'.

Reading the Campus as Frontier

For those new to campus (e.g. potential students, or potential faculty and staff), the central working idea of campus is that it is a *frontier* to be explored and experienced. As visitors to campus, they actually see it with fresh eyes. Marcel Proust famously said, 'The real voyage of discovery consists in not seeking new landscapes but having new eyes.' But in the case of visitors to campus, it is both a new landscape and new eyes to see it with. Consequently, they may have the most accurate view of what really *is*, as well as what might be, since they are looking for a 'fit'. For visitors, the value of the campus landscape is perceived at several levels. First, there is the notion of first impressions. As previously mentioned, many students make their decision of where to apply to an institution within the first 20 to 30 minutes of their visit. The first impressions of campus and the campus tour are essential in this time frame. Next, students are looking for a 'fit' – does the campus appear to them as a place they would feel 'at home' in? Does the appearance of campus meet their expectations of what a campus is supposed to look like? Lastly, as visitors read the campus, they take away messages (some intended and some not) about what the institution values and has established as priorities. Some of these messages are apprehended consciously, some unconsciously below the threshold of awareness. An unkempt landscape with litter, dead plants, and brown turf transmits several potential messages such as 'this institution does not have enough money to take care of the landscape, let alone a student'. To the contrary, a well-landscaped and well-maintained landscape communicates safety, security, well-being, and care – for both the place and its inhabitants.

Conclusion

A campus is like a small city. All the factors that make for complexity in urban planning are there: economics, policy, power differentials, open space, architecture, transportation, parking, utility infrastructure, residential areas, recreational areas, and business areas. But the campus also has unique attributes that significantly differentiate it from most urban areas. Architectural critic Allan Temko describes it this way:

> To visualize the potential unity, order, and richness of the . . . environment, which is now so tragically marred by disunity, disorder, and poverty, one must go to our more handsome colleges and universities. For it is on the campus, as virtually nowhere else in the country, that architectural permanence, rational organization of diverse activities, generous provision of open space, liberal respect for the arts and sciences, and – in some ways most significant of all – freedom from the automobile and from advertising, can be seen acting together to provide an organic milieu for civilized life … the campus, at its finest, embodies principles of design which may be fruitfully employed throughout our civilization.
>
> (Temko 1993: 137)

Like a city, where some residents do not care and cannot be bothered to be involved in the process of planning and designing the city, on a campus, some 'residents' do not care about their environment. But others will care, and care deeply, and choose to exercise their rights as citizens to speak their minds and work to better the campus. It behooves those of us who work, learn, and play on campuses to know that different users will not read the campus in the same way that others do. Especially important is campus planning and design that strives for clarity and certainty in the embedded communication of both symbolic and functional messages so that all users receive the same message. This striving for awareness and clarity in designed communication will go far to reduce the power imbalance inherent in the structure of built environments.

Note

1   APPA used to be the acronym for the US Association of Physical Plant Admin-istrators. In 1991 they changed their name to The Association of Higher Education Facilities Officers, but retained the name APPA. In 2007 they adopted the letters 'APPA' only, without reference to what the letters mean and only a tag line that states 'Leadership in Educational Facilities.'

References

APPA (2012a) *Thought Leaders Report 2012: Campus Space . . . an Asset and a Burden*, available at: www.appa.org/Research/CRDM.cfm (accessed 3 August 2013).

APPA (2012b) *Buildings . . . the Gifts that Keep on Taking*, available at: www.appa.org/Research/CRDM.cfm (accessed 3 August 2013).

Becker, F. (1977) *Housing Messages*, Stroundsburg, PA: Dowden Hutchinson & Ross.

Biemiller, L. (2008) 'To college employees, the work environment is all-important', *The Chronicle of Higher Education*, 54(45), 3–12.

Boyer, E. (1987) *College: The Undergraduate Experience*, New York: Harper & Row.

Gigerenzer, G. (2007) *Gut Feelings: The Intelligence of the Unconscious*, New York: Viking Press.

Howard, P. (2006) *The Owner's Manual for the Brain*, Austin, TX: Bard Press.

Kaiser, H. and Davis, J. (1996) *A Foundation to Uphold: A Study of Facilities Conditions at U.S. Colleges and Universities*, Alexandria, VA: APPA, available at www.appa.org/Research/CRDM.cfm (accessed 3 August 2013).

Kaplan, R. and Kaplan S. (1998) *With People in Mind: Design and Management of Everyday Nature*, Washington, DC: Island Press.

Kenney, D., Dumont, R. and Kenney, G. (2005) *Mission and Place: Strengthening Learning and Community through Campus Design*, Westport, CT: Praeger Publishers and The American Council on Education.

Lang, J. (1987) *Creating Architectural Theory: The Role of Behavioural Sciences in Environmental Design*, New York: Van Nostrand Reinhold Company.

LeDoux, J. (1996) *The Emotional Brain: The Mysterious Underpinnings of Emotional Life*, New York: Simon & Schuster.

Marsh, W. (1964) *Landscape Vocabulary*, Los Angeles, CA: Miramar Publishing.

Meinig, D. (1979) *The Interpretation of Ordinary Landscapes: Geographical Essays*, New York: Oxford University Press.

Mlodinow, L. (2012) *Subliminal: How Your Unconscious Mind Rules Your Behavior*, New York: Pantheon Books.

Ojeda, O., O'Connor, J. and Kohn, W. (1997) *Campus and Community*, Rockport, MA: Rockport Publishers.

Strange, C. and Banning J. (2001) *Educating by Design: Creating Learning Environments that Work*, San Francisco, CA: Jossey-Bass.

Temko, A. (1993) *No Way to Build a Ball Park and Other Irreverent Essays on Architecture*, San Francisco, CA: Chronicle Books.

Van Yahres, M. and Knight, S. (1995) 'The neglected campus landscape', *Planning for Higher Education*, 23(4), 20–6.

Zaltman, G. (2003) *How Customers Think: Essential Insights into the Mind of the Market*, Boston, MA: Harvard Business School Press.

6

Sustainable Development
Impacts on Space and Place in Higher Education

MARCELLA UCCI

Introduction

The global, wide-ranging debates on sustainable development have had an increasingly direct impact upon the design, management and use of the built environment. In common with higher education institutions worldwide, those in the UK have, over the last decade, given increasing attention to the sustainability of their activities, spaces and places. Pressures from international and government policy, funding bodies and a wide range of stakeholders have brought the sustainability agenda – especially 'green issues' – to board level, so much so that most UK universities now have at least one 'sustainability officer' (or its equivalent), and publish their sustainability policy on their websites. These demands for sustainability are bound to change approaches to university design and use, and are also likely to affect the perceptions of the campus as a place. Due to the complexities associated with the notion of sustainable development and to the variety of stakeholders, inevitably the concept of a 'sustainable university' is a complex, multifaceted one that means different things in different contexts. While the majority of initiatives and debates focus on 'environmental sustainability' (e.g. minimising demands on natural resources, reducing harmful emissions, protecting biodiversity), broader aspects of sustainability are now being addressed, or at least debated, in the UK higher education sector, such as: equity, empowerment, global citizenship, education for sustainable development, and stakeholder/community engagement. While the majority of sustainability projects focus on energy efficiency, and on carbon emissions or waste reduction, the varied nature of the sustainability agenda inevitably has wide-ranging impacts on the physical university.

This chapter discusses how the sustainability agenda is impacting upon the physical university, taking as a case study the UK's higher education context. Starting with an overview of the main drivers shaping the sustainability debate in UK higher education, the chapter then illustrates the sector's current sustainability approaches and its related performance, with a particular focus on issues pertinent to space and place. This is followed by a discussion on the potential pedagogical value of the physical university with respect to sustainability principles, highlighting the complexities of this appealing yet problematic notion. In the conclusions, this chapter provocatively questions whether, within the context of the UK sector, the physical university should be considered as a means or as a barrier for delivering sustainability. Although in the past five to 10 years, UK higher education has witnessed an unprecedented flurry of activity to address its sustainability – particularly for energy efficiency and carbon emissions reduction – a significant step change is still required to meet crucial targets. This chapter argues that, while commendable and essential, this action-oriented focus on changing the physical infrastructure may have also provided an opportunity to avoid addressing more crucial (and more difficult) questions.

Setting the Context: Drivers for Sustainability in UK Higher Education

This section provides an overview of the key factors driving the spreading and widening of the sustainability agenda in UK higher education. The main drivers can be summarised as: national and international policies; funding councils' policies; stakeholder pressures (staff, students, funding councils, local and international communities); and market forces (including globalisation and the resulting need for new research and teaching initiatives). In terms of the role of funding councils, the English one (HEFCE) is taken as a case study.[1]

The area of environmental sustainability with the greatest amount of policy and regulation in Europe and the UK relates to energy use and carbon emissions. The UK government's target for an 80 per cent reduction in carbon emissions by 2050 compared with 1990 has resulted in a large amount of policy, legislation, grants and financial incentives. While some of these initiatives are not specific to the university sector, they have an inevitable impact on its activities. European Union legislation has also played an important role, for example with the EU Emissions Trading Scheme and with the Energy Performance of Buildings Directive, which resulted in changes to UK regulations – now requiring new buildings and major refurbishment works to meet minimum energy performance standards (Part L of Buildings Regulations). Furthermore, public buildings with floor area exceeding 1,000 m^2 – including universities – have to show a Display Energy Certificate (DEC), which rates the building's operational performance (based upon actual energy use derived primarily from meter readings) against sector-specific benchmarks, as well as against the building's performance in previous years. The DEC is also accompanied by an advisory report with recommendations for performance improvement. Another relevant piece of UK regulation is the Carbon Reduction

Commitment Energy Efficiency Scheme (CRC). This scheme aims to tackle CO_2 emissions not already covered by Climate Change Agreements and the EU Emissions Trading Scheme. The CRC is a mandatory UK-wide trading scheme covering large business and public sector organisations. It requires businesses to report on and pay a tax on energy used, and ranks businesses in a performance league table, which provides a further reputational incentive to improve their energy efficiency.

The UK government's commitment to sustainable development, demonstrated via several strategic papers, has also affected the higher education funding councils. For example, in England, a formal, system-wide approach began in early 2005 with a consultation by HEFCE. This was followed some time later by a policy statement (HEFCE 2009) prepared after consultation with the higher education sector. Some of the key policy objectives for HEFCE itself were identified as:

- continue to raise the profile of sustainable development so that it becomes a mainstream part of university and college activities;
- seek 'win–win' opportunities by helping to identify sector-wide business cases and benefits for individual institutions;
- fully integrate sustainable development into our strategic plan and policy-making through sector impact assessment and being open about the reasons for policy choices; and
- facilitate a carbon reduction culture to significantly reduce carbon emissions across the sector.

As a result of the UK government's carbon reduction targets, HEFCE has identified a sector target of 43 per cent reduction to be achieved by 2020 against a 2005 baseline. Institutional targets are not required to be the same as the sector target, as HEFCE acknowledges that each institution will be able to make a different contribution to the target. Performance against the sector level target is to be published annually using data collected nationally through the Estates Management Statistics. Prior to publication, institutions are given an opportunity to check their data and to provide a short contextual statement (HEFCE 2013a). It is unclear whether, in future, funding to institutions may be linked to their carbon performance.

Stakeholders' pressures have also played an important role in the uptake of sustainability in UK higher education. The student organisation People and Planet, campaigning on world poverty, human rights and the environment, has had a pivotal role with its 'Green League', which receives attention in UK higher education through publication in the weekly *Times Higher Education*. Established in 2007, the Green League offers a ranking of UK universities based on their 'environmental' performance. While it gives prominence to carbon performance and energy use, other criteria are included, such as a publicly available environmental policy, comprehensive environmental auditing, the number of environment management staff, or an ethical investment policy. The campaign has been very effective in placing sustainability on the agenda of university managements. In addition, the campaign has also succeeded in helping to widen the notion of sustainability in the sector. For example, in its recent versions, the Green League has included the explicit commitment to integrating sustainability into the curriculum as one of the factors contributing to the score. Unsurprisingly, the Green League initiative has sparked some controversy over its methodology. For example, in awarding points for carbon emissions per head, the Green League does not adjust for factors such as age of the buildings or institutional profiles. Also, the methodology is adjusted every year, making it difficult to make comparisons over time.

The campaign from People and Planet highlights a key aspect related to stakeholder pressure: reputation. Reputational gains or damage are often quoted as a reason to 'go green'. At present, there is mixed evidence on the importance that students give to green credentials when choosing a university. A Forum for the Future (2008) survey indicated that in 2007–8, only 5 per cent of students considered the environmental credentials of an institution as very important when choosing a university. However, the Sodexo (2008) university lifestyle survey showed that 64 per cent of students thought that there should be more green initiatives at their university. More recently, a survey found that nearly 80 per cent of first and second year students agreed or strongly agreed with the statement, 'My university/college practices and promotes good social and environmental skills' (Drayson *et al.* 2011). These findings suggest that even though 'green credentials' might not be a major determining factor in university selection, once students are accepted into a university, they do appear to care about its environmental performance.

In the context of stakeholder pressure and engagement, the Environmental Association for Universities and Colleges (EAUC) should also be mentioned. This is a membership organisation that shares information and best practice for stimulating and delivering sustainability in the sector. Among other activities, EAUC is a forum for discussion for environmental managers and sustainability officers of higher and further education institutions. The Green Gown Awards scheme, run by EAUC since 2004–5, is an example of how drivers for sustainability can emerge from stakeholders within higher education institutions.

Finally, it is worth mentioning that market forces also affect the sustainability agenda in UK higher education. First, organisations cannot afford to ignore the financial risks associated with rising energy prices and increasing legislation on carbon emissions reduction. Furthermore, it could be argued that employers will eventually play a more pivotal role in driving the Education for Sustainable

Development (ESD) agenda, due to the need for a workforce able to deal with environmental crises, ethical dilemmas and long-term planning for sustainability. In addition, a survey of university students shows that over two-thirds of first and second year respondents believe that sustainability should be a goal of their university (Drayson *et al.* 2011). Also, with globalisation, the financially rewarding opportunity of attracting international students is now a common strategy for most UK universities. While this can be seen as beneficial in driving changes to the curriculum and pedagogy, the air travel implications can also have significant impacts on the carbon footprint of universities. In this case, the balance between financial, environmental and reputational risks/rewards is a complex one.

Delivering Sustainability: Approaches and Performance of UK Higher Education

The role of UK universities in sustainable development and the characteristics of a 'sustainable university' are still being debated. The most obvious and frequently addressed areas of responsibility are the environmental aspects of resource depletion and resulting environmental impacts, largely associated with campus-related activities. On the other hand, increasing numbers of UK universities have acknowledged that they have a wider role to play in sustainable development. A brief review of environmental/sustainability policies available on the websites of various UK higher education institutions reveals that they mostly address environmental concerns relevant to carbon, waste, pollution and biodiversity, as well as sustainable procurement (ethical purchasing, 'fair trade' and so on). However, some institutions have developed even wider-ranging policies. For example, the University of Plymouth's sustainability policy was developed to address the whole institution with a '4C approach', acknowledging the relevance of the sustainability agenda to: Curriculum, Campus, Community and Culture. Similarly, Oxford Brookes University's (2010) 'Sustainability report' identifies six key areas relevant to its corporate responsibility programme: community, curriculum, environment, marketplace, research and workplace. This widening of the sustainability agenda is confirmed on the HEFCE website, with a statement on sustainable development:

> Our vision is that, within the next 10 years, the HE sector in England will be recognised as a major contributor to society's efforts to achieve sustainability – through the skills and knowledge that its graduates learn and put into practice, its research and exchange of knowledge through business, community and public policy engagement, and through its own strategies and operations.
>
> (HEFCE 2013b)

Since the broadening of the sustainability agenda in institutional policies is a fairly recent phenomenon, details of policy translation into practice are sometimes scarce.

Given the size of the higher education estate and the large number of people using it – 2.5 million students and just under 400,000 members of staff – the sustainability impacts of UK universities are potentially wide-ranging. However, very few objective data are available, except in relation to energy use and carbon emissions, as well as waste/recycling and water use. Here, a national data collection project, Estates Management Statistics (EMS), gathers premises-related data from all UK higher education institutions, and then shares it with them for benchmarking purposes to help improve the management of physical infrastructure. Environmental sustainability is now a key area for EMS, which reports energy use,[2] water use and percentage of waste recycled.

Ward *et al.* (2008) used EMS data to review the energy consumption of UK higher education institutions, using data for the period 2001 to 2006. They showed that, in 2006, the reported total energy consumption from all sources in the funded HE institutions was 706.23 ktoe (kilotonne of oil equivalent, a unit of energy), or 8.32 million kWh – the equivalent consumption of 365,953 average UK households, or 30 per cent of households in Wales. Also, the paper highlights that the energy consumption in the sector has increased in the six years up to 2006, rising by about 2.7 per cent above the 2001 levels. It should be emphasised, however, that the data analysis was not adjusted for changes in weather conditions over the years. The study highlighted that this increase in energy use is not evenly distributed across all institutions, since the high energy-consuming institutions appear to be increasing their net consumptions, relative to other institutions. Also, gross internal area, and staff and research student full-time equivalent numbers (FTEs) have the highest correlation with energy consumption. Other factors, such as building age, do not have a strong correlation with energy use, presumably because factors such as building services also play a role – whereby the age and type of building services, such as heating systems, is not necessarily correlated with the age of the building due to renovations. However, details of building services information are not available in the EMS data.

The EMS Annual Report 2010 (HEFCE 2011), which refers to the 2008–9 financial year, highlights that:

- Overall, space is being more efficiently used than it was 10 years ago, with gross internal area (GIA) per student and staff (FTE) falling from 9.6 m^2 to 8.8 m^2 per person. However, this period has also witnessed rapid growth in student numbers and a decline in the number of students could reverse this improvement. In addition, little progress has been made in terms of bringing the amount of academic space into line with the norms found in other sectors.

- With the exception of notional CO_2 measures, which have not been included in the EMS report due to an inconsistent time series owing to changes in methodology, environmental performance has seen an improvement over the last 10 years against all key metrics. However, the sector will need to go much further in reducing energy consumption if it is to meet emissions targets for 2020 and 2050.

- Over the last 10 years (1999–2009), the median energy consumption per student and staff FTE has gone down from 2,764 kWh to 2,446 kWh, and the difference between the upper and lower quartile values has decreased from 2,609 kWh to 2,337 kWh – meaning that results across the sector have become more consistent. However, these figures have not been normalised to account for weather conditions.

- The EMS report also shows a decrease of 27 per cent in median non-residential water consumption per student and staff FTE between 1999 and 2009. On the other hand, median waste per FTE was constant at 0.11 tonnes per person (staff and students) between 2004 and 2009, while the median percentage of non-residential waste recycled increased from 13 per cent in 2004–5 to 33 per cent in 2008–9.

The People and Planet 'Green League' 2012 (People and Planet 2012), which ranked 145 UK universities using a combination of EMS data, as well as data directly provided by the institutions, provides an even more recent picture of the sector's performance. It reveals that:

- Sector-wide carbon emissions are down 4 per cent on the previous year (although it appears this data may not have been adjusted for weather effects).

- There has been an 86 per cent rise in universities employing at least one member of staff with sustainability responsibilities.

- In 2011, only 24 universities had an explicit commitment to integrating sustainability into the curriculum within their approved Teaching and Learning Strategies. In 2012, this has risen by 96 per cent to 47 universities – so just under one-third of the sector now has this formal commitment in place.

Clearly, there are some discrepancies on the exact magnitude of energy and carbon savings achieved by the sector so far. This is partly due to the use of different baselines and data inclusion/exclusion criteria, as well as methodological limitations such as the lack of weather adjustments. Undoubtedly, regardless of the exact size of energy saving, the sector has to make significant changes to its energy/carbon reduction approaches in order to help meet the UK government targets.

Altan (2010) provides a review of energy efficiency intervention schemes between 2001 and 2007, from carrying out a survey of UK higher education institutions. The study examined technical, non-technical and management interventions. It found that the largest aggregate percentage of interventions was related to the installation of control systems. However, the single most adopted intervention was sub-metering (over 90 per cent of respondents). Equipment efficiency improvement initiatives were rated as recording the highest level of success, followed by insulation interventions and switching of electric power source. Green electricity purchasing was reported by 65 per cent of respondents, while combined heat and power (CHP) plants and photovoltaic (PV) systems were reported by 26 per cent, respectively. A variety of non-technical, behaviour-change schemes were also reported, as well as new energy procurement strategies. The study identified major barriers to interventions, including lack of methodology, lack of clarity in energy demand and consumption issues (i.e. specific drivers for energy demand are unclear, as the exact distribution of energy by end use is largely unknown), difficulty in establishing assessment boundaries and so on. It should also be highlighted, however, that the survey responses represent only 18 per cent of the 131 institutions that were the subject of this study. It may also be argued that there was some self-selection bias, as, presumably, organisations with the greatest levels of energy saving projects may have been more likely to respond to the survey. Overall, the study concluded that it is important to develop systems for effectively measuring and evaluating the impact of different policies, regulations and schemes.

In addition to the energy-saving strategies identified in Altan's study, it is also worth mentioning that many UK higher education institutions are now pledging to achieve minimum standards in BREEAM[3] ratings (e.g. an 'Excellent' rating for new buildings and 'Very Good' for all major refurbishments). In some cases, this is a legislative requirement: the Scottish Funding Council requires that all new builds and major refurbishments to further and higher education buildings in Scotland must achieve a BREEAM 'Excellent' rating. However, it should be noted that data on the education sector (including schools) show that there can be dramatic discrepancies between predicted and actual energy use in buildings, with the actual use being as much as double the predicted use (CarbonBuzz 2013). Furthermore, energy efficient buildings often use innovative technology and design strategies, which can require additional resources and careful procurement approaches (especially in the commissioning phase) in order to deliver energy saving without compromising performance or comfort. For example, the new building of the School of Slavonic and East European Studies (SSEES) at University College London adopted passive downdraught cooling to deliver a low-energy ventilation and cooling strategy within the context of London's urban heat island. This required a complex control regime with several modes of operations. The performance of the building was extensively modelled at the design stage to ensure occupant comfort combined with energy efficiency. Despite this, a considerable and unexpected effort was required at the commissioning stage for the identification and remediation of defects, as well as tuning of the control strategy (Short *et al.* 2009). The management of this process presumably also required considerable resources from the in-house project and facility management teams.

A critical area that requires further data gathering and analysis is the exact distribution of energy by end use (lighting, heating, cooling and so on), as well as further information on 'scope 3' emissions.[4] Within this context, it is particularly important for UK universities to establish the carbon emissions associated with strategic areas of universities' operations, such as information and communication technology (ICT), as well as those arising from student and staff travel. Some studies highlight the importance of transport in the carbon footprint of UK higher education. For instance, carbon emissions from commuting can be significant, especially for those universities relying heavily on cars for access: the University of Bradford found that commuting had a significant role in its carbon footprint, with building energy use accounting for around 45 per cent of its calculated daily CO_2 emissions, commuting 45 per cent and waste to landfill 10 per cent (Hopkinson and James 2005). There are fewer data on carbon emissions associated with academic and business travel in UK universities. However, the Environment Institute at University College London (UCL) carried out a survey of its staff and research students to assess the carbon emissions associated with commuting and business travel. It found that the total transport emissions for the 2007–8 academic year amounted to an average of 2.5 tonnes per person. Of the total, approximately 23 tonnes (77 per cent) were as a result of air travel, and 5.5 tonnes (18 per cent) were due to rail travel (Fahrni *et al.* 2009). In this case, business travel significantly outweighed commuting in terms of its role in carbon emissions. While UCL's urban location results in high public transport usage and the Environment Institute only has a small number of staff and students, this study suggests that the globalisation of university activities could result in a significant growth in carbon emissions. On the other hand, a carbon footprint study of De Montfort University (Ozawa-Meida *et al.* 2013), which addressed scope 1, 2 and 3 emissions, revealed that scope 3 emissions comprised around 79 per cent of the total university's greenhouse gas emissions. Procurement emissions were 38 per cent of the overall estimated footprint and 48 per cent of total scope 3 emissions. As for travel, international and UK-based student travel was 8 per cent of the total emissions, staff and student commute was 18 per cent, and business and visitor travel 3 per cent. It should be noted that this footprint includes energy use in private halls of residence (9 per cent). On the other hand, a UK student organisation states that 'preliminary research shows that carbon equivalent emissions from flights by international students studying in the UK are similar to or greater than carbon emissions from the whole HE sector's building stock' (People and Planet 2009). Clearly, the exact magnitude of carbon emissions associated with travel types varies across the sector and nearly all institutions are now gathering more detailed data on this issue. Since the work of nearly all UK universities is enmeshed with global economies for teaching and research, limiting air travel would, accordingly, have major implications.

Carbon emissions arising from the use of ICT are also significant. It is estimated that ICT use in UK further and higher education generates over 500,000 tonnes of CO_2 per year (JISC 2009). Figures for individual institutions are not widely available. However, one case study at the University of Sheffield shows that annual use of electricity by ICT equipment is about 18 per cent of non-residential electricity consumption (Cartledge 2008). Several projects are under way UK-wide to assess the energy saving and carbon reduction potential of various technologies, including videoconferencing. Especially for research-intensive universities, there is the potential for a serious strategic tension between reducing their carbon footprint and the need for computing power. In relation to the carbon emissions associated with ICT and travel, the issues of home working and of distance learning should also be considered. While an extensive discussion on this topic is beyond the scope of this chapter, it is worthwhile mentioning the results of a study comparing the estimated carbon emissions arising from campus-based full-time HE courses versus part-time or distance learning courses (Roy *et al.* 2008). The study concluded that:

> Distance learning HE courses involve 87 per cent less energy and 85 per cent lower CO_2 emissions than the full-time campus-based courses. Part-time campus HE courses reduce energy and CO_2 emissions by 65 and 61 per cent, respectively, compared with full-time campus courses ... Existing HE sustainability programmes should be broadened beyond considering campus site impacts and 'greening the curriculum'. Indeed, were HE expansion to take environmental impacts seriously, then part-time and distance education should be prioritised over increasing full-time provision.

It must be emphasised that these conclusions are not necessarily widely applicable, as results are based on a specific methodological approach derived from a survey of 20 courses: 10 full-time campus-based courses; three part-time campus-based courses; three part-time distance taught, mainly print-based Open University (OU) courses; and four part-time distance taught courses (of which one was a non-OU course), delivered partly or wholly online. In order to allow comparisons in a systematic manner, results were normalised in terms of energy consumption per student per 10 CAT points, whereby under the UK Credit Accumulation and Transfer system (CAT), 1 CAT point is equivalent to 10 hours of total study, with 360 points required for an undergraduate degree and 180 for a masters degree.

Aside from reducing carbon emissions associated with campus-related and wider activities, the sustainability debate in the UK higher education sector is, unsurprisingly, also focusing on the Education for Sustainable Development (ESD) agenda. This also overlaps at times with debates on global citizenship and with the internationalisation of the curriculum – both of which are driven by educational and economic motivations (Haigh 2008). A discussion on this topic is beyond the scope of this chapter. However, it should be acknowledged that while modelling good practice through campus-related activities can be considered a teaching tool for sustainable development (as discussed in following section), the impact of ESD on the sector can be potentially broader, both in terms of curriculum content and pedagogical approaches (Cotton et al. 2009).

The Physical University as a Living-Learning Laboratory for Sustainability

The previous sections highlighted the finding that UK universities are becoming increasingly aware of the relevance of the sustainability agenda to all aspects of their operations. This not only applies to the physical university context, but to wider issues related to teaching, research, and engagement with local and international communities. Nonetheless, arguably, those aspects related to the physical university provide quite literally the most 'visible' opportunities to showcase sustainability, and to let stakeholders experience sustainability in practice. The pedagogical value of places is clearly articulated by Gruenewald (2003: 621):

> Places are profoundly pedagogical. That is, as centers of experience, places teach us about how the world works and how our lives fit into the spaces we occupy. Further, places make us: As occupants of particular places with particular attributes, our identity and our possibilities are shaped.

There is an opportunity, therefore, for the physical university to become a living-learning laboratory for sustainability principles, addressing both students and staff, and, potentially, the wider community. The notion of a living-learning laboratory for sustainability raises questions of how sustainability can be communicated through spaces and places, as well as how interactions between the physical university and its 'users' can be oriented towards more sustainable practices. Furthermore, it might be appropriate to consider whether there is a relationship between users' perceptions of spaces and places, and their commitment to making those spaces/places more sustainable.

On the issue of how sustainability can be communicated in buildings, it is appropriate to address the following questions: (1) When using a teaching space, how can university staff or students understand if and how that space is sustainable?; (2) When walking around the university campus, what features indicate its sustainability? Hence, the question arises as to whether sustainable architecture has its own aesthetics, which would clearly communicate its agenda to users – possibly even letting them learn about specific sustainability principles in practice. In a recent book, several authors debate this issue (Lee 2011). Overall, their answers indicate that there is not a unique or universally recognised aesthetic for sustainable architecture, and that this very notion is problematic. This is partly because sustainable architecture is torn between the aims of delivering change (implying a radical or unconventional aesthetic) versus the need to mainstream sustainable architectural approaches (which requires a neutral approach that works well within the prevailing aesthetic). On some occasions, the unconventional aesthetic in sustainable architecture has been achieved by attributing an intrinsic aesthetic value to technological (environmental) innovation. However, this approach has been criticised by some as lacking in 'beauty'. In addition, it has also been argued that since all buildings should be sustainable, there might be no case for a specific aesthetics of sustainable architecture (Hill 2011). Therefore, sustainable buildings suffer from the dilemma inherent in sustainable development: the tension between delivering and communicating dramatic change, and working within the architectural status quo. In fact, Hill goes as far as highlighting that most sustainable architecture to date is still colluding with the prevailing consumption-dependent model of growth. Despite acknowledging that the aesthetic dilemma of sustainable architecture can have no simple resolution, Hill remains (vaguely) optimistic about its future.

Since sustainable buildings have no intrinsic way of communicating their sustainability agenda, how can universities ensure that their spaces and places become an opportunity to communicate, learn and apply sustainability principles? Some universities are offering their buildings as case studies for student or research projects focused on sustainability. While this approach may be an effective learning strategy, it is perhaps not particularly efficient since it targets a selected group of students/researchers. An alternative approach is wider behaviour-change campaigns: this approach has gained the attention of the research community, as well as of policymakers, who have become aware that technology alone does not always deliver the expected efficiencies or savings. Users are often more creative in using innovative products/technologies than technologists would like. While behaviour-change campaigns do not directly change the physical infrastructure, they have the potential to affect aspects of place-making.

Within the UK university sector, the most well-known behaviour-change campaigns originally focused on student residences. For example, the 'Student Switch Off' is a not-for-profit campaign encouraging student action on climate change. Winner of the 2012 Ashden Award, which is presented to groundbreaking green energy champions in the UK, the campaign focuses on energy-saving competitions within halls of residences at 54 UK universities, achieving average reductions in electricity usage of 7 per cent (National Union of Students 2013). Another example is the HEFCE-funded 'Moving Towards Zero Waste' project, primarily focused on reuse schemes in halls of residences. It is perhaps not surprising that behaviour-change campaigns addressed, at first, student residences, as non-domestic buildings are more complex – due to the variety of both users and building controls or operational practices. However, the 'Green Impact for Universities and Colleges' is an environmental accreditation and awards scheme aiming to support teams of staff and/or students representing, for example, a university department to make tangible changes in behaviour and policy, through an online workbook criteria that lists a number of ways in which points can be gained, for example by demonstrating the team has had a basic energy audit in the last 12 months, or that all plain A4 white copier paper bought by the team meets certain environmental criteria. The workbook also explains how, for each criteria, auditors would check the validity of the team's claims. In 2011–12, the scheme engaged 152 organisations and 5,907 team members across the country, collectively, to take 58,834 actions, with 25,185 actions taken as a direct result of the programme, and over 800 students trained and supported to audit the teams (National Union of Students 2012). While the scheme has been successful in engaging a number of staff and students, as well as in improving the interaction of Green Impact Teams with their buildings, the time needed to complete the online workbook should not be underestimated. Furthermore, it is debatable whether all the 'actions' that are taken as a direct result of the programme produce energy saving. For example, one of the criteria includes the requirement of having posters and stickers encouraging staff and students to switch off lights/equipment when not in use. However, the energy-saving effectiveness of posters/stickers has not been demonstrated.

While environmental behaviour-change campaigns are now being initiated in non-residential university buildings, their impact on actual consumption is, for now, not easy to measure. There is, however, a growing number of academic institutions who are embarking on energy usage feedback projects, which have the potential to bridge the gap between behavioural approaches and performance-based approaches linked to the inherent characteristics of specific buildings. These projects utilise energy/carbon data (primarily through meter-reading data) to provide feedback to building users on their energy performance. The data are manipulated and presented, often in a 'dashboard' fashion, in an understandable format that also stimulates behaviour change for the target users. Like broader behaviour-change campaigns, energy feedback projects provide opportunities for new, more sustainable interactions between buildings and their users. In university contexts, the most common approach to energy-use feedback is competitions, whereby groups such as halls of residences or university departments compete against each other in saving energy over a certain period. In this case, the energy usage information provides incentives and also guidance on how well each group is doing. A small number of universities are now also piloting projects where some of these approaches are combined with direct or indirect incentives for departments. For example, at the University of Manchester, the Carbon Credit Scheme is a pilot project compiling energy consumption data with an aim to 'develop a model for the devolvement of responsibility for energy consumption to schools/directorates through a system of annual target setting for carbon emissions from energy consumption' (University of Manchester 2013). A similar approach seems already operational in some parts of the University of Cambridge, where incentives are provided to departments to save energy. In particular:

> Baseline allowances for each Department's electricity usage are based on historic data from previous years and are converted to a financial value at year end using the prevailing average price. The value of any difference between the actual units consumed and the allowance will represent either a saving to be delivered to, or an extra cost to be recovered from, Schools or Institutions.
>
> (University of Cambridge 2013)

While an extensive discussion on the efficacy of these approaches is beyond the scope of this section, it should be emphasised that their long-term impact is still debated. Competitions can lose their novelty factors – although this is truer for staff than for the more transient student population. On the other hand, incentives or penalties based on the performance of individual departments may, for now, be of limited financial value (and hence bring little added interest to the environmental agenda). This may change, should energy prices rise significantly, or should universities decide to charge departments for their energy use. However, this last option would be very controversial, as the energy consumption of departments is affected by the intrinsic characteristics of the building itself (for which departments have little choice), or by high student numbers and/or research-intensive activities (whereby departments could argue they are being penalised for doing well). While weighting factors could be applied to account for these issues, these may end up diminishing the effects of energy-charging schemes and, potentially, still cause some resentment. Crucially, it must also be emphasised that energy-feedback projects and energy-charging schemes are still in their infancy within the UK university sector, particularly for those institutions with a large and varied building stock. This is because the quality of the energy data is still a considerable challenge. While technologies for gathering and displaying energy data are now available, in practice, their deployment can be complex and expensive – particularly if one wishes to consider data disaggregated by departments (which can often share buildings), by end use (lighting, small power, etc.), or by different user groups (such as students, researchers, administration).

Earlier in this section, it was highlighted that, when considering the 'pedagogical value' of the physical university within the context of sustainability, one may need to address the potential relationship between users' perceptions of spaces and places, and their commitment to making those spaces/places more sustainable. In particular, it is important to consider the role of spaces/places in relation to issues such as social cohesion and identity. It has been postulated that 'sustainability is not possible without a well-established social fabric that allows people to recognise themselves as a group or as a community sharing prototypical features and having achieved certain levels of social cohesion' (Pol 2002). Based on this approach, two neighbourhoods in England were studied to test the hypothesis that 'socially cohesive communities that have a strong sense of social and place identity will be more supportive of environmentally sustainable attitudes and behaviours compared with those communities in which cohesiveness and social and place identities are weaker' (Uzzell *et al.* 2002). The study concluded that sustainability cannot be considered in isolation from either its social or place-related context. In particular, 'place-related social identity as expressed through both collective social relations and individual and collective relationships with place may form an important dimension of environmental attitudes' (Uzzell *et al.* 2002). This issue is particularly important when considering the concept of 'salience of identity', based on the fact that people can choose between several identities (male or female, mother or professional, etc.) and only a salient identity will be operative in a specific moment, based on the context. Different identities can compete with a specific place identity, for example in the university context, a person's salient identity might range from: university staff, to faculty member, or member of the university library, etc. Because of the important and contextual nature of the salient identity, 'environmental management should create conditions to make sustainable values prototypical elements of the salient identity' (Pol 2002).

In the university context, there are not only various groups at play (staff, students and others), but also each individual or group can have several social or place-related identities. For example, a student will have several identities related to his or her department, discipline, country of origin or special interests (which may relate him or her to a specific student organisation), halls of residence, buildings where most of his or her lectures take place, buildings hosting the library or canteen, and so on. Similarly, research staff will have different identities related to their disciplinary background, research group, department, faculty, any university-wide activities they may be engaged with, the building where offices are located and/or lectures given. The complexity of these issues is highlighted further when considering a study that followed an academic department at three points in time, where both organisational and spatial changes took place (Sailer *et al.* 2012). The study concluded that there are some spatial factors that clearly affect interactions and collaboration – for example, being split across floors was a major barrier to interaction. In fact, for all weekly and daily networks, co-location on the same floor was an even stronger driver for tie formation than group affiliation. On the other hand, for other aspects, it was more difficult to disentangle the relative contributions of space and organisational change to network structures. The authors argued that this is not simply due to the nature of the case study (where spatial and organisational changes took place at the same time), but, more broadly, it is because organisational change, spatial change and collaboration networks all affect each other with various dynamic feedback and feed-forward loops. Hence, the transient and multifaceted nature of social and place-related contexts within complex structures such as universities means that addressing salient identities for sustainability purposes is not a simple task. Yet, such a task is often delegated to 'sustainability officers' (sometimes in a fairly junior role within the organisation) with limited experience and understanding of these complex issues, and little power to influence key players.

The Physical University: A Means or a Barrier to Delivering Sustainability?

This chapter has discussed how, due to a number of drivers, the sustainability agenda is becoming more of a priority for UK higher education institutions. In this context, the legislative and financial risks (such as rising fuel prices) accompanied by reputational and financial rewards (such as stakeholder pressures or potential savings thanks to resource efficiencies) are a compelling argument for addressing sustainability. While carbon emissions and energy use are at the heart of the debate with a plethora of existing and emerging initiatives, the widening of the meaning and applications of sustainability in UK higher education must also be noted. Increasingly, the term (and comparable notions such as corporate social responsibility) has developed a wider scope pertinent to several higher education activities – teaching, research and community engagement. For now, however, the focus of most sustainability initiatives is on win-win solutions, addressing, for example: saving energy while saving money; increasing research in the sustainability field, thus also increasing research income; and addressing sustainability in the curriculum, hence also meeting students'/employers' expectations. Most institutions have not yet addressed the most controversial aspects of the sustainability agenda, such as how to balance a reduction in carbon emissions associated with student and business travel against the needs for economic growth, or how to reduce emissions arising from ICT without compromising the computing power needed to support growing student numbers and research income. Even more controversial is perhaps the 'green' value of distance learning and home working, and to what extent this should be considered as a suitable 'greening' strategy.

A review of current sustainability performance and approaches in the UK higher education sector revealed that: (1) the amount of effort that the university sector as a whole and individual universities are putting into addressing the sustainability agenda is now considerable and still rising; and (2) there is still a lack – in terms of robustness and granularity – of baseline performance data, as well as insufficient systems for assessing the effectiveness of sustainability initiatives. This is a somewhat perverse situation where, due to time constraints and stakeholder pressures, the sector is compelled to implement sustainability projects, without necessarily knowing exactly which areas should be targeted first, nor having systems in place to properly monitor the impact of such initiatives. Inevitably, many of these projects still focus on various aspects of the physical university, with many institutions investing in more efficient technologies and 'greener' buildings – as well as initiating behavioural-change programmes. While these efforts are commendable, their effectiveness is not necessarily as great as might be expected. For example, the previous sections highlighted that buildings designed to be 'green' are often not so green once they are in use, either because of technological failures or due to the behaviour of building users. In addition, the application of innovative technologies in buildings often requires carefully framed procurement mechanisms, a special attention to commissioning, and additional time and expertise from facility managers, as well as – in some cases – changes in users' expectations and/or behaviour. It might be argued that estates and facilities departments in many universities do not have the capacity (in terms of resources and training) to deal with some of these complex issues. Furthermore, the varied nature of activities occurring in university buildings, together with the complexity of governance structures and the variety of building users, mean that meeting or changing users' expectations can be extremely complex.

In addition, despite the flurry of activities, a large number of stakeholders and university users remain oblivious to such initiatives. This is partly because sustainability projects or sustainable buildings do not necessarily have intrinsic ways of communicating their sustainable aims. Furthermore, the varied and dynamic nature of social and place-related 'salient identities' in university communities, combined with the complex interactions between individual, organisational and spatial factors, mean that facilitating more sustainable interactions between the physical university and its community is not a simple task. Yet, the vast majority of sustainability projects are initiated and implemented by a relatively small number of environment/sustainability managers, who seldom have training in communication or social sciences, and are often not in strategic positions within their organisational structures.

Perhaps even more crucially, when considering the targets that the UK, as a whole, and its higher education sector, in particular, have to meet, it is apparent that the size of carbon emission reduction achieved by higher education so far is still small, and a significant step change is required. This means that more radical solutions than those currently employed are needed. These solutions may eventually dramatically affect the physical university, as well as several other aspects of universities' operations. Inevitably, this will mean going beyond win-win solutions and tackling the most controversial aspects of sustainability in higher education. In fact, the biggest challenge does not lie in the lack of robust data or of systems for assessment, nor in the amount/ type of projects and initiatives that the sector is dedicating to sustainability. The real challenge is deciding whether, and to what extent, the current sustainability targets can and should be met without compromising the status quo (including university spaces/places) and without considering alternative models of 'growth'. Dunphy *et al.* (2007: 14) argue that three phases can be identified in the evolution of corporate sustainability. The first 'wave', in their terminology, is characterised by rejection and non-responsiveness. The second wave focuses on compliance first, then efficiency (for example, opportunities for cost saving) and then 'strategic proactivity' (sustainability used to gain competitive advantage). The third wave is defined as the 'sustaining corporation', whereby the sustainability agenda is internalised and profit is not the only driver for actions. The wave model does not assume that each organisation will go through every phase in a linear fashion, and, in fact, some organisations might move 'backwards' in some cases. Based on what has been discussed so far, it appears that UK higher education can be considered within Dunphy and colleagues' 'second wave' phase, characterised by a continuum running from compliance to 'strategic proactivity'. Increasingly, perhaps, institutions are moving along this continuum, as they gradually identify advantages that may result from achieving green credentials. In fact, it might be argued that most UK universities are now at least in the compliance or efficiency phase – especially for carbon emissions and energy use. One can also argue that a small number of institutions are in the 'competitive advantage' phase, where some universities may have seen sustainability as an opportunity for differentiation and branding. We are not aware of any UK university that can currently be considered as a 'third wave' organisation with a fully internalised sustainability agenda. Yet, universities might appear to be particularly suited to becoming third wave organisations: for one thing, they are usually thought to have (and themselves usually think that they have) distinctively high ethical standards – more so than the generality of organisations: it is sometimes said that they should be 'schools for ethical understanding' (Keohane 2006: 93).

While the physical university has been the main focus of sustainability projects for some time, one must wonder if its places and spaces should be considered as a mean for delivering sustainability, or possibly even as a barrier to the whole process. Currently, university spaces and places fail to 'teach' what sustainability is and how it can be accomplished in reality. The sustainability 'message' is not evident or pervasive enough; it does not address all higher education communities, nor does it save enough energy/carbon. This is partly because changing space and place takes time and effort: for example, replacing old buildings with new, 'more efficient' ones is costly and time-consuming, and technical innovations require extra efforts – especially if they are expected to save energy while delivering the same levels of comfort/performance. This is all even more difficult for refurbishment projects of existing buildings. So it might seem unsurprising that, despite the noticeable level of activity in this field, significant step changes are still needed for these initiatives to make a real difference, both in terms of actual performance as well as in relation to the interactions with the university community. On the other hand, however, it may even be argued that the focus on action and on changing the physical infrastructure has provided an opportunity to avoid addressing the more crucial (and more difficult) questions.

When considering the inherent contradictions embedded in sustainability and sustainable development, the lack of an evident step change in the current approaches to sustainability in the UK university sector is unsurprising. The preference for win-win solutions that do not significantly compromise the status quo is an example of these contradictions: growth first, sustainability must follow. While these contradictions are not unique to the university sector, it could be argued that universities have a unique position in this context. This is clearly articulated in a document by Universities UK (UUK) – the major representative body for UK universities – which has produced a university leaders' statement of intent on sustainable development (UUK 2010). The document states that:

Universities are in a unique position to support society in addressing the challenges of sustainable development through their missions of innovation, transferring knowledge through research, scholarship, teaching and learning as well as through organisational activities as campus managers and employers and as key bodies in local communities.

Hence, it might be argued that universities have the moral duty to lead on the debates on sustainability, not simply from the perspective of research, but addressing what it means to them as institutions. In this sense, the real challenge for UK universities is not deciding how to operationalise via technological and/or behavioural approaches the currently (limited?) notions of sustainability, but questioning whether universities should undergo a radical rethinking of their role in society and economics – including whether the university community is prepared to question its role as appearing to be yet another profit-making business. For universities to be schools for wisdom rather than simply distributors of knowledge, the UK university community should openly debate whether the current approaches for delivering a sustainable physical university are in fact an attempt to save the status quo, which is no longer sustainable (nor the only possible one?). Should these questions be explicitly addressed, then universities as a whole, including their physical component, may undergo a truly radical and tangible change – in ways that are, at present, hard to discern.

Notes

1   Policy and funding for public higher education in the UK are managed separately in England, Scotland, Wales and Northern Ireland. While this chapter mostly examines the case of England (which has over 80 per cent of the UK's higher education institutions), the situation elsewhere in the UK is similar. HEFCE allocates public funding to support teaching and research in universities and colleges, which institutions supplement from tuition fees, research grants, consultancy, donations and any other earnings.

2   For now, this generally excludes indirect emissions occurring from sources not necessarily owned or controlled from the institution (e.g. commuting, business travel, emissions from suppliers, etc.).

3   BREEAM, standing for the Building Research Establishment Environmental Assessment Method, is a method for rating the sustainability of buildings. There are different versions of BREEAM, depending on the building type, its geographical location and whether it is a new build, a refurbishment or an in-use project.

4   'Scope 1' emissions are direct emissions that occur from sources owned or controlled by the organisation (e.g. emissions from combustion in owned or controlled boilers/furnaces/vehicles); 'scope 2' accounts for emissions from the generation of purchased electricity consumed by the organisation; and 'scope 3' covers all other indirect emissions that are a consequence of the activities of the organisation, but occur from sources not owned or controlled by the organisation (e.g. commuting and procurement).

104 · Marcella Ucci

References

Altan, H. (2010) 'Energy efficiency interventions in UK higher education institutions', *Energy Policy*, 38, 7722–31.

CarbonBuzz (2013) 'CarbonBuzz', available at: www.carbonbuzz.org/evidencetab.jsp (accessed 24 February 2013).

Cartledge, C. (2008) 'Sheffield ICT footprint commentary', available at: www.susteit. org.uk/files/category.php?catID=4 (accessed 9 March 2013).

Cotton, D., Bailey, I., Warren, M. and Bissell, S. (2009) 'Revolutions and second-best solutions: education for sustainable development in higher education', *Studies in Higher Education*, 34(7), 719–33.

Drayson, R., Bone, E. and Agombar, J. (2011) 'Students attributes towards and skills for sustainable development', *National Union of Students and Higher Education Academy*, available at: www.heacademy.ac.uk/assets/documents/esd/Student_attitudes_towards_and_skills_for_sustainable_development.pdf/ (accessed 22 February 2013).

Dunphy, D., Griffiths, A. and Benn, S. (2007) *Organizational Change for Corporate Sustainability*, Abingdon: Routledge.

Fahrni, L., Rydin, Y., Tunesi, S. and Maslin, M. (2009) 'Travel related carbon footprint: a case study using the UCL Environment Institute', available at: www. ucl.ac.uk/environment-institute/News/Work%20Related%20Travel%20report.pdf (accessed 22 November 2009).

Forum for the Future (2008) 'Future leaders survey 2007/08', available at: www.forum forthefuture.org/sites/default/files/project/downloads/futureleaders0708.pdf (accessed 9 March 2013).

Gruenewald, D. (2003) 'Foundations of place: a multidisciplinary framework for place-conscious education', *American Educational Research Journal*, 40(3), 619–54.

Haigh, M. (2008) 'Internationalisation, planetary citizenship and higher education', *Compare: A Journal of Comparative and International Education*, 38(4), 427–40.

HEFCE (2009) 'Sustainable development in higher education: 2008 update to strategic statement and action plan', available at: www.hefce.ac.uk/Pubs/HEFCE/2009/09_03/09_03.pdf (accessed 9 March 2013).

HEFCE (2011) 'Performance in higher education estates: EMS Annual Report 2010', available at: www.hefce.ac.uk/media/hefce1/pubs/hefce/2011/1117/11_17.pdf (accessed 9 March 2013).

HEFCE (2013a) 'Carbon reduction targets for institutions', available at: www.hefce.ac. uk/whatwedo/lgm/sd/carbon (accessed 9 March 2013).

HEFCE (2013b) 'Sustainable development on HEFCE website', available at: www. hefce.ac.uk/whatwedo/lgm/sd/ (accessed 9 March 2013).

Hill, G. (2011) 'The aesthetics of architectural consumption', in S. Lee (ed.), *Aesthetics of Sustainable Architecture*, Rotterdam: 010 Publishers, pp. 26–40.

Hopkinson, P. and James, P. (2005) 'How Yorkshire and Humberside Higher Education can help to minimise the region's carbon dioxide emissions', available at: www. heepi.org.uk/documents/final%20dcarb%20Report%20-%20May%2017.doc (accessed 22 November 2009).

JISC (2009) 'Green ICT: managing sustainable ICT in education and research', available at: www.susteit.org.uk/uploads/DOCS/55-BP-GreenICT-v1-06-AB.pdf (accessed 11 June 2010).

Keohane, N. (2006) *Higher Ground: Ethics and Leadership in the Modern University*, Durham, NC: Duke University Press.

Lee, S. (ed.) (2011) *Aesthetics of Sustainable Architecture*, Rotterdam: 010 Publishers.

National Union of Students (2012) 'Green Impact Portfolio 2011–2012', available at: www.green-impact.org.uk/wp-content/uploads/2012/09/GI-portfolio-final_low-res.pdf (accessed 24 February 2013).

National Union of Students (2013) 'Student switch off', available at: www.student switchoff.org/ (accessed 22 February 2013).

Oxford Brookes University (2010) 'Sustainability report', available at: www.brookes.ac.uk/about/sustainability/docs/sustainabilityreport2010/ (accessed 2 August 2010).

Ozawa-Meida, L., Brockway, P., Letten, K., Davies, J. and Fleming, P. (2013) 'Measuring carbon performance in a UK university through a consumption-based carbon footprint: De Montfort University case study', *Journal of Cleaner Production*, 56, 185–96, available at: http://dx.doi.org/10.1016/j.jclepro.2011.09.028 (accessed 20 November 2013).

People and Planet (2009) 'Green League Methodology 2009', available at: http://peopleandplanet.org/greenleague2009/methodology (accessed 9 March 2013).

People and Planet (2012) 'People and Planet Green League 2012', available at: http://peopleandplanet.org/green-league-2012/tables (accessed 9 March 2013).

Pol, E. (2002) 'The theoretical background of the City-Identity-Sustainability Network', *Environment and Behavior*, 34(1), 8–25.

Roy, R., Potter, S. and Yarrow, K. (2008) 'Designing low carbon higher education systems: environmental impacts of campus and distance learning systems', *International Journal of Sustainability in Higher Education*, 9(2), 116–30.

Sailer, K., Marmot, A. and Penn, A. (2012) 'Spatial configuration, organisational change and academic networks', *Conference for Applied Social Network Analysis*, Zurich, Switzerland, 4–7 September 2012.

Short, A., Cook, M. and Lomas, K. (2009) 'Delivery and performance of a low-energy ventilation and cooling strategy', *Building Research and Information*, 37(1), 1–30.

Sodexo (2008) 'The university lifestyle survey 2008', available at: http://uk.sodexo.com/uken/Images/ULS%20Summary%202008_tcm15-185165.pdfm (accessed 22 November 2009).

UUK (Universities UK) (2010) 'A university leaders' statement of intention on sustainable development', available at: www.eauc.org.uk/universities_uk_statement_of_intent (accessed 10 June 2010).

University of Cambridge (2013) 'Incentives for the economic use of electricity', available at: www.admin.cam.ac.uk/offices/em/sustainability/energy/electricity.html (accessed 22 February 2013).

University of Manchester (2013) 'Carbon Credit Scheme', available at: www.sustainability.manchester.ac.uk/carboncreditscheme (accessed 22 February 2013).

Uzzell, D., Pol, E. and Badenas, D. (2002) 'Place identification, social cohesion and environmental sustainability', *Environment and Behavior*, 34(1), 26–53.

Ward, I., Obbonna, A. and Altan, H. (2008) 'Sector review of UK higher education energy consumption', *Energy Policy*, 36, 2939–49.

7

Place-Making and Other Purposes

Public Art on Campus

LORNA HARDS, SIAN VAUGHAN
AND JAMES WILLIAMS

Introduction

Public art is a traditional element of a university's physical environment. Campuses are adorned with legacies of historic artworks in the form of sculptures, fountains and murals, among which new works appear sporadically and haphazardly; yet the intentions and messages behind these works of art have largely been overlooked. Universities' use of public art has largely been subsumed within broader parameters and not been investigated as a phenomenon itself. In the UK, for example, recent research by the Public Monuments and Sculpture Association and the Public Catalogue Foundation have included, to varying degrees, artworks owned by universities in their published catalogues (Merritt *et al.* 2010; Roe 2008). While such work records and analyses the works themselves, they give very little attention to the universities' motives for commissioning or installing public art works, instead focusing on the artists' own intentions in creating art works. However, in the context of current changes in the higher education landscape, notably funding diversification and widening participation, public art that is owned and commissioned by universities has the potential to play a significant role in engaging the public in higher education and requires scrutiny. In this chapter, we begin to explore this potential in relation to the specific context of UK higher education.

Public engagement is currently a major concern in UK higher education. HEFCE's Strategic Plan 2006–11, including its support for initiatives such as the 'Beacons of Public Engagement', has emphasised that universities need to engage more fully with the 'public' (HEFCE 2009: 9). Underlying this strategy is the work of such scholars as David Watson, who has highlighted ways in which universities are engaging with a range of publics (Watson 2003, 2007). In this context, 'public engagement' is understood as activities in which universities promote themselves and encourage wider participation in higher education (National Coordinating Centre for Public Engagement, 2010.). Thus far, public engagement has largely been understood without substantial reference to the spaces within which it takes place or the artefacts that often occupy that space.

As well as the changing political and economic landscape of higher education in the UK, which is emphasising engagement, the current flurry of building of and relocation to new campuses provides opportunities for universities to define and present themselves through public art. These opportunities can be identified by the local planning authority, which makes a requirement of the university that, among other measures to mitigate the negative effects of development, there is a public art contribution. There is also evidence of recognition by universities that public art can contribute to wider agendas. Examining recent public art strategies by UK universities is therefore very revealing of the prevailing definitions and conceptualisations of the higher education sector. Are the physical spaces of university campuses seen as public? If so, who are the 'public' for universities' public art? In defining the aims and functions of public art on campus, what messages about the university's own aims and function are being communicated?

Examining the public art strategy documents also reveals the definition and conceptualisation of public art held by the university. Concomitantly with the changing political and economic landscape of higher education, discourse and practice on public art has matured and evolved so that the term is now widely recognised as defining a contested practice that can encompass virtual, per-formative and socially engaged practice as much as more traditional sculptural and painted objects and street furniture (Cartiere 2008: 7–17). In particular, the roles played by public art commissioning in urban regeneration have been problematised in terms of the blurring definitions of public and private, corporate and cultural capital. Drawing on other disciplines, notably social geography and urbanism, public art critique and practice has broadened concepts of space from the physical to encompass the temporary, performative and experiential in public spheres of activity and interrelationships. The growing sophistication in the understanding of space as a socio-politico-economic production in contemporary public art has been mirrored by a recognition of 'public' not as a singular homogenous mass, but itself as a contested and complex concept in which there are multiple, diverse publics for public art (Miles 1997). As centres of knowledge and innovation, are uni-versities benefitting from contemporary public art critique in both reflecting on and developing multiple uses of public art and in rethinking higher educa-tion's role in its multiple and diverse communities?

Strategising Public Art as Part of Campus Development

A common prompt for the production of a university public art strategy is the development or redevelopment of an institution's campuses. Oxford Brookes

University's Public Art Strategy was written by Artpoint, an external public art agency, but fits into a wider master plan published in 2006 to redevelop its Gypsy Lane and Headington Hill campuses (Oxford Brookes University 2007). It is essentially a traditional public art strategy of the kind prepared for large-scale public and private developments since the early 1990s. It is intended as 'a guide for architects, designers, maintenance staff and anyone involved with the commissioning of artworks', and provides some simple methodological guidelines for commissioning. Beyond this, it identifies opportunities for the provision of public art, the purpose of which it states is to 'enhance the environment, celebrate the university and contribute to its distinctive character' (Artpoint 2008: 4).

The strategy focuses on traditional forms: physical, spatial and permanent works. Temporary works only serve the purpose of engaging the student population through the redevelopment process, 'providing points of vibrancy and celebration through an otherwise disruptive process' (Artpoint 2008: 21). The strategy offers a vision of public art that is tied in with the architectural and landscape design of the new spaces and advocates that art be integrated into the development, with works being site-specific and artists ideally engaged at an early stage. These are principles of best practice in public art commissioning first codified in the late 1980s and early 1990s in the UK (Arts Council of Great Britain 1991; Petherbridge 1987), after the reaction to the non-site-specific, generally abstract works put into urban spaces as part of modernist developments, encapsulated by the various negative descriptions, the 'turd in the plaza' or 'plop art' (Freedman 2004).

The strategy divides the campuses into 15 defined character areas, for each of which an individual approach to public art is described, with analysis of the use and character of each space informing the subsequent recommendations for suitable artistic interventions. The intention is evidently to interpret physical public art broadly. A range of approaches is suggested, including art on different scales from iconic works to design-based contributions to digital interactive pieces and often a multilevel approach in a single location, such as sculpture paired with lighting, landscaping and artist-designed street furniture.

The role of artworks in enhancing the space and contributing to its distinctive character is clearly both practical and ideological, as it has been in city strategies since the early 1990s. For example, orientation is a key function of artworks in the development, especially for pedestrian routes running through this space. Artworks here are seen as playing a vital role in assisting visitors' navigation and understanding of the site, through signage, lighting and paving. As well as helping people to navigate effectively and reach underused parts of a campus, artworks will also encourage people to linger in spaces. At the Student Centre and Catering, artworks need to 'endorse the wider aim to keep students on campus and promote the desire to spend time in open areas' (Artpoint 2008: 13). This aim stems from the university's master plan, but is reflective of the wider trend in UK higher education to make more use of space and commercial use of facilities. The strategy reflects the desire for a cohesive identity among sites that is shared by many multi-campus universities. The current campuses, the strategy observes, are poorly designed, disparate and unconnected. It suggests that lighting, signage and planting could assist in creating a recognisable, coherent identity. It also suggests that commissioning through an agency or lead artist would be more coherent in itself, and thus better help to create a unified image.

Conveying the right image and the university's brand is fundamental to the public art programme. The strategy claims that 'public art should seek to support this effort [preparing a new strategic plan and to rebrand] and help to reinforce identity' (Artpoint 2008: 23). This is, unsurprisingly, most evident in the case of the entrance square, one of the 15 character areas. This is the main entrance to the campus, and the artwork must welcome and announce arrival. The space is identified as important for branding since it is close to the main route from Oxford to London. Thus, the suggestion is that a large iconic artwork – a 'beacon on the hill' – should represent the university's ethos and that consultation would be undertaken with 'stakeholders involved in the image and future marketing of Brookes to ensure the university as a whole benefits from this new identifier' (Artpoint 2008: 7).

This raises two issues. First, there are a number of other stakeholders in the university, beyond those engaged in its marketing. University staff, students and local communities are stakeholders in the university, its campus and the art commissioned for it, although this appears to be recognised only on the last page of the strategy, where it is noted that staff, students and local communities should be consulted in order to encourage a sense of shared ownership. Second, it raises the question of what is distinct about the university's ethos. The strategy states that 'any artworks should reflect Brookes' distinctive voice and contemporary view' (Artpoint 2008: 23). It recommends that the core values of the university should be represented to the outside world by artworks. However, the core values listed are actually rather generic and vague.

The strategy gives the example of *Aspire*, an artwork installed in Nottingham in 2008, designed to act as a landmark and an 'identifier' (Figure 7.1). It was commissioned by the University of Nottingham from architect Ken Shuttleworth for its new Jubilee Campus. At 60 m tall, it is the tallest free-standing art work in the UK. It makes an announcement about the 'ambition, knowledge and world leading innovation' of the University of Nottingham, according to the university's publicity (University of Nottingham n.d.). Whether

Figure 7.1 Ken Shuttleworth, *Aspire*, 2008, University of Nottingham Jubilee
 Campus, photograph copyright Chris McMurray.

this is how the work is perceived by those who see it is another question, and
one might also ask how the values it displays are distinguishable from the core
values of an institution such as Brookes, which seem to be remarkably similar.

Arguably, one further sense in which this strategy is traditional is by being
prescriptive. Other contemporary strategies advocate open briefs, as we will
discuss – at Bristol University and North West Cambridge, for example.
Brookes' strategy, by contrast, determines the location, form and theme of
public art. The use and character of the 15 character areas is not to be understood through artist research or consultation with users, nor was it taken
from the university's master plan for campus development (Oxford Brookes

University 2007). It is a notion developed by the Public Art Strategy, which consulted only a focus group of five students. This process was narrow: the students were given a range of examples of physical art forms, introduced to the 15 predefined areas and asked what art they thought would suit each. While the five students supplied qualitative data about spaces and gave their opinions about the best form and theme for works, the consultative process does not represent an open conversation. The strategy falls foul of criticism first voiced in 1988 (Deutsche 1988), which questions the legitimacy of remotely prescribing the nature of space. It does not seem that Oxford Brookes's strategy is engaged with this literature, or with the understanding of creating democratic space it offers.

Part of the Wider Cultural Offering

Durham University provides a useful example of a UK university taking a different strategic approach to public art as part of an overall cultural offering. The university proclaims that 'culture has been identified as one of the strategic priorities for Durham University' and that the Durham University Cultural Strategy was 'devised to formalise the university's offering, to create a coordinated approach and reduce the duplication of activity and resources needed to deliver and publicise the cultural offering' (University of Durham 2009: 1). However, the strategy demonstrates the conscription of public art by a university to a cultural agenda that has primarily non-cultural objectives.

The Cultural Strategy is prefaced with the recognition of a potential contribution to social and economic regeneration in the surrounding region. It notes that the university's 'cultural activity has an important role in the economic well-being of the community', providing 'an opportunity to actively engage with the local population creating a sense of community and reducing isolation'. According to the strategy:

> A well-developed cultural identity is one in which university students, staff and the wider community engage with each other to enjoy artistic, social, recreational and educational activities. It is through this process of meeting and learning that the strength of the community is enhanced.
>
> (University of Durham 2009)

There has been a long tradition of viewing higher education institutions as vehicles for economic regeneration (Kitson *et al.* 2009; Robinson and Adams 2008), and there are obvious resonances here with the engagement agenda with higher education.

However, the conceptualisations of culture and community are not interrogated or explored, nor are the evidence base or evaluation for these potential economic and community-enhancing contributions hinted at. The strategy document is relatively brief, and although one of the seven stated cultural strategic goals is 'to utilise the university as cultural space for the display of public art', there is little specific detail on this goal. The goal to 'display' public art and a desire to 'host exhibitions, concerts, sculptures, etc.' reveals a traditional concept of public art as the exhibition of art objects. While a deliverable is set to build a budget for public art into new build and renovation projects, there is no sense of how this budget would be utilised. Other strategic goals include overcoming barriers to participation, but they also strongly emphasise promotion, enhancing profile and building national and international partnerships with high-profile organisations. The final strategic goal is perhaps the most revealing of the drivers behind Durham's desire to take a more strategic approach to culture: it is a 'means of attracting students and staff and enhancing the overall student and staff experience'.

In this context, the display of public art is primarily intended as part of the demonstration of the cultural capital of the university for marketing and recruitment purposes. There is no mention of existing public artworks in the audit of cultural assets, and the online 'What's On' and 'Visitor Attractions' sections of the university website make no mention of public art. Thus, although seeming to have a high profile, public art's inclusion in the Cultural Strategy appears to be superficial. This is somewhat strange, as later the same year as the publication of the Cultural Strategy, Durham University publicly celebrated the unveiling of a new piece of public art. *Vessels of Life* by Ranjitsinh Gaekwad (Figure 7.2), then a Distinguished Fellow and artist in residence at the Institute of Advanced Study, was commissioned by Durham University for its Botanic Gardens and sponsored by Northumbrian Water. Admittedly seeming to prefer traditional sculpture objects, Durham University is actively adding to its public art. There is little detailed consideration evident in the strategy of exactly how the university might use public art in either exploring contemporary concepts of public art or capitalising on the use of Durham's existing art works.

Sculpture Trails: Managing and Marketing Existing Public Art on Campus

Other universities capitalise on their existing public artworks by creating public art trails. The sculpture trail at the University of Birmingham is relatively small scale, though illustrious, incorporating a collection built up through the twentieth century. It includes works from the university's Research and Cultural Collections and also includes items from the Barber Institute of Fine Arts Collection (the University Gallery), such as the *Equestrian Statue of King George I*; gifts to the university, such as Bernard Sindall's *Girl in a Hat*; and abstract modernist works by well-known artists, such as Anthony Caro

Figure 7.2 Ranjitsinh Gaekwad, *Vessels of Life*, 2009, Durham University Botanic Gardens (press photograph courtesy of Durham University).

and Barbara Hepworth, on long-term loan to the university. Beyond free-standing works, the trail includes the traditional-style works incorporated into the main university buildings built in the first decade of the twentieth century, such as the frieze above the main entrance of the Aston Webb Building representing 'great men from the worlds of art, philosophy, science and industry' by Henry Pegram. A very late piece by Eduardo Paolozzi, *Faraday*, was commissioned from the artist to mark the centenary of the University of Birmingham's Royal Charter in 2000.

By presenting works as a trail, the university gives an insight into the art that it owns or hosts, which otherwise would not be known to the public. In this way, it is an extra marketing tool for the university. Early works, such as the Pegram reliefs, themselves convey the message that the university, even when it was newly formed, was part of the tradition of European culture and learning. They can therefore be seen as an early form of branding. Later works do not make such a clear statement, and there is no sense in which, as a collection, these works tell a specific story about the university, except in the fact that a significant proportion of the artists are very well-respected and the presence of works by them suggests that the university is of a similarly high quality, with a high level of cultural capital.

The Sculpture Trail is aimed at a non-specialist audience, judging by the light and anecdotal tone of the trail leaflet. The leaflet does not, however, present an entirely useable trail (University of Birmingham 2008): it lists art both inside and outside campus buildings, some of which are not publicly accessible, at least not at all times. For example, the library is only open to library users, although a sculpture on the fourth floor is listed; a work by Jacob Epstein located in the Medical School is included, but is only accessible by prior appointment. This raises questions about whether the trail, by including these items, goes further towards making more of the campus accessible, or whether it lessens the sense of the openness – and 'publicness' – of the university; a university that allows the public to know what it has but still not to see it in person. It seems that it is marketing unknown collections to scholars as much as drawing in a wider constituency to use the campus as a cultural facility. Ultimately, it is an uncomfortable combination of the two functions.

By contrast, the University of Warwick's sculpture trail is clearly aimed at the wider community. The university's large and well-developed collection numbers around 800 abstract works from the second half of the twentieth century and the twenty-first century. A guide, which takes the form of an iPad/iPhone app entitled *Art at Warwick*, has been produced, allowing users to browse the collection by artist, location, medium, or decade, read information about the artist and the artworks and make their own gallery of favourite artworks, and, 'For those who are at the university or planning to visit, the location facility allows you to find actual works on the campus and view them in-situ' (University of Warwick 2012). Thus, it is a facility for a whole range of possible visitors to the university, from scholars, to members of a wider public – though only those with a particular brand of smartphone. A brief sculpture trail leaflet is available for those without (University of Warwick n.d.). In addition, launched in January 2013, the university has produced two trails for children that can be self-directed or accompanied, with accompanying resources for teachers (Figure 7.3). The availability of this level of expertise and service stems from the presence and resources of the university's Arts Centre. This organisation brings with it its own impetus for engaging the wider community, in particular young people, and providing educational materials for schools as it is funded as an Arts Council National Portfolio organisation. This is an Arts Council funding scheme, introduced in 2012, intended to ensure that more people experience and are inspired by the arts and that 'Every child and young person has the opportunity to experience the richness of the arts' (Warwick Arts Centre n.d.), in line with the aims of the Arts Council.

The original act of collecting abstract works by the university could be seen as a branding exercise, that is to say, an exercise in building the visible cultural capital of a newly created university. However, the exercise does more than market the university. It is possible to argue that this fits into the broader higher

Figure 7.3 Warwick Arts Centre Sculpture Trail (photograph courtesy of Warwick Arts Centre).

education concern that university resources should be used more effectively to the benefit of the wider community, with a public art collection seen as resource for both university and community.

Building a Contemporary Public Art Collection

Building a collection is an aim in itself of both the University of Bristol International Public Art Programme (Situations 2008) and North West Cambridge Public Art Strategy (University of Cambridge 2011). Bristol's programme states that the aim is that, by 2020, 'the university and its environs will not simply be enhanced by a set of artistic interventions, but that it will have built an outstanding international collection of public artworks', while North West Cambridge aims to create a 'distributed collection' through new commissioning.

The cultural strategies of Bristol and Durham Universities are comparable in that they do not relate to one specific development. However, Bristol's is created within the framework of a university master plan (University of Bristol 2006), meaning that there is a specific awareness of future development. In this context, it aims to 'articulate a cohesive and inspirational vision for an on-going public art programme'. It then describes a commitment to best practice in public art, and dedicates a page to the discussion of the question 'What is public art?'. This, then, is the most explicitly critically engaged document that we consider. That this should be the case is no surprise. The document is written by Situations, a public art research and commissioning organisation then affiliated with the University of the West of England (independent from 2012). It is therefore rooted in an understanding of both public art and the academic environment. It pushes for a broad understanding of public art: the physical collection being accompanied by 'an exceptional series of temporary events, residencies and debates which contribute to the enhancement of its international reputation as a centre of excellence'. Rather than trying to encapsulate the core values of the university, it calls for art that represents the university by being the best of its kind – 'just as ambitious, innovative and internationally acclaimed as the university's teaching and research'.

The aims of the programme cover the same ground as at Oxford Brookes, promoting orientation, creating distinctive environments and interventions, and contributing creative and imaginative ideas to the design and development of the university's buildings and public realm. However, the Bristol strategy moves on to recommend a complex engagement with the work of the university 'drawing out distinctions and connections between different academic strands of activity'. Engagement should be with what the university does, not only the image it is trying to convey. Ian Davenport's *Everything*, commissioned by the Contemporary Art Society's Special Collections Scheme for the Warwick University Mathematics Institute foyer, is given as an example of conceptual art exploring the theoretical ideas of abstract mathematics.[1] The desired effect of such work in Bristol is to create meeting and talking points that 'nurture creativity and independence of mind'. The aim is not, then, to broadcast a message, for example, of the university's modernity, as in the case of Oxford Brookes. Rather, it is to encourage debate.

As well as permanent art, at Bristol, temporary works are advocated as a means of improving and enhancing the urban realm, and engaging staff, students and the general public. Indeed, the final aim listed is for the university to become a centre of 'excellence in public engagement'. It does not go further to suggest that this will improve the image of the university or attract students: any instrumental value is to be inferred. In fact, the university is well aware of this potential, and in its Cultural Strategy it states that the 'well-being, and hence the recruitment and retention of students and staff, is influenced by the quality of the university's cultural life' (University of Bristol 2006).

North West Cambridge Public Art Strategy, written by the Contemporary Art Society, is specifically linked to the large-scale development of research facilities and accommodation in a new area adjacent to the village of Girton. Like the Bristol strategy, it presents a broad understanding of public art.

Elements of the programme are more defined here, due to the specific nature of the site and Development Plan, though it, too, provides a range of models for commissioning to accommodate a long and varied development process. By far the largest proportion of the allocated budget is to support the 'dispersed collection' formed of new commissions. These might be developed through residencies and design collaborations, where artists work with design teams to influence creatively or contribute to designs. Residencies are listed as the first programmatic strand, emphasising that the engagement of artists with the site over time takes preference over the specific nature of the outcome. Indeed, the strategy identifies the need for 'open minds and open briefs', and anticipates residencies having multiple and varied results including events, talks, performances and publications during its course (University of Cambridge 2011). Just as the Bristol strategy advocated artists connecting with the work of different university departments and disciplines, it is through the residencies that connection to the work of the university is made in Cambridge.

The aims of the dispersed collection are all related to users of the new site. These aims are: legibility and way-finding to encourage usage of the development site; developing a distinctive cultural identity that contributes to sustainable future communities; an ongoing platform for community engagement and interaction as commissions are developed; and access to great art and cultural activity for diverse communities. Thus, we see familiar aims for public art such as legibility and identity, but with a community spin that sees the potential social value of the programme greatly emphasised. The strategy states that the new development will 'encourage investment in Cambridge and will help to recruit and retain the best staff and students from around the world'. It is not in the service of these goals that public art is primarily employed, however; community and social benefits take precedence. The first public art principle listed is 'The provision of sustainable and diverse opportunities for existing and future communities to engage and benefit from the public art programme, contributing to social cohesion and community building.'

It is worth interrogating the rationale behind this. First, the scale of the development is greater than the others we have considered so far, incorporating 66 hectares of land, currently part of Cambridge's green belt. On it there will be academic and research facilities, accommodation for 2,000 undergraduate students, 2,000–2,500 dwellings for staff, as well as hotel and conference facilities. There will also be community facilities, public open space and nature conservation areas. This will provide 'living and research accommodation needed to grow the university's research capabilities and to retain its world class position'. It is not the development of an area of existing campus, but the development of a new urban centre and a new community. It therefore has more in common with normal city development than university development. The strategy responds both to the university's master plan and the North West Cambridge Area Action Plan, which states that 'a strategy for public art is required' (Cambridge City Council 2009).

Unsurprisingly, then, when concern with local community has been minimal in the strategies discussed so far, the Cambridge strategy is suffused with this notion. It lists engagement activities as: community participation in specific projects; contribution to conceptual and content development; public access to the project website; public presentations, seminars and events during each residency year; participation in temporary event programmes; school and community education programmes; consultation on developed proposals; and access to archive and legacy materials.

One strand of the programme, 'Making Place – Creating Local Identity', consists of a series of commissions designed to contribute to the naming of 'site identity elements', with the intention that these should be meaningful in local terms. An artist will lead a programme of community engagement and creative dialogue allowing local people to 'contribute their thoughts, memories and stories of the area'. This is intended to build ownership of the development. The artist will also work with the marketing team, and the naming of identity elements must also support branding. The project is thus dual purpose, assisting with ownership and marketing the new area and the university generally. There is potential conflict here, as we will discuss.

Another strand of the programme is temporary work, characterised as 'activation', or 'bringing life to the proposed development at early stages and encouraging public use of the Application site'. This implies that it is short-termist, though it is intended to 'build a platform for sustainable programmatic partnerships with local and wider creative agencies'. It also aims to bring people into the space and engage them with the development, and through this engagement to create local identity.

Like Durham, the university space is perceived as a cultural space. However, in Cambridge, the purpose of this exercise is not recruitment; the development is at too early a stage and the audience is too local for the international recruitment Cambridge University is aiming at – though organised events might provide good marketing images. By comparison with Bristol, Cambridge's temporary programme is nevertheless much more instrumental in its aims. In Bristol, these are intended only to attract and engage visitors and passers by, with no explicit agenda. Community engagement can be seen as a desire to ensure that the university is not seen as placeless. In the Cambridge strategy, there is enthusiasm for tapping into the actual place, with themes including the history, archaeology and ecology of the site.

This strategy is one of a large institution building a large development on to a village. Cambridge University is taking measures to make this a new local centre with a range of facilities, and these provisions are intended to create a vibrant new area, mitigating the negative effects of development suffered by existing residents. However, this new university area is extremely significant, having a direct impact on the lives of local people, but not necessarily benefitting them. This situation would explain the statement early in the document: 'Community engagement is built into every strand of the public art programme through a creative approach that aims to build understanding and support for the proposed development and generate a widespread sense of ownership and connection' (University of Cambridge 2011: 2). This implies that the art programme is essentially instrumental. It may be described as inclusive, but it also serves the purpose of easing the path of the development by reducing potential local resistance. It does not offer local people the opportunity to influence the development fundamentally; rather, it offers a token level of involvement. It appears democratic, but it could also be read as allowing a small space in the overall development for community expression as a form of appeasement.

Developing Strategies with Transparency and Community Focus

A less problematic community-focused engagement approach is evident in Robert Gordon University's (RGU) development of a public art strategy for its Garthdee campus. Over the past 10 years, RGU has undertaken extensive development on this campus and has a plan to relocate the whole university to it. While it is a plan encompassing the creation of a new single campus, it is nevertheless on a much smaller scale than Cambridge's plans.

The local context of Aberdeen and RGU has undoubtedly influenced the approach taken. Local interest in and support for public art is demonstrated by the 2012 launch of Aberdeen City Council's Public Art Aberdeen website, dedicated to public art in the region, including news and other resources for artists, communities and organisations, as well as a guide for the various stages of commissioning public art (Aberdeen City Council n.d.). As in Bristol, the university has relevant academic expertise in public art. Gray's School of Art is a constituent of RGU, and has a long-standing and active research interest in art in the public sphere.

There is a high degree of transparency and desire for community engagement evident in how RGU is making publicly available online the process of the strategy development (with the usual caveat that the mere availability of documentation online cannot be read as evidence that it is widely accessed and used). RGU have published not only the brief and application details for production of the strategy (RGU 2012a), but also three clarification and response documents resulting from the tender process. Thus, it is possible to explore the aims and motivations of RGU, as well as details of the budget allocation – confirmation of only a somewhat meagre one-off allocation of

£60,000 for implementation of the strategy (RGU 2012b). As with Bristol and Cambridge, the wider policy context at RGU is evident, as the public art strategy has to relate to an architectural master plan in the form of an Estate Development Plan, in which the key issues are identified as a 'compact academic facility with an end-to-end walking time of 2 minutes', providing visual links with the river and reinforcing the existing primary arrival point/entrance (RGU 2012c). There is also acknowledgement of a cultural engagement strategy being under development that will take the broad premise of 'Enriching lives through culture, in which the university will be advocate and facilitator of cultural engagement and enrichment in its local and regional communities' (RGU 2012d).

The community and regional aspirations of RGU are equally evident in the brief for the public art strategy. The background information provided emphasises the history of the institution and its role in the community and the brief calls for the development of a vision as to how the arts 'may engage with both academic activity and the campus development', and identifies three core constituencies of 'students, staff and visitors', emphasising that this vision should promote RGU as 'respectful and welcoming of its immediate neighbours'. It describes as cultural assets, not only the university collections that have museum accreditation, but also individuals within the university community who have 'various relationships with the cultural community within the city and shire'. This demonstrates recognition by the university that engagement agendas can operate at all levels, from the institutional to the individual.

The brief recognises the complexity of the proposed single campus in terms of its physicality, multiple functionality, diverse user groups and the symbolic messages it will embody and communicate, aiming for the art to contribute to 'portraying a clear statement of the focus and ethos of the university as a whole'. The stated aim is to develop a series of art projects, rather than art works, and envisages elements that may be permanent, temporary, durational or performative, 'ranging from those dealing specifically with the architectural and landscape environment to others aimed at creating collaboration between the disciplines or interaction with local communities and partners'. Health and safety concerns and stipulations regarding low maintenance do reveal a lingering emphasis on traditional, project-based work. Ian Banks, of art and architecture practice Atoll Ltd, the consultant appointed by RGU, collaborating with a new media artist and a lighting consultant, has expanded the university's community focus within strategy development activity. A blog site, Public Art and the Riverside Campus, has been created as a reference and tool for developing the strategy (PARC n.d.). This includes an online questionnaire that was originally sent to 54 largely internal RGU stakeholders, as well as a summary report and analysis of the results received from these internal stakeholders, with a 54 per cent response rate (PARC n.d.). Obviously, the small sample size means that the survey cannot be read as evidence of consensus among the university community. The survey is further limited in that it primarily canvassed RGU stakeholders, not representatives of the wider community. It is significant, however, in that it demonstrates that the university wished to engage and publicise a community focus in the production of its public art strategy.

The survey also asked respondents to identify priorities for spaces and sites for public art development by indicating a personal or professional preference for each of 13 theoretical 'artistic outcomes' in terms of their importance in the short, medium or long term. Though there was some confusion reported with this question as to whether 'importance' was to do with desire or urgency, it was aimed at establishing thinking about the need for a comprehensive, long-term approach, plus the focus of deciding what sort of artistic programmes should be pursued as a first priority. The top three responses were: the campus riverside and ecology; creative engagement – community arts and well-being; and school identity. The consultant concluded: 'What is clear is a desire and a need for RGU to up its game both artistically and practically, and for it to use such a public art programme to attempt to "bridge" with the city much more than before' (PARC n.d.).

Alternative Approaches Using Public Art

Our final example is one where the focus is not so much on intentions or the formulating of policy and strategy documents, but illustrates instead alternative approaches to the traditional sculptural object that a UK university has explored. Anglia Ruskin University has campuses in Chelmsford and Cambridge, and is therefore, like Oxford Brookes and RGU, a former polytechnic sharing a city with a far older university institution. Like the majority of the public art strategies we have considered, Anglia Ruskin's Visualise programme links campus development with a desire to engage the wider community. The university is developing a new site near its main Cambridge campus to house its Faculty of Health, Social Care and Education, and aims to take an innovative public art approach:

> Rather than taking the traditional public art approach of sculptures in public spaces, Visualise is embracing the university's centre of excellence in fine art, media arts and digital technologies to create projects that will enable us to explore the public spaces within Cambridge and Anglia Ruskin University in new ways.
>
> (Anglia Ruskin University 2012)

The Visualise art programme ran through 2011 and 2012, and was managed by FutureCity, a culture and place-making consultancy (FutureCity n.d.). Anglia Ruskin claimed through Visualise to be providing 'a valuable cultural contribution to Cambridge through the significant investment generated through the university's Cambridge Campus redevelopment'. Unlike Oxford Brookes, Bristol or Cambridge, it does not make public the finance or mechanisms for realising the programme, nor does it take RGU's approach and reveal the processes that led to the formulation and adoption of the programme. Yet, we can discern common themes in the publicity and marketing for the programme – a relationship to the university's academic and research activities and desire for wider community engagement.

The Visualise brochure refers to bringing together different communities in the context of the digital age (Visualise n.d.). The focus on new media and the digital undoubtedly reflects the research activities of the university. The Cultures of the Digital Economy (CoDE) Research Institute is a multidisciplinary initiative at Anglia Ruskin University working in, among other topics, media theory and network culture, media archaeology, digital music and video, fine arts, video games, audio engineering, and computer design and animation. The Ruskin Gallery, a public gallery within the Cambridge School of Art, the oldest constituent part of the university, prides itself on an innovative digital gallery.

The Visualise programme consisted of three types of projects: a public art commission by artists 'Circumstance', art and technology collaborations, and a programme of exhibitions and events. The latter included a series of talks and discussions at the university open to the general public, which covered a wide range of contemporary art practice under the general heading 'Negotiating New Spaces for Art'. The combination of art, science, technology and ways of seeing were the themes at the heart of the events and exhibitions programme, bringing internationally known artists such as Liliane Lijn to work with the digital screens in the Ruskin Gallery, as well as in unusual public spaces, including shops in Cambridge city centre and the grass lawns of the Cambridge Institute of Astronomy.

For the public art commission, 'Circumstance' (artist Duncan Speakman and collaborators) was commissioned to create a major new project for Cambridge Campus students, staff and local residents in a 'pervasive experience' using combinations of art, sound and performance with portable and online technologies to connect different sites across Cambridge. In the first phase of the commission, apps for smartphones were released that guided participants through the streets of the city as if they were in a film. For a week in June, Circumstance ran a participatory event (Figure 7.4) in which participants were encouraged to pick up a hand-crafted wooden speaker box from a secret location in Cambridge:

Figure 7.4 Circumstance, *Of Sleeping Birds*, Cambridge 2012 (photograph copyright Sophie Wainwright).

Of Sleeping Birds is a pedestrian symphony. We built 40 location sensitive portable loudspeakers, each one plays a different element of the music we composed. The speakers are carried by the audience through a city, the GPS position of the speaker causes different sections of the composition to be played, and the movement of the people in the group changes the acoustic qualities, the audience become the orchestra.

(Circumstance n.d.)

Thus, the public art commission from the Visualise programme did not result in an object for display in the university or a design feature in the campus landscape. It was temporary and durational, involving the use of sound art and media technologies. It was participatory and performative, although we might debate the level of mass engagement given the limited numbers of speakers and the requirement to actively become an insider in identifying their secret locations.

It is the third element of the programme – the art and technology collaborations – that hint, perhaps, at ways that universities might start to use public art to meet current policy agendas. These collaborations were created to enable artists to work on research and development projects with Cambridge-based technology companies. This is typical of much knowledge transfer activity across the UK, where universities and local technology companies work together to develop new products (Abreu *et al.* 2010). The university acknowledged that 'under a theme of "public intervention", the collaborative projects will be encouraged to exploit the opportunities provided by pervasive computing and wireless technologies – a real business strength in Cambridge' (Anglia Ruskin University 2012).

Three collaborations were initiated. Arts organisation Proboscis was commissioned to undertake a collaborative research and development project with Phillips R&D in Cambridge to look at innovation around NFC (near field communications) and personal health care. The short-term aim of the project was to explore the way personal health data could be reinterpreted. In the second collaboration, artist Bettina Furnee and Cambridge company Optricks Media explored the potential of augmented reality games in engaging with a public realm space in the city. The site chosen, Reality Checkpoint, is a large lamp post in the middle of Parker's Piece located at the intersection of the park's diagonal paths. A local landmark, it is believed that it was on this green that the foundations of the modern rules of association football were first set out. In July 2012, Furnee and Optricks Media ran an augmented reality game, *New Rules for a Fair Society*, in which participants were invited to come to Parker's Piece to place their own rules, and vote for others, using the free augmented reality browser, Wikitude, for smartphones, or alternatively to submit and vote for rules via the website. In the third collaboration, artist Eduardo Kac, winner of the 2009 Ars Electronica Prize for Hybrid Art, was to undertake research and development on two new projects, including a new audiovisual experiment intended to be the first in the world using MBed (embedded systems) made by ARM in Cambridge. Kac was also commissioned to collaborate with sound engineer Rob Toulson in the CoDE research centre at the university and test a 'bio-conductive ink' invented by Bare Conductive Ink Ltd. Thus, we see a direct merger of the public art programme with the generation of research outcomes for the university.

Conclusions

Examining universities' use of public art can be revealing of the prevailing definitions and conceptualisations of both higher education and public art. Our snapshot examination of strategies and practice in the UK reveals a prevailing conservatism and the predominance of traditional (late twentieth-century) conceptualisations of the nature (object) and function (place-marketing) of public art. The review of publicly available and recent public art strategies by UK universities has revealed primarily instrumental uses of public art. In particular, these reflect the changing political and economic landscape of higher education in the UK, with an emphasis on engagement and the current flurry of building of, and relocation to, new campuses. The physical roles played by public art in the built environment of the campus are emphasised, particularly in terms of orientation, navigation and understanding of the campus through iconic objects, as well as artist-designed signage, lighting and paving. Public art is seen as a contribution to identity and community creation for new campus developments, but we can also possibly infer a role as part of strategies to ensure consent for development that may otherwise be problematic. The issues around the involvement of art in development and regeneration have received significant attention in contemporary public art discourse. In a higher education context, these issues draw attention to the problematic position of universities in the UK, public institutions of learning that increasingly also have to operate as commercial enterprises.

The potential for contribution to higher education engagement agendas is also a key driver in universities' approaches to public art. We can discern a distinct confusion between community engagement and marketing the university, another signifier of the confusion between a university's role as both a public and a commercial organisation. Thus, the engagement agenda operates on two levels. As in Durham, the display of public art can be primarily viewed as part of an overall cultural offering, as the demonstration of the cultural capital of the university for marketing and recruitment purposes. With Oxford Brookes, this is taken further: the art is not only a demonstration of general cultural capital, but is also to embody and broadcast the core values of the institution. Unsurprisingly, a more critical consideration and conceptualisation of public art is evident at higher education institutions with research expertise in the field. Thus, at Bristol, the aspiration is for an international programme of public art that builds a collection as an asset in itself, a strategy that advocates a programme of excellent public art as, in itself, representative of a great university.

So are universities benefiting from contemporary public art critique in both reflecting on and developing multiple uses of public art and in rethinking higher education's role in its multiple and diverse communities? Examination of the second level on which public art is being seen as contributing to the engagement agenda suggests that there is benefit. Despite a prevailing conservatism, we can identify the broadening of concepts of university space from the physical to encompass the temporary, performative and experiential from contemporary public art practice and discourse. Concurrent with this is a consideration of the public for university public art, thinking of 'public' as not a singular homogenous mass, but as multiple, diverse publics. The majority of the public art strategies that we have considered explicitly state the intention to engage with the institutions' wider communities. This in itself is problematic: the public art strategies reveal the complexities and pragmatic considerations universities face when determining levels of access, the definition of spaces and activities that take place in them, and even in recognising and defining their multiple communities.

Our research has revealed some interesting areas of development. Several institutions are viewing their public art holistically, as collections rather than as individual commissions. There are resonances here with university special collections and museums, which have traditionally navigated, to varying degrees, the boundaries between academe and public. The development of sculpture trails, while still coloured with the marketing agenda, hints at ways universities might learn and capitalise from museum practices in outreach and community engagement in using their public art as a collection.

Alternative approaches to traditional sculptural monuments are being explored by universities, and the strategies indicate a desire to expand the concept of public art to encompass temporary, performative and socially engaged practices, although in practice these are still very much in the minority. Anglia Ruskin's Visualise programme provides a good example of these possibilities, and of a university using public art beyond the campus. Visualise also provides an interesting cross-disciplinary approach, linking art collaboratively with sciences and technologies, particularly the digital. Visualise's commissioning of 'art and technology collaborations' hints perhaps at ways that universities might start to use public art to meet current policy agendas around knowledge transfer and impact with more creative interpretations that bridge disciplines and combine both business and community engagement.

It is worth briefly considering what an examination of universities' use of public art has *not* revealed. What current UK policies for higher education are conspicuous by their omission in this context, or at least by the scant attention they receive? While the staff community of a university is taken into account, the student voice is largely missed. With the introduction of fees, and consequent emphasis on the student experience and employability, this is a significant omission. Similarly, the strategies make little mention of the use of their public art in terms of learning, although perhaps this is felt to be so self-evident that it does not require development. Undoubtedly, there is more that universities in the UK could do in reflecting on and developing multiple uses of public art. In research terms, the use of public art has proved a fruitful lens to examine the UK higher education and its developing agendas, in particular the related but very different concerns of marketing and social engagement.

Note

1   For further details, see the University of Warwick Art Collection entry on the University's website: www2.warwick.ac.uk/services/art/artist/iandavenport/wu0817 (accessed 21 November 2013).

References

Aberdeen City Council (n.d.) 'Public art', available at: www.aberdeencity.gov.uk/ PublicArtAberdeen (accessed 28 February 2013).

Abreu, M., Grinevich, V., Hughes, A. and Kitson, M. (2010) *Knowledge Exchange between Academics and Business, Public and Third Sectors*, Cambridge and London: University of Cambridge and Imperial College.

Anglia Ruskin University (2012) 'Visualise', available at: www.anglia.ac.uk/ruskin/ en/home/microsites/visualise.hmtl (accessed 28 February 2013).

Artpoint (2008) *Oxford Brookes University Redevelopment: Public Art Strategy*, Oxford: Oxford Brookes University, available at: www.brookes.ac.uk/spacetothink/docs/ public-art-april-09.pdf (accessed 27 February 2013).

Arts Council of Great Britain (1991) *Percent for Art: A Review*, London: Arts Council.

Cambridge City Council (2009) 'Northwest Cambridge area action plan', available at: www.cambridge.gov.uk/north-west-cambridge-area-action-plan (accessed 28 February 2013).

Cartiere, C. (2008) 'Coming in from the cold: a public art history', in C. Cartiere and S. Willis (eds), *The Practice of Public Art*, Abingdon: Routledge, (7–17).

Circumstance (n.d.) 'Circumstance', available at: http://productofcircumstance.com/ new/index.php/project/of-sleeping-birds/ (accessed 27 February 2013).

Deutsche, R. (1988) 'Uneven development: public art in New York City', *October*, 47(Winter), 3–52.

Freedman, S. (ed.) (2004) *PLOP: Recent Projects of the Public Art Fund*, London: Merrell.

FutureCity (n.d.) 'FutureCity', available at: http://futurecity.co.uk/home (accessed 28 February 2013).

HEFCE (Higher Education Funding Council for England) (2009) *Strategic Plan 2006–11: Updated 2009*, Bristol: Higher Education Funding Council for England.

Kitson, M., Howells, J., Braham, R. and Westlake, S. (2009) *The Connected University: Driving Recovery and Growth in the UK Economy*, London: NESTA.

Merritt, D., Greenacre, F. and Eustace, K. (2010) *Public Sculpture of Bristol*, Public Monuments and Sculpture Association Public Sculpture of Britain Series, Liverpool: Liverpool University Press.

Miles, M. (1997) *Art, Space and the City*, London: Routledge.

National Coordinating Centre for Public Engagement (2010) *The Engaged University: A Manifesto for Public Engagement*, available at: www.publicengagement.ac.uk/sites/ default/files/Manifesto%20for%20Public%20Engagement%20Final%20January%202 010.pdf (accessed 26 February 2013).

National Coordinating Centre for Public Engagement (n.d.) 'What is public engagement?', available at: www.publicengagement.ac.uk/what (accessed 26 February 2013).

Oxford Brookes University (2007) 'Oxford Brookes University', available at: www. brookes.ac.uk/spacetothink/docs/masterplan.pdf (accessed 27 February 2013).

Petherbridge, D. (1987) *Art for Architecture: A Handbook on Commissioning*, London: HMSO.

Public Art and the Riverside Campus (PARC) (n.d.) 'PARC blog', available at: http:// publicartandtheriverside.blogspot.co.uk (accessed 27 February 2013).

RGU (Robert Gordon University) (2012a) 'Public art & the Riverside Campus, development of a University Public Art Strategy: brief and application details' available at: www4.rgu.ac.uk/files/One%20Campus%20Final%20Brief.pdf (accessed 27 February 2013).

RGU (2012b) 'Public Art Strategy clarification and response 16th February', available at: www4.rgu.ac.uk/files/Clarification160212.pdf (accessed 27 February 2013).

RGU (2012c) 'Public Art Strategy clarification and response 21st February 2012', available at: www4.rgu.ac.uk/files/Clarification210212.pdf (accessed 27 February 2013).

RGU (2012d) 'Public Art Strategy clarification and response 24th February 2012', available at: www4.rgu.ac.uk/files/Clarification240212.pdf (accessed 27 February 2013).

Robinson, C. and Adams, N. (2008) 'Unlocking the potential: the role of universities in pursuing regeneration and promoting sustainable communities', *Local Economy*, 23(4), 277–89.

Roe, S. (2008) *Oil Paintings in Public Ownership in Birmingham*, London: The Public Catalogue Foundation.

Situations (2008) *The University of Bristol International Public Art Programme*, Bristol: University of the West of England, available at: www.situations.org.uk/media/files/University_of_Bristol_public_art_strategy_.pdf (accessed 27 February 2013).

University of Birmingham (2008) *Campus Sculpture Trail*, Birmingham: University of Birmingham.

University of Bristol (2006) 'Cultural Strategy', available at: www.bristol.ac.uk/university/governance/policies/cultural.html (accessed 27 February 2013).

University of Cambridge (2011) 'North West Cambridge Public Art Strategy', available at: www.nwcambridge.co.uk/PA-PDFs/Full/20_Public_Art_Strategy/20_NWC_Public_Art_Strategy.pdf (accessed 27 February 2013).

University of Durham (2009) 'Cultural strategy document', available at: www.dur.ac.uk/culture/strategy (accessed 19 February 2013).

University of Exeter (n.d.) 'Sculpture Walk', available at: www.exeter.ac.uk/sculpture/site1/frames.htm (accessed 28 February 2013).

University of Nottingham (n.d.) 'Aspire', available at: http://aspire.nottingham.ac.uk (accessed 27 February 2013).

University of Warwick (2012) 'Art at Warwick (iPad)', available at: www2.warwick.ac.uk/newsandevents/interactive/mobileapps/artatwarwick/ (accessed 1 March 2013).

University of Warwick (n.d.) 'Sculpture Trail', available at: www2.warwick.ac.uk/services/art/resources/sculpture (accessed 28 February 2013).

Visualise (2013) 'Visualise', available at: http://visualisecambridge.org/?page_id=33 (accessed 28 February 2013).

Warwick Arts Centre (n.d.) 'Warwick Arts Centre', available at: www.warwickarts centre.co.uk/news/news/national-portfolio-funding (accessed 27 February 2013).

Watson, D. (2003) 'Universities and civic engagement: a critique and a prospectus', Keynote address for the 2nd biennial 'Inside-Out' Conference on the civic role of universities – 'Charting uncertainty: capital, community and citizenship', University of Queensland, Ipswich, 3 July 2003.

Watson, D. (2007) *Managing Civic and Community Engagement*, Buckingham: McGraw-Hill/Open University Press.

Part II
Space and Place in Context

8

The Idea of a University and its Concrete Form

ANTHONY OSSA-RICHARDSON

The aesthetic appreciation of our past goes in recognisable, if not always predictable, cycles. This is most evident perhaps in our architecture: as recently as the 1960s, the Victorian legacy was so despised that one of its greatest treasures, the Midland Grand Hotel at St Pancras, London, only narrowly escaped demolition, and while Scott's opulent hotel is now Grade I listed, refurbished and lionised, the era that scorned him is taking its turn in the shade. Among the most important works of that decade are the university campuses that mushroomed in neglected vales and marshes outside cities across England – Brighton, York, Colchester, Canterbury, Lancaster, Warwick, Norwich. Few young scholars at such places, one suspects, now notice their built environs: the drabness of precast concrete, of point-blocks and terraces, of repetition, speaks of mere functionality and blends into the background. Later additions to the sites have done their best to turn away from the old mood; the contributions of Norman Foster and Will Mather to East Anglia are a case in point, as are the recent phases at York.

At the time of construction, however, these structures were animated not only by concerns for cost and utility, though these were undoubtedly prominent, but also by less quantifiable considerations: beauty, visual drama, history, and, above all, ideals of higher education old and new. The architecture, at once art and machine, aimed both to embody utopian principles and to facilitate their realisation: that is, to provide a place that gave memorable expression to a philosophy. If the talk was of revolution, of a bright start, tradition and memory continued to maintain a central presence.

This chapter, then, seeks to examine the ideas behind the physical forms of three English new universities of the era: the University of Sussex, designed by Sir Basil Spence; the University of York, built by Andrew Derbyshire at Robert Matthew Johnson-Marshall (RMJM); and the University of East Anglia (UEA) by Denys Lasdun. The material facts are now well established, thanks to a number of recent works of scholarship both general (Muthesius 2000) and specific, especially on UEA (Dormer and Muthesius 2001; Sanderson 2002). I want here to consider instead the intellectual context and reception of the architecture and of the rhetoric behind it, adding to a clutch of smaller studies that have moved, to a greater or lesser extent, in this direction (e.g. Campbell 2008; Darley 1991; Hill 2012; Smith 2008).

*

The university was created in the Middle Ages by a religious elite with the aim of producing a literate class for work in the courts and chanceries. The highest education, however, led to theology: in principle, to the reform and cultivation of self for God. Post-war Britain could hardly have been a more different world, and yet, when plans were drawn up for a slew of new universities in the late 1950s, a kernel of the old ideal had survived; in addition to training a new and teeming generation for middle-class life, education was to produce less tangible benefits – the discovery and reform of the self. This was perhaps most succinctly expressed by Asa Briggs in *Bias*, the student journal at Sussex, where he served as professor of history and later vice-chancellor: 'My ideal is an independent student, helped to discover not only new knowledge but himself, becoming increasingly self-reliant (and self-critical) as he becomes more knowledgeable' (quoted by Hawkins in Daiches 1964: 200).

From the early 1940s, prominent voices called for reform and renewal in higher education (Silver 2003). Among these voices, perhaps the loudest was that of Sir Walter Moberly, whose 1948 *The Crisis in the University* offered a potted history of the university, espousing a return to the ideals of liberal education put forward a century before by John Henry Newman. Such an education, he wrote, would train the student 'to recognize, to respect and delight in, what is intrinsically true, good and beautiful. It does so simply because this is a want of man's nature and in its satisfaction he fulfils himself.' Without such a want, he added, a man 'would be less than fully human' (Moberly 1948: 31). Self-realisation, by this light, is associated with learning for its own sake rather than for practical or vocational ends, and, as a corollary, with an apprehension of the unity of intellectual disciplines. Newman had insisted, in explicitly Christian terms, that 'all branches of knowledge are connected together, because the subject-matter of knowledge is intimately united in itself, as being the acts and the work of the Creator'. Again, 'all Knowledge is a whole and the separate Sciences parts of one'. Education was itself best understood as 'a work of self-reformation', as Newman had experienced at Oxford (Newman 1859: 2). The religious connotations remained explicit in Moberly's book, published by the Student Christian Movement, in which he had been active through the 1940s (Silver 2003: 100–26).

A decade later, the most public philosophical concerns about higher education had become more narrowly focused on the arts–sciences divide. The Crowther Report of 1959, although it defended the specialisation of English schooling, objected to the starkness of the division between the sciences and the arts among school-leavers, that is, between 'literacy' and 'numeracy' – a term it coined (Crowther 1959 I: 25, #397–415). This division it identified as a modern malady, noting that 'when John Henry Newman was an undergraduate, the honours course at Oxford demanded proficiency in both classics and mathematics' (Crowther 1959 I: 25, #378). More famous than the Report was C. P. Snow's rather lopsided (and conceptually unoriginal) broadside against the disengagement of the two cultures (Snow 1959); what began as a Rede lecture achieved a very rapid dissemination in printed form, sparking a good deal of controversy, notably from F. R. Leavis, but also affecting key policy decisions, most of all among the university planners (Muthesius 2000: 102; Perkin 1991: 298). The impact of Crowther and Snow can be discerned throughout the articles and debates in *Universities Quarterly* over the following decade, for instance in a 1962 piece, 'The integration of knowledge', suggesting a revival of the medieval liberal arts curriculum to solve the fragmentation of academic disciplines (Vereker and Wilson 1962: 280). A similar revivalism had been at the heart of American reforming efforts 30 years earlier, in the form of the 1935 Virginia Plan, following the work of Richard McKeon and Scott Buchanan (Haarlow 2003). Robert Maynard Hutchins, so influential in the reshaping of American academia, could write in 1936:

> The medieval university had a principle of unity. It was theology ... The medieval university was rationally ordered, and, for its time, it was practically ordered, too. But these are other times; and we are trying to discover a rational and practical order for the higher learning of today.
>
> (Hutchins 1936: 96)

In the United States of the 1930s, and in 1950s Britain, *something* was felt to be missing from modern education – something where religion had been in the Middle Ages, and was still in Newman's *Idea*. Snow, above all, helped to crystallise the *desideratum* as a unity between the disciplines, now seen as the defining philosophical problem of the new universities (Brawne 1967: 10; Cross and Jobling 1969: 175).[1] Newman was a frequent point of reference, alongside Mill and Arnold (Muthesius 2000: 99–100), but even without these names, the principles held. Even as early as 1957, the architect Lionel Brett could assert that 'we have grown in this country to think of a university not as vocational but as a place designed to produce (as far as possible) the Universal Man' (Brett 1957: 240). And as Michael Brawne observed, the attempt to solve this problem, to bring about wholeness, 'had considerable architectural implications' (Brawne 1967: 10).

John Fulton, the first vice-chancellor at Sussex, made clear the spiritual and political dimension of their endeavour, referring in 1964 to 'the ideal of an educated democracy in which the citizen is raised through contact with the man of learning to a higher level of personal development' (Daiches 1964: 14). Sussex had admitted its first 50 students in 1962; the campus opened the following year, a few miles north of Brighton, on the south coast of England. From the first, the intention there was to overcome the boundaries between subjects: departments and faculties were abolished in favour of 'Schools of Study' bringing together related subjects, and all students were to take both major and minor subjects for their degree. Fulton agreed with Spence that Falmer House, the main student centre on campus, would provide space for the 'vital process of cross-fertilization between members of differing faculties' (Daiches 1964: 202). Lectures, finally, were also rejected for small seminars to encourage personal involvement and debate. Despite this, some felt that not enough had been done to lessen the disciplinary divide. Michael Beloff, after extensive discussion with the students at Sussex, commented that 'in many instances the bridges between subjects are not as numerous, or not as well-constructed, as the syllabus implies. Where he is told to find bridges, the student instead finds chasms' (Beloff 1968: 86). Likewise, Granville Hawkins, an early Sussex undergraduate, remarked in 1964 that one of the main problems remained 'to get some kind of exchange between the arts and science students', and that seminars had not been successful in this direction: the 'accumulated traditions of separateness that the older universities and particularly the schools have helped to create and sustain' were simply too strong. Moreover, the physical isolation of the subjects in discrete buildings allowed students and staff alike 'still to think of separate disciplines'. As a solution, Hawkins recommended 'the establishment of joint projects where scientists and arts students must work together, although doing different and quite precisely defined jobs, in a concrete partnership' (Daiches 1964: 195).

Fulton's counterpart at UEA, Frank Thistlethwaite, wanted his university to pursue 'the truth in fundamental matters for its own sake', and most members of his Academic Planning Board agreed, sharing the Victorian ideal of liberal education (Sanderson 2002: 68). On the board, Noel Annan and Edgar Williams were especially keen on interdisciplinary arts-sciences courses for the undergraduates, with Snow in mind; only the chemist Christopher Ingold was sceptical about bridging the divide. Like Fulton and others, Thistlethwaite wanted Schools of Study, rather than departments (Brawne 1967: 37), which he explained as 'an effort to guard against the dangers of excessive specialisation in undergraduate study and reflects a desire to break down the kind of departmental barrier that often stands in the way of properly integrated courses incorporating two or more traditional "subjects"'. Hence, at UEA, there would be Schools of Biological Sciences, of Chemical Sciences, of English Studies, of European Studies, of Fine Arts, of Mathematics and Physics, and of Social

Studies, each offering a variety of integrated courses. It was important, finally, that each of these schools 'be given appropriate embodiment in architectural terms' (LaD/143/2, 28/2/66).

Lasdun, whose work Thistlethwaite fervently supported, acknowledged the philosophy: 'Our academic brief was concerned with the striving towards unity of knowledge and the common identity of the whole university' (Lasdun 1965: 219). The architect was appointed in 1962, and began building in 1964 to plans unveiled the previous year. The University Grants Commission (UGC) expressed some trepidation on the appointment after Spence's reckless expenditure at Sussex: 'prestige architects', as Thistlethwaite reported their view in 1963, 'were to be avoided like the plague' (LaD/83/1, Memo 6/2/63). The site had been chosen on a former golf course to the west of Norwich, and before Lasdun's first buildings opened in 1966, university life was conducted in prefabs, subsequently demolished. UEA's bristling residential ziggurats remain the most recognisable icon of the new universities, and yet it was his 'Teaching Wall' that properly embodied the philosophical concerns of his brief. Lasdun sought to avoid precisely what Granville Hawkins had lamented at Sussex, namely the physical separation of the disciplines, by splicing all subjects into a single, south-facing sausage of concrete and glass running along the north side of the campus. He later denied that the integration of the Teaching Wall was practical, since actual interdisciplinary activity was to happen not within the Wall, but elsewhere: this aspect of the design, rather, was a symbolic gesture, in the service of a sense of place. Tellingly, Lasdun would be quoted as saying of UEA: 'it's not even a building, it's a place' (Duckett 1968: 58). Other campuses of the period, notably Essex and Lancaster, though they differed in their actual form, took a similar approach to UEA in presenting the university as 'one vast building'; as one recent monograph has put it, this basic plan was intended to embody 'the unity of the institution and its aims, academic and educational co-operation' (Dormer and Muthesius 2001: 64; on Essex, cf. Sloman 1963b: 980). As always, there were sceptics:

> Many people feel that the concept of interpenetration of disciplines by means of architectural union is unattainable and almost as soon as the Chemistry School had moved in, it was decided to fit heavy doors to prevent students from the School of English and American Studies from straying into it. Now they are kept locked.
>
> (Birks 1972: 82)

Of all the new vice-chancellors, it was Eric James (Lord James of Rusholme) at York whose thoughts on education were the most fully developed. James had, in fact, contributed to the Crowther Report, and his guiding mood was a hostility to academic specialisation, promoting instead a 'power to think effectively in general terms', following Newman (Smith 2008: 32). Like Moberly and Richard Livingstone in the 1940s, James lectured on Plato's theory of education in 1975; that philosopher had evidently been another source for the era's focus on intellectual unity. At York, James rejected the Redbrick model of organisation, supporting a return to a quasi-collegiate system, where students of different disciplines might both live and work together, profiting from each other's ideas. This, again, followed Newman, who had noted:

> An assemblage of learned men, zealous for their own sciences, and rivals of each other, are brought, by familiar intercourse and for the sake of intellectual peace, to adjust the claims and relations of their respective subjects of investigation. They learn to respect, to consult, to aid each other.
>
> (Newman 1859: 138; cf., in James's era,
> Halsey 1961: 55)

For Andrew Derbyshire, too, the integration of the arts and sciences was of primary importance. Unlike his RMJM colleague Hugh Morris, who worked on the University of Bath in the same period, Derbyshire came from a scientific background, reading natural science at Cambridge, with a special interest in the physics of light and sound. Just as the 'sensual aspects of science' most appealed to him, so it was the sensory quality of architecture that struck him from early on: 'I loved the smell of building' (Saint 1984a). After the war, he spent time at the Building Research Station in Garston, where he recalled figures such as the Canadian architect Bill Allen, 'who were deeply devoted to the idea of integrating art and science in architecture, and had some very good ideas about how to do that'. These experiences proved foundational, plainly shaping Derbyshire's designs for York.

The university opened in 1963, initially based at Heslington Hall, a mile and a half to the east of the city, and at the old King's Manor, in the city centre. The first new buildings in Heslington (Phase II) opened two years later, using steel frames with grey concrete cladding; these included two colleges and the chemistry labs. On the campus, the subjects were housed in buildings largely distinct from one another, as at Sussex, but Derbyshire, by integrating study and residence at each college within a small radius, and with multiple intersections in the paths between the colleges, aimed to stimulate interaction between students of different disciplines. The sciences and arts buildings were deliberately arranged in such a way as to effect encounters between students walking between them. As expressed in the innovative York Development Plan, drawn up by Derbyshire with two associates in 1962: 'it should ideally be impossible to go from one unit of accommodation to a similar one without coming into contact with at least one of completely different academic or social character on the way' (YDP 1962: 13). We shall touch on this again below, but it is worth noting one index of successful integration at York. A 1983 student survey produced, among other things, a set of statistics about friendships across the disciplines (Derbyshire 1984):

- 80 per cent of Arts students had friends in Science Departments.
- 90 per cent of Science students had friends in Arts Departments.
- 91 per cent of Arts students had friends in Social Science Departments.
- 95 per cent of Social Science students had friends in Arts Departments.
- 89 per cent of Science students had friends in Social Science Departments.
- 87 per cent of Social Science students had friends in Science Departments.

The architect commented, 'This result is enormously gratifying and full of encouragement for the future. York appears to have succeeded in this realm beyond our wildest dreams.' But the survey demonstrates only social, not intellectual bonds, which would be far harder to quantify, let alone evaluate. Nor did any of the new architects or planners ask why bridging the arts and sciences, or the disciplines more generally, should be a good thing; those such as Ingold who objected to the new methods grounded their criticisms on practicality, not on the fundamental aim of the endeavour. Doubt, when it arose, arose elsewhere. The educationalist Stuart Maclure, for instance, considering the programme of study at UEA in 1965, wondered if its generalism really *was* 'liberal':

> It keeps options open longer and forces students to be free from the narrower forms of specialization. But at what cost? The course credit system and the seminar system involve a great deal of direct teaching. Will undergraduates who are forced to be liberal students enjoy as much freedom as those who can bury themselves from choice in some all-consuming yet lopsided study?
>
> (Maclure 1965: 750)

The idea implicit in new universities was that in the study of diverse fields lay the promise of enlightened selfhood: in Briggs's terms, the discovery not only of new knowledge, but of oneself. As Moberly had already made clear, that idea was historically and essentially a religious one, and, in a secular age, quasi-religious impulses and connotations kept returning at the young institutions. This came in the curriculum, but also in the architecture: more fundamental than the arts-science divide was a romantic concern for the self, and its striving for identity and realisation within a built environment.

*

The siting of the new universities, on campuses distinct from regional town centres, was already a nod to the older model, rejecting the urban integration of the late nineteenth- and early twentieth-century 'Redbricks'. Some contemporary critics deplored the isolation of these locales: 'Any activity . . . that takes itself out of the city or refuses to come into it, impoverishes the city and impoverishes itself' (Brett 1963: 258; cf. Banham 1966b). But the planners themselves demanded a secluded space for the benefit of private contemplation, even alluding to the religious origins of the move. In a 1960 interview, responding to a question on the 'monastic' character of his design for Sussex, Spence said:

> That is quite right. It is the sort of monastic idea which, of course, was the basic idea of Oxford and Cambridge; the quadrangle, whose space induces meditation and discussion and solitude and quietness.
>
> (Spence 1960: 471)

At York, Derbyshire and his team referred to the peculiar corridors of his early buildings as 'cloisters'. Similarly, the influential photographer John Donat, concluding a survey of new university building around the world, asked 'Do secular monasteries necessarily provide the right environment in which to grow up?' (Donat 1966: 632a). And 25 years later, one historian commented:

> In this country our vision has, inevitably, remained that of the Oxbridge collegiate model. Linked to the monastic pattern, which in turn was taken by the medieval hospice and almshouse . . . it offered the enclosure of community but also protection from change, a place where ideas fix and institutions atrophy.
>
> (Darley 1991: 355; cf. Bendixson 1967)

The new university thus offered seclusion both in its *place* (campus away from town) and its *space* (quiet within the campus); both aspects were associated, via the Oxbridge model, with medieval religious communities. Seclusion and community, in turn, promoted the peaceful development of self by learning. This was the simple first step towards the idea of the university. But the particular designs and plans of the buildings on campus also served to articulate philosophical principles, to reiterate historical allegiances, and to foster interconnection and academic unity. That the architecture should instantiate educational ideals was always the intention. Frank Thistlethwaite wrote to Lasdun in 1964:

> We always knew you would give us a university of outstanding originality; we could not have anticipated the full depth and meaning of the design

nor the faithful way in which it embodies in architectural terms both the general idea of the University and the particular wishes of the users of individual buildings.

(LaD/83/3, 15/09/64)

No comment on function, practicality, cost-efficiency, or even visual attractiveness; Thistlethwaite writes about the plan only as a higher work of art, defined by its 'originality', 'meaning' and expression of the 'idea of the [symbolically capitalised] University'. Although expressed with a particular succinctness, this message was no aberration; we may compare, for instance, a public lecture given by Eric James in 1966: 'the buildings have got to express fundamental ideas about the nature of a university' (James 1966: 37). All of the new campuses were conceived by those involved, and by many contemporary observers, as bearers of meaning, of an idea.

It is worth asking, then, what physical forms were best suited to conveying this idea. The architectural journals of the early 1960s were awash with ideas, sketches, diagrams, possibilities, and we see already hints and anticipations of the forms later realised on campus – a water tower at Örebro, Sweden (*AR* 762 (1960): 100), much like that which turned up at York; a drawing of Arne Jacobsen's design for St Catherine's College, Oxford (*AR* 767 (1961): 5), its slender belfry sticking up in similar proportions to Spence's later 'symbol of incompleteness' at Sussex; and a plan for a stepped residential block at Birmingham (*AR* 767 (1961): 11), which to any later observer would only recall Lasdun's ziggurats at East Anglia. The built shapes themselves triggered imitations; for instance, the concrete arches of Spence's Falmer House (1963), quoted from Le Corbusier, reappeared in the 1974 additions to the Carnatic Halls at Liverpool. More importantly, form was a problem of growing concern to contemporary theorists; the historicism of the past century was in crisis, and there was, from many quarters, a call to establish a new 'language' or 'vernacular' for modernity, referential but not reverential to the past. The linguistic metaphor was, in some places, banal, reaching its nadir in an earnest article expounding the relevance for architects of Chomsky's 'deep structure' linguistics (Greene 1969). But elsewhere it had a greater intellectual weight. Most famous on this front, perhaps, was the Norwegian critic Christian Norberg-Schulz, whose *Intentions in Architecture* (Norberg-Schulz 1963) demanded a new, humanistic response to architectural style, one that gave 'visual expression to the constitutive ideas of a community or to the social structure', and manifested 'a common basis which may counteract the loneliness of modern man' (Norberg-Schulz 1963: 17). But Lasdun, especially, had already made much of this 'semiotic' attitude to architecture in his 'Thoughts in progress' articles of 1957, published as an anonymous monthly dialogue in *Architectural Design*. Much like Norberg-Schulz, he complained:

> Architectural languages have existed in the past and they may be very
> desirable, but at present we have simply not got anything like a clearly-
> defined architectural vocabulary. To-day, every building has to be solved
> within its own terms.
>
> (Lasdun 1957a: 301; cf. Lasdun 1957b)

One possibility as a source of 'vocabulary' was some variant on or descendant
of classical form, and thoughts in this direction were stimulated especially
by Rudolf Wittkower's *Architectural Principles in the Age of Humanism* (1949),
and by Wittkower's student Colin Rowe. Even the most modernist practice,
such as that of Le Corbusier, could appear cognate with the principles of
classicism, given a full understanding of the problems and solutions involved
(Banham 1966a: 15). Among the university architects may be found a range
of attitudes towards this historicism, as will become apparent. Spence's
idiom at Sussex was perhaps the most overtly referential, with its fine red
brick and concrete accents, especially the horizontals and vaults, derived from
Le Corbusier's houses in Paris, the Maisons Jaoul; this turned out to be a style
having more in common with Oxbridge collegiate architecture of the 1960s
than with the other new campuses. Furthermore, the architect maintained that
his first and most important building there, Falmer House, alluded to the
Colosseum, which, in its rigid but ruined geometry, mediated between the
monumental and the personal: it 'cosseted the individual in spite of its vast
size' (Spence 1964: 210). He used the same verb of his own plans, hoping that
students would leave Sussex with 'a consistent feeling of enclosure, and a
consistent feeling of having been cosseted in the architectural sense' (Brawne
1967). The significance of antiquity for Spence was specific, even idiosyncratic:
elsewhere, he named the Acropolis as the 'first symbol of the new idea of
democracy – a wonderful example of beauty following the function' (Spence
1966: 202). Beauty followed function, but both were essential. Immediately
before citing the Acropolis, Spence spelled this point out. Protection and
convenience, he argued, were necessary in all building, but insufficient for a
work of architecture:

> Human beings demand this extra dimension, this extra dimension of
> beauty. One says beauty in a bland way, but it is a very intricate and subtle
> thing, because a beautiful environment is tied up with convenience, with
> an understanding of the individual and how one can embrace and envelop
> the individual.

Spence's invocation of beauty was pointed. In a functionalist era that overtly
rejected aesthetic criteria, the word required a special disclaimer, as he later
recognised:

With a sickening thud it is borne in on one that officially 'aesthetics' is a dirty word and any one who openly speaks of beauty as a necessity is to be treated with caution and, if possible, restrained. Beauty is only acceptable as a by-product not a necessity. Yet the level of aesthetic appreciation usually marks the standard of achievement of a civilization.

(Spence 1964: 203)

His colleagues experienced the same tension. Derbyshire recently admitted: 'I was reluctant to use the word "beautiful" but always lived in hope that [York] would be so in a subconscious sort of way' (Derbyshire 2012). Likewise, when Noel (now Baron) Annan wrote to congratulate Lasdun on the UEA design, he remarked, 'above all – to use a word which is totally out of fashion today – it seems to me to be a singularly beautiful complex of buildings' (LaD/143/4, 3/7/67). Whatever form it took, and whether acknowledged or not, beauty was always important alongside function. In his 1975 lecture on Plato, Eric James maintained the correlation between moral and aesthetic virtues, insisting that education worked best in fine environs: 'Beauty is not peripheral; art is not an adornment, an optional extra. They are integral to the whole educational enterprise' (James 1975: 20). As an aesthetic virtue, meanwhile, memorableness was as important as beauty. The University of Kent's master planner, Sir William Holford, when asked for a word that encapsulated his design, chose 'memorable' (Brett 1963: 264). Spence, too, intended Sussex to 'leave a lasting visual memory' (Brawne 1967: 27). Derbyshire later spoke of his desire to create at York something 'beautiful . . . memorable . . . an aesthetic experience of value' (Derbyshire 1977). His aesthetic impulse was perhaps most pronounced, and most elaborated, in a 1984 interview with Andrew Saint:

> The retreat in the face of economic pressures – from wringing the absolute architectural *ultimate* out of a prefabricated system, in the earlier phases of the university, to gradually shedding bits of it because we couldn't afford them towards the end – is a very good description in physical terms of what's happened to the idea. If you compare the last college with the first college you can actually see it in front of your eyes, the retreat from the ideal to the pragmatic and inconsistent and ideologically impure.
>
> (Saint 1984a, italics indicate vocal emphasis)

Lasdun, for his part, cited Le Corbusier's dictum that 'architecture is a thing of art, a phenomenon of the emotions, lying outside questions of construction and beyond them', and asserted for himself that 'The architect's aesthetic judgement is a function of myth and reason, a link between the emotional and the rational and the necessary means of entry into the realm of ideas' (Lasdun 1984: 135–7). As Lionel Brett later noted of the period, the functionalists – the

'System Boys', in Leonard Manasseh's phrase – were never so far away from artistic considerations (Esher 1981: 67).

Like Spence, Lasdun embraced some form of the classicism characteristic of the 1950s (Hill 2012: 16), and later cited as influences the famous texts of that era: Wittkower, Geoffrey Scott's *Architecture of Humanism* and John Summerson's *Classical Language of Architecture*, as well as the built works of Hawksmoor (Lasdun 1984: 135). As for antiquity itself, he returned not to the Acropolis and Colosseum, but to the amphitheatre at Epidauros, a site that provoked the remark that a sense of place was 'one of the most profound impulses in architecture'. However, as Jonathan Hill has shown in a magnificent recent essay (Hill 2012), Lasdun's primary allegiance at UEA was not to antiquity, but to the tradition of the picturesque, that is, the loose, informal grouping of buildings in a vivid landscape. The buildings, ideally, should in fact become *part of* the landscape, as if natural themselves. To this end, colour was essential. In 1967, E. R. Crane opined of UEA that colour was 'most lacking at present', seeing in the pine and concrete 'a very puritanical treatment' (Crane 1967, at LaD/143/4). But Lasdun was after subtler effects of shade. He had initially declared that his concrete would be 'cathedral-coloured', as if alluding not only to the continuity of architectural tradition at the campus, but also to the religious origin of universities as a whole. He later proposed another rationale, noting that 'concrete in its natural grey state appears to enhance the colours of the landscape to the greatest advantage', and adding that, after weathering, the concrete 'will streak, it will become part of nature (Dormer and Muthesius 2001: 70; Hill 2012: 14).[2] Lasdun's aim was architecture as a natural object, 'making what is virtually an outcrop of stone on the side of a hill leading down to a river' (Lasdun 1966: 221). Spence at Sussex, though he used a different palette, had a related notion in mind, advocating 'materials 'sensitive to the location': local red brick, concrete, knapped flint, copper, timber, white paint. 'The whole precinct', he explained, 'should have the "sense of a university" and should, if possible, grow out of the soil of Sussex to become a natural part of this beautiful site' (Spence 1964: 203–5).

Again, something similar happened at York, albeit by happy accident. Derbyshire and James shared a passion for Siena Cathedral, and initially mocked up a prototype of banded fluorspar and green granite as a cladding for their concrete; when this proved too expensive, they had to settle for drab grey gravel dredged from the Trent River near the factory. 'I console myself', the architect said to Saint, 'with the thought that it was actually the colour of the earth that you dig up from the site in Heslington. Do you know, there's something to be said for the fact that buildings, if they're the colour of the ground they're standing on –'. Saint, interrupting, recognised the fancy: 'the Arts and Crafts phrase is "racy of the soil"' (Saint 1984b; cf. Saint 2010: 309).

It must be recorded that Derbyshire has since rejected such concerns as too whimsical; but in the mid 1960s, the dream of an architecture rising organically from its natural surroundings, at one with the landscape, was far from unusual.

Lasdun is often associated with the New Brutalism championed above all by Reyner Banham in the 1950s. One Swedish critic saw in UEA a fulfilment of Brutalism in its earliest form, bearing the stamp 'of anti-provincialism, of striving for a maximum use of new techniques, of scorn for idyll and individualistic self-assertion, of respect for [that] which is robustly simple and of the vision of a total environment' (Segerstad 1968). It was a movement with an ambiguous relation to the picturesque evident at the campus. Although Banham himself rejected the picturesque, he vaunted qualities in Brutalist design that had much in common with it, especially its aformalism and its 'memorability as an image'. What he wanted was a new sort of architecture, or, as he put it, an 'architecture autre', raw, loose and informal, in response to the *art autre* of the late expressionists, *art brut* and *musique concrete* (Banham 1955, 1966a: 68–9; Stalder 2008). But while Banham sought to escape classicism in favour of a futuristic, technological architecture, Lasdun grasped the historical significance of the new style, an insight appreciated by many of his admirers – notably Frances Yates (Hill 2012: 16). In particular, it afforded him the possibility of expressing at UEA the ideal of free, natural growth implicit in the 'striving towards unity of knowledge and the common identity of the whole university'.

*

Of all the aesthetic language put forward at the new universities, perhaps the least predictable was the rhetoric of incompleteness, of the unfinished. Spence, again, theorised this most explicitly, and in his pronouncements on Sussex we find a constant tension between the complete and the incomplete. Already in 1960, he pointed to ancient Greek thought, as embodied in the Athenian Agora: 'The Greeks accepted, as matter of philosophy and wisdom, the idea of incompleteness, but they tried to get as much perfection as possible into each part of the development' (Spence 1960: 470). To support this claim, he gave no references, and none could have been given; it would be easy to dismiss such language as vapid, but in hindsight the manoeuvre was gestural rather than scholarly. It was important, Spence suggested. to provide areas of completeness in the evolving campus, but also to preserve the open-endedness of the whole, so that further change remained possible: 'as soon as a building is completely finished, it must begin to die. The idea of a living, growing thing made a deep impression, and in our university at Sussex this condition was bound to prevail for many years', although 'small cells of completion should be quite possible' (Spence 1964: 204). To represent this principle, Spence added to Arts A a huge sculpture resembling a tuning fork, which was in fact 'a symbol of incompleteness in raw concrete, breaking the skyline like two arms stretched skyward'. As an incomplete construction, the campus could be seen as a free organism, adaptable to circumstance – 'frog-spawn', as he memorably called it in one place (Brawne 1967: 27). The fullest statement came in 1966:

> I thought that what was necessary was a method of building which allowed the greatest possible freedom when the time came . . . So in my mind's eye began a picture of something like a rock plant that grew quite naturally in between the rocks, sending out leaves of a pattern that was in character and predetermined from the seed that was sown. There should be little areas of completeness, where students could go and realise that this was complete and this was their little world.
>
> (Spence 1966: 206–8)

Incompleteness was manifest in the free, undesignated spaces that Spence fought for, against the cost-consciousness of the UGC: the provision of such spaces, he later proclaimed, 'lifts a mere group of buildings to the level of a place of higher learning' (Spence 1964: 203). The old metaphor of 'higher learning', reanimated by the word 'lifts', draws the allocation of physical space into a tight association with the ideals of education, the one both embodying and promoting the other. As one recent scholar has pointed out, the 'Great Court', Spence's open green between the buildings, was intended, like the Agora he admired, to facilitate intellectual life and the free exchange of ideas (Campbell 2008: 100).

Lasdun used a similar rhetoric in 1965, before beginning work at UEA: 'What we shall build in East Anglia is an organism which is architecturally complete and incomplete, which can grow and change but which does not produce a wilderness of mechanisms' (Lasdun 1965: 219). Where *incompleteness* had been Spence's master trope, Lasdun's was *organism*. The Earlham landscape was itself one (Lasdun 1965: 219), and when he came to muse on the fluidity of architecture a year later, he reached for the same term:

> The word that comes to me is organism. It somehow helps me to dismiss fixed images of what buildings should look like, and to think about the needs of the building, both now and in the future, so that we are beginning to think of an organization which may be fixed in a certain place next to a historical building, but which already has the seeds coded into it of change, both as to the use of the rooms in the building and – more important perhaps – anticipating what the surroundings may become in, say, twenty years' time.
>
> (Lasdun 1966: 220)

Given this later language, one must feel a measure of sympathy for Lionel Brett, who praised UEA in 1963, a month after the plans had been unveiled, as 'a deeply felt and imaginative concept', adding that 'The veins of this beautiful organism are to fill with blood, pumped systematically from the heart' (Brett 1963: 263). A letter to *Architectural Review*, under the initials of two of Lasdun's team, scowls unsent in the UEA archive, dismissing Brett's analogy for its suggestion of rigidity, and proposing instead the metaphor of a 'microcosm which by adherence to certain basic principles then follows a continually changing pattern of growth' (LaD/143/1, undated).

This cento of overlapping quotations should evoke a broader rhetorical view of university planning in the mid 1960s. Of course, such talk of organic growth and incomplete arrangements was not unique to campus design in the period; rather, it was a staple of civic planning in England and elsewhere, deriving most of all from the biologist Patrick Geddes and the urban theorist Lewis Mumford, whose *Technics and Civilization* (1934) was still widely read by aspiring architects after the war. The metaphors and drawings of the campus designers may be well compared to contemporary utopianists, such as Constantin Doxiadis, who wrote of a 'dynamic city consisting of static cells' (Doxiadis 1966: 57), just as the Smithsons had drawn evocative 'sociometric diagrams', schematising their work in terms of molecular and cellular biology (Muthesius 2000: 88). The critics who came to see the campuses, no less than the architects and planners, used the same metaphors (e.g. Dober 1965: 49; Birks 1972: 19).

But if the language of Spence and Lasdun reflected a more widespread discourse, it was nevertheless of particular relevance to the new universities, for two reasons. First, on a pragmatic level, the campuses had to be built very rapidly, and cope with changing and unpredictable numbers of students over a longer period of time. There was, then, a particular need for buildings that could go up fast and cope with unforeseen needs and uses. In concrete terms, this necessitated large quantities of precasting; even so, the first students at Sussex were housed in offsite accommodation, while UEA made extensive use of temporary structures while Lasdun's were being realised.

However, the rhetoric of organism had deeper resonances – it connected to the picturesque aesthetic at UEA and, to an even greater degree, at York; and more importantly it echoed, or rather *embodied*, the revived pedagogical discourse cradling the new universities from their inception. This had been a discourse about freedom, the concept etymologically at the heart of a *liberal* education. Lasdun alluded to a 1963 radio broadcast by the Liverpool sociologist Dennis Chapman, aiming to get a handle on post-war youth culture; Chapman had spoken, to Lasdun's delight, of a 'dislike of forced formality', a 'romantic puritanism' and a 'greater independence due to better homes, health and education', noting finally that the young 'wished to choose their own ethic by which to live' (Lasdun 1965: 219). These were the principles instantiated at UEA; as Lasdun's biographer William Curtis has expressed it, the architect's aim was 'to create an image of openness and freedom' (Curtis 1994: 99).

Derbyshire's ideas for York had a similar impetus, but were still more radical in device and execution. He came to York after designing a hypothetical urban project called 'The Zone' as part of a joint final thesis at the Architectural Association in 1952. David Gray, in his notes to a 1971 AA exhibition, remarked that The Zone was the single project that best summarised British students' architectural interests of the period, referring to their 'determination that architecture should be an instrument of social as well as physical reconstruction' (Gray 1971: 20–1). Although Derbyshire was reluctant to express party-political views as an architect, he nonetheless admitted to a socialism as incarnated in his buildings (Saint 1984a). The Zone had been planned against hierarchic centralisation, and the same would be true at York, which was explicitly conceived, like UEA, in organic terms: the Development Plan, drawn up by Derbyshire at Welwyn in 1962, speaks of the building units as 'the cell of the growing organism' (YDP 1962: 45). The plan, in now familiar terms, sought 'provision for easy growth and flexibility of use' (YDP 1962: 13), implicitly associated with the freedom of personal movement within the campus: 'from each unit all the other components of the complex are directly accessible'. Such a plan prompted the historian Stefan Muthesius to see in York a cohesive whole: not 'an assembly of separate units', but 'a kind of complete and "anti-diagrammatic" organism' (Muthesius 2000: 136). The term 'anti-diagrammatic' is an unfortunate one, given the well-known diagrams in the Development Plan, which resemble those of Doxiadis and the Smithsons, and, in their detail and elegance, possess an aesthetic merit in their own right (Figure 8.1).

Almost all architectural decisions at York were made, in one way or another, for reasons of flexibility. Again, this was partly practical. If both Spence and Lasdun used precasting, much of York was system-built using the CLASP method of light concrete panels arranged on a pin-jointed steel frame, which allowed all such buildings to come in on time and on budget in readiness for the arriving students: at first, 1,000 in three years. The deployment of CLASP was suggested by Stirrat Johnson-Marshall, who had used a prototype in his Hertfordshire schools of the previous decade (Saint 1987: 162); Derbyshire later recalled prefabrication as a sort of 'religious belief' on his colleague's part, and he had himself demanded good arguments for its use: 'I'm not doing this as a matter of faith, I'm doing it as a matter of reason' (Saint 1984a). Not all contemporaries saw it as the most cost-effective solution; at a meeting in early 1963, Lasdun and Thistlethwaite agreed that CLASP would take 18 months to develop for university use and was thus as expensive as any other method (LaD/83/1, Memo 6/2/63). At Essex, meanwhile, CLASP was rejected for its height limitations (Sloman 1963b: 982). As Michael Brawne pointed out

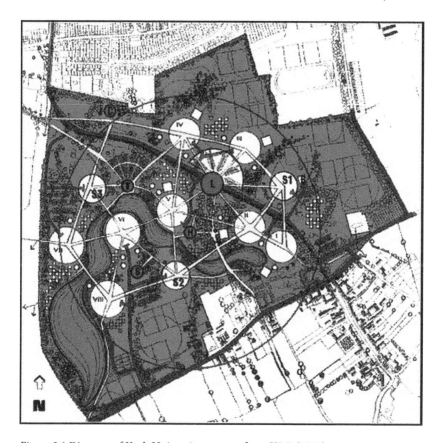

Figure 8.1 Diagram of York University campus from YDP (1962).

in 1965, RMJM used CLASP again at Bath, while their peers chose other methods: perhaps, he suggested, there was some 'emotional bias' in its favour (Brawne 1965: 410).

It is clear that CLASP was chosen at York for practical reasons above all. But the decision was not incompatible with an aesthetic appreciation, which in this instance came not from RMJM, but rather from Reyner Banham, writing as early as 1962, before seeing it in practice at the university. Was CLASP construction architecture at all? His answer is worth quoting at length:

> It is clearly a long way from the conception of architecture that is embodied in even something as superficially similar as the SPAN housing designed by Eric Lyons – indeed, CLASP's penchant for the tried and available material to do any particular job has done much to disguise its truly revolutionary content from professionals as well as laymen . . . Is it, then,

an *architecture autre*, an *other* architecture? If this concept is defined on radical grounds, not the purely formalistic ones that have been advanced so often of late, the proposition has some force. This is not, in any visible sense, architecture considered as one of the accepted fine arts; not architecture as the expressed will of a highly developed personality. And yet it carries its own visual conviction, the air of being the expressed will of something or some body of things, the product of some sort of highly developed creative force.

(Banham 1962: 352, emphasis in original)

CLASP, remarkably, seemed the answer to Banham's old problem. Its flexibility, then, was not only economic and practical, it was also, potentially, philosophical. Indeed, much of the rhetoric around York concerned freedom, in all manner of aspects; the architect and the critic had much in common. Most of all, Derbyshire, like Banham, took no interest in the nostalgic historicism of his peers. Asked to recall his early influences, he mentioned not Wittkower and Scott, but Mumford's *Technics* and, still farther afield, *On Growth and Form* (1917) by D'Arcy Wentworth Thompson, an exquisite and monumental treatise on the mechanics of biological growth (Derbyshire 2012). Banham, too, was fascinated by Thompson's images of topological transformation (Stalder 2008: 268, 271). Despite these similarities, in 1966 Banham biliously dismissed the new universities as the 'outhouses of academe' – elitist crutches for cathedral cities, 'parasitic on existing works of landscape art', or, in other words, a 'great social sell-out' (Banham 1966b). In a contest of socialisms, Banham's was the bitterer.

If the UEA campus was picturesque, it was York that more frequently invited this word (e.g. Banham 1966b: 547; Brawne 1965: 409). It is no surprise that Pevsner, the period's greatest advocate of the picturesque, admired the campus. The first aspect that merited this label was the setting of buildings in an especially lush landscape to counterpoint their grey cladding: willows pour into the snake of a lake, a 'stroke of genius' holding together the campus (Pevsner 1974: 464), delicate bridges in a variety of materials curve over the water, and black swans and other birds teem throughout. Derbyshire had sought 'a weaving of built forms in and out of a strong landscape matrix' (Derbyshire 1986: 3), and critics approved; Christopher Mitchell observed that 'the variety of external spaces is added to by the uncompromising collision of building and nature' (Mitchell 1965: 1446; cf. Mitchell 1972: 422).

The second and more important echo of the picturesque at York lay in its plan. The arrangements of its first building phase (Phase II), incorporating Derwent and Langwith Colleges, as well as the boiler house and what would become the chemistry labs, remain powerful, despite the increasing blandness of the later phases around them. In these first colleges, and to a lesser extent elsewhere, the visitor will notice no particular doors or entrances, no 'front' or 'back', and the same applies to the campus as a whole, in marked contrast to Sussex and UEA. Between Derwent and Langwith stretches the 'cloister', a passage ambiguously surrounding the walker now on both sides, now on one, first enclosed as a corridor and then opening out into a colonnaded path around a shallow, rectangular fountain. To reach the library, sited on a hill across the main trunk road dividing the site, one follows the cloister past a semi-covered courtyard (Market Square), up a winding ramp open in the middle, and across a stepped bridge, suddenly open and stilted over the road. Around the lake, the cloisters become covered bridges and walkways, the roofs of which also convey service ducts, connecting the four central colleges and related buildings through the whole. It added up to a 'spatial brilliance', in the words of the historian Paul Thompson, an early supporter of CLASP on functional grounds (Thompson 1965: 119; cf. Thompson 1963: 5). John Donat, a year later, found that the campus had 'already achieved the appearance of an instant place' (Donat 1966: 605). Michael Beloff was less impressed, describing the open common rooms produced by the cloister as it threaded through Derwent and Langwith:

> High cavernous roofs, a multitude of entrances . . . draughty gusts whistling through wind-tunnel shapes, these are the recurrent qualities, or defects, of the rooms.
>
> (Beloff 1968: 167)

Criticisms aside, the campus is informal, asymmetrical, unpredictable, and – like the tousled clothes that the art student takes an hour to ready – meticulous. What holds it together is not an order with clear boundaries between buildings, but rather a visual motif that signals the appearance of a college, as well as the relation of the colleges to the place as a whole. This motif is the pyramid, present in the colleges as roof lights and echoed by the spire of the nearby Heslington Church – an unexpected but 'happy harmony' (Derbyshire 1977). The roof lights serve as a visual relief to the horizontals of the CLASP blocks, and were much admired by contemporary visitors. For Thompson, in a lyrical mood, their 'icy-grey and silver emphasise the frosty, early morning delicacy of the building'. Others preferred to call them 'romantic' (Mitchell 1965: 1446; Storm-Clark 1981: 307). The intention was indeed romantic, or picturesque. At night, the roof lights, together with other lit windows, would serve to guide the walker from centre to centre: 'you could still see the stars, so that . . . you walked along footpaths from one target light to another target light, and it was pretty dark in between' (Saint 1984b).

The recurrent motif, by its symbolic distribution of space, thus serves to highlight the looseness of the campus plan. Finally, it is recapitulated at the heart of the campus as Central Hall, a monumental half-octagon raised on cantilevered supports beside the lake. The hall, intended as a one-off 'demonstrative architectural statement' (Derbyshire 1986: 3), and most frequently reproduced on commercial postcards of the site, achieves for the entire campus what the Development Plan advised for each college: 'Identity is given to the complex as a whole by the presence of the unique central building . . . to which all the other units are symmetrically related' (YDP 1962: 45).[3]

In its verdancy and spatial fluidity, York may recall the utopian fantasy of Frank Lloyd Wright, notably an influence on Spence's landscaping at Sussex (Spence 1964: 206–7). Wright, in articulating his second vision for Broadacre City towards the end of his life, had written:

> See the architecture of heavy enclosure for human life (the fortification) vanishing! A new kind of building to take its place comes to view – like magic – building now more natural to our time. In spite of all untoward vicarious circumstance, man is now to be less separated from nature . . . The hard-and-fast lines between outside and inside (where he is concerned) tend to disappear.
>
> (Wright 1958: 154)

But the utopianism of the York campus was more specifically socialist in character, as realised for a community of scholars working towards a unity of knowledge. The Development Plan emphasised the social and intellectual benefits of the collegiate system: the colleges, it claimed, should be understood 'as an extension of the opportunities for meeting new people and making contact with fresh ideas and experiences which are a *raison d'être* of the university itself' (YDP 1962: 11). The walkways and the layout of the colleges served a similar purpose in the scheme:

> Meeting, both accidental and deliberate, must be provided for by the greatest possible number of intersections en route (without producing congestion) and it should ideally be impossible to go from one unit of accommodation to a similar one without coming into contact with at least one of completely different academic or social character on the way.
>
> (YDP 1962: 13)

Lasdun had a like justification of his elevated walkways at UEA, separated from motor traffic so that pedestrian interaction encouraged a sense of identity with the whole. The campus, he said, was to be 'a map of human relationships . . . where activities merge', or again, 'a map of social relationships describing a geography of human inquiry and freedom' – 'Instead of closed courts there would be an image of availability, movement and interchange' (Curtis 1994: 91, 95). As precursors, he pointed to Le Corbusier and the Futurists (LaD/143/5,

Lasdun to Jackson, 19/11/68). The model was appreciated by contemporaries, such as Nicholas Taylor, for whom the design enhanced 'the freedom of the inhabitants of what must be a completely unpredictable community' (Taylor 1967). Harold Perkin, in a reflection on the utopian 'myth' at the founding of the new universities, has written of the architecture of Sussex, Essex, York and UEA as 'contriving those casual collisions between minds which are the spark of university life' (Perkin 1991: 301). The visiting critic Richard Dober saw in these designs a potential solution to the anonymity and human isolation of the American campus (Dober 1965: 96). This was, indeed, the old idea of the university in its social aspect, manifested in a natural setting in harmony with the principles of the picturesque. But, paradoxically, freedom had to be 'contrived', or imposed, and the architect Michael Cassidy was not the only critic to note that such 'coercive social planning' had yet to be proven beneficial (Cassidy 1968: 504; cf. Banham 1966b: 546).

One downside of the open linear structures at York and UEA was their exposure to the English climate, as Albert Sloman at Essex pointed out: 'no one is more irritable than a wet don' (Sloman 1963b: 980). Another issue was the difficulty of navigation, and this was a frequent complaint at UEA (Muthesius 2000: 287). Likewise, at York, many critics noted the site's 'open-endedness'; Brawne decried its 'lack of graspable organization' (Brawne 1965: 410), while Christopher Mitchell, returning to the campus in 1972, expressed an ambivalence on the matter:

> There is a casualness in the way the buildings relate to each other, and also in the way in which people become involved with the individual buildings. If one is living as part of the university, and moving frequently from building to building, this is probably both acceptable and appropriate; to a visitor, it has the slightly unsatisfactory feeling of never having arrived, accentuated by the multiplicity of external doors frequently without any associated entrance hall.
>
> (Mitchell 1972: 422)

This last observation, distinguishing between the experiences of the inhabitant and the visitor, shows a greater perspicacity than many responses of the time. Most remarkably, it turned out to reflect the architect's intentions. A misfiled and misthreaded reel-to-reel tape in the Morrell Library, containing a 1977 lecture delivered to the Visual Arts Society at York, offers a moment of revelation:

> We realised pretty early on that this was going to be a difficult place to find one's way about in ... One wants to be able to explore. I don't like situations that expose themselves immediately, reveal all their secrets.
>
> (Derbyshire 1977)

The voice is wistful, undramatic, but the admission is astonishing. Not only has an abstract principle been allowed to dominate the functional needs of the university – the project has deliberately encouraged mystery and disorientation. Pressed on the remark, Derbyshire later remembered his childhood spent between the Peak District and local coalfields, always curious as to what lay around the corner; exploration, crucially, became tantamount to possession and belonging. This was the campus as an 'open work', to use a contemporary expression (Eco 1962), one whose meaning or significance was completed only by the individual's active engagement with it. In geographical terms, such concerns echo the revolutionary manifestos of 1950s Paris – Ivan Chtcheglov's 'Formulary for a new urbanism', published in 1952 under the pseudonym Gilles Ivain, and Guy Debord's 1958 'Theory of the dérive'. The two essays were complementary – the one planning a magical, imaginary city, the other proposing ways to explore and interact with what already existed – both against rigid urban structures, against the rationalism of Le Corbusier, both extolling transience and plasticity. Those who *dérive* or wander 'let themselves be drawn by the attractions of the terrain and the encounters they find there' (Debord 1981: 50; Kaufmann 2001: 164–78). And modernity, added Debord, offered great potential for such an exercise of poetic freedom:

> Within architecture itself, the taste for dériving tends to promote all sorts of new forms of labyrinths made possible by modern techniques of construction. Thus in March 1955 the press reported the construction in New York of a building in which one can see the first signs of an opportunity to dérive inside an apartment.
>
> (Debord 1981: 53)

What Derbyshire provided, with this context in mind, was the opportunity to *dérive* inside a campus. We may seem to have wandered far from the idea of the university. But all these spatial features of York – the collegiate arrangements, the loose groupings of buildings in nature with many interconnecting paths, and the incipient aesthetic of mystery – were intended to generate a particular relationship between the student and his or her environs, a freedom from restraint and an opportunity to cultivate selfhood. The common rhetoric of incompleteness had always been double, applying both to the self and to the architecture it inhabited, and so at York the individual was to develop as a whole in his or her endeavour of private and shared discovery, the intellectual exploration symbolised by the physical. These effects had not been contemplated by those who thought about the role of space in higher education, but Derbyshire, if he had a new solution, was addressing an old problem.

*

The early 1960s saw a renewed interest in architecture as something *experienced*. This can be seen both in practical studies such as Gordon Cullen's influential 'Townscape' column in *AR* (and 1961 book), and in works of high theory and hermeneutics, from Gadamer to Norberg-Schulz. Derbyshire preferred to speak of 'memorableness': it was this quality, he said, 'which seems to express, as well as any other, the particular identity of place and experience which we believe must be sought' (YDP 1962: 14). He has since denied Cullen's impact on his own work, seeing in *Townscape* a mere set of observations without analysis; and yet York's mystery of corners, of the slow reveal, is an obvious match for Cullen's aesthetics. As for the theorists, experience was what gave meaning to architecture, although it was recognised that such experience was always mediated (e.g. Norberg-Schulz 1963: 86).

The experiential perspective, above all, stands in contrast to the objective, a priori god's-eye view of the architect or planner, a turn with two major implications. First, it offers only temporary and fragmented views, never the whole; it takes pleasure not in the symmetry or order of a total plan, but in local effects, closures and openings – both embrace and release, in Frank Lloyd Wright's terms. And so its theorists are naturally drawn to a sense of incompleteness. In a recent book, Lindsay Jones has applied the approach of Gadamer and Norberg-Schulz to sacred architectures around the world. His experiential description of certain religious structures will remind us of York's inchoate cloister:

> The labyrinthine passages at once welcome visiting initiates and force them to admit that their acquaintance with the structure will always remain incomplete; the cryptically complex labyrinth will reveal itself only by increments and never fully.
>
> (Jones 2000: I.25)

Likewise, as at York, a building 'might evoke a sense of belonging and inclusion among some social groups and, simultaneously, a sense of exclusion among others' (Jones 2000: I.32). But if the meaning of a building derives from affect, from experience, what is 'evoked', then the doors are open to private judgements and associations that the architect has no power to control: what he or she represses from above may always return from below. Thus, the CLASP prefabrication to be used at York was a shock to its more conservative benefactors who, we learn, 'wanted a more traditional setting of stonework, gothic arches and ivy' (Storm-Clark 1981: 307). But another contemporary eye, John Donat, found in the York concrete a 'longing for nostalgic associations with Oxford stone, moss and ivy' (Donat 1966: 608). Those who look cannot help seeing the old in the new; experience, then, inevitably enriches a built place with meaning beyond or even counter to intention. Architecture lives. For this reason, Jones warns his reader against the attempt to reconstruct original 'meaning':

> The notion of interpreting or exploiting a religious building in order 'to get back into' the consciousness of their creators or users – to somehow 'look through' an artistic form into the historical context of its origin – is problematic in the extreme because works of art and architecture are, in an important sense, perpetually new. Regardless of how much we are able to learn about the architect, the original users of a building, and the situation to which it was tailored ... we will never be able to reconstruct or re-establish that bygone 'world' to which the monument first belonged; we will never be able to retrieve that which 'brings back the circumstances of the situation and restores it 'as it was'.
>
> (Jones 2000: I.143–4, quoting Gadamer 1960: 148–9)

The post-war campuses are not works of religious architecture, but they have in common a sense of higher purpose, the embodiment of an ideal. It may be, as Jones argues, impossible fully to recover that ideal; but we can, nonetheless, with patience, re-establish a living tradition, just as the planners and architects themselves did 50 years ago. To glance at Lasdun's scribbled notes, or to hear Derbyshire's recorded voice, warm and humane, is to raise the possibility of empathy, that is, to be able to imagine the bricks and concrete not as a mere charming souvenir of the dead, but as a message of value, grown less legible with age but not yet obliterated, and demanding interpretation. It is the latter that makes sense of experience, as Norberg-Schulz insisted; but experience must be the initial step, and must remain the last. Wonder, said Plutarch, is the beginning of enquiry. Where at first the York roof lights only excited my curiosity, now they play their part in a system of ideas: the wonder is explained, but not explained away. Asked by Lionel Brett for his own word to sum up his design, Derbyshire responded, 'Identify' (Brett 1963: 264). Those at York, or Sussex or the rest, who can experience the campus as a place in its own right, with its own history and meanings, have the opportunity of finding their own part in a community and in a tradition – of participating in the idea of the university.

Notes

1   It was, of course, not only a problem for the universities, but for schools as well, which were, if anything, even more important. Albert Sloman, vice-chancellor of Essex, expressed this point with characteristic vividness: 'however imaginatively a university may try to supplement the education of victims of specialization, its efforts can only be palliatives. As cures they are about as effective as parking an ambulance at the foot of a cliff' (Sloman 1963a: 875).

2   This principle was not unique to UEA. Compare, for instance, Lasdun's testy reply to the scholar Anthony Jackson, who had criticised the weathering on his Royal College of Physicians (1964): 'The concrete has weathered, as stone does, and this was deliberate. It has not weathered "badly"' (LaD/143/5, Lasdun to Jackson, 19/11/68). Jackson objected to the layout of UEA, although he found its shapes exciting; as he later put it, the campus was guilty of 'stretching functionalism to gain an architectural experience' (Jackson 1970: 194n.).

3   Central Hall may have influenced the American critic Richard Dober's idea of 'place-marking' on campuses: 'Erected as icons of aesthetic supremacy, stylized elegance, the uplifting *grand projects* are usually intended to signify institutional advancement, solemnize special causes three dimensionally, ennoble benefactors, and provide publicity, if not prestige, to the sponsoring college and university' (Dober 1996: 177, emphasis in original).

References

Material from the archive of Denys Lasdun's papers, held at the British Architectural Library, Victoria and Albert Museum, London, is denoted by the box number, beginning 'LaD'.

Banham, R. (1955) 'The New Brutalism', *Architectural Review*, 118(708), 354–61.

Banham, R. (1962) 'CLASP', *Architectural Review*, 131(783), 349–52.

Banham, R. (1966a) *The New Brutalism*, London: Architectural Press.

Banham, R. (1966b) 'The outhouses of academe', *New Society*, 210, 546–7.

Beloff, M. (1968) *The Plateglass Universities*, London: Secker & Warburg.

Bendixson, T. (1967) 'Lasdun's harbour in East Anglia', *The Guardian*, 5 December.

Birks, T. (1972) *Building the New Universities*, Newton Abbott: David and Charles.

Brawne, M. (1965) 'University of York: first and second phases', *Architectural Review*, 138(826), 409–11.

Brawne, M. (ed.) (1967) *University Planning and Design: A Symposium*, Architectural Association Paper Number 3, London: Lund Humphries.

Brett, L. (1957) 'Universities 2: today', *Architectural Review*, 122(729), 240–51.

Brett, L. (1963) 'Problems of planning the new universities', *Architectural Review*, 134(800), 257–64.

Campbell, L. (2008) '"Drawing a new map of learning": Spence and the University of Sussex', in P. Long and J. Thomas (eds), *Basil Spence: Architect*, Edinburgh: Edinburgh University Press, pp. 97–104.

Cassidy, M. (1968) 'Who was right?', *Official Architecture and Planning*, 31(4), 496–504.

Crane, E. (1967) 'University of East Anglia: some reflections', held at LaD/143/4.

Cross, M. and Jobling, R. (1969) 'The English new universities – a preliminary enquiry', *Universities Quarterly*, 23, 172–82.

Crowther (1959) *15 to 18. A Report of the Central Advisory Council for Education (England)*, 2 volumes, London: HMSO.

Cullen, G. (1961) *Townscape*, London: Architectural Press.

Curtis, W. (1994) *Denys Lasdun: Architecture, City, Landscape*, London: Phaidon.

Daiches, D. (ed.) (1964) *The Idea of a New University: An Experiment in Sussex*, 2nd edition, London: André Deutsch.

Darley, G. (1991) 'Visions, prospects and compromises', *Higher Education Quarterly*, 45(4), 354–66.

156 · Anthony Ossa-Richardson

Debord, G. (1981) 'Theory of the dérive', in K. Knabb (ed.), *Situationist International Anthology*, Berkeley, CA: Bureau of Public Secrets, pp. 50–4.

Derbyshire, A. (1977) 'The architecture of the University of York', reel-to-reel recording of a lecture given to the Visual Arts Society, York, 14 November. (*Note*: In 2004, this item was held in the J. B. Morrell Library at York, misfiled under 'Darbyshire'; it appears to have since vanished from the catalogue.)

Derbyshire, A. (1984) 'Architectural implications of the York campus survey (synopsis)', unpublished document, author's collection.

Derbyshire, A. (1986) *Explorers in an Unknown Land: Making a New University*, unpublished pamphlet, King's Manor Library, York, shelfmark K 8.42741 DER.

Derbyshire, A. (2012) Private communication with the author.

Dober, R. (1965) *The New Campus in Britain: Ideas of Consequence for the United States*, New York: Educational Facilities Laboratories.

Dober, R. (1996) *Campus Architecture: Building in the Groves of Academe*, New York: McGraw-Hill.

Donat, J. (1966) 'Living in universities', *Architectural Design*, 36(12), 589–632.

Dormer, P. and Muthesius, S. (2001) *Concrete and Open Skies: Architecture at the UEA 1962–2000*, London: Unicorn Press.

Doxiadis, C. (1966) *Between Dystopia and Utopia*, Hartford, CT: Trinity College Press.

Duckett, M. (1968) 'Moving away from matchboxes', *Daily Telegraph Magazine*, 217 (29 November), 56–62.

Eco, E. (1962) *Opera aperta: Forma e indeterminazione nelle poetiche contemporanee*, Milan: Portico.

Esher, L. (1981) *A Broken Wave: The Rebuilding of England 1940–1980*, London: Allen Lane.

Gadamer, H.-G. (1960) *Wahrheit und Methode*, Tübingen: Mohr.

Gray, D. F. (1971) 'The zone', in James Gowan (ed.) *Projects – Architectural Association 1946–71*, AA Cahiers Series No. 1. London: Whitefriars Press.

Greene, J. (1969) 'Lessons from Chomsky', *Architectural Design*, 39(9), 489–90.

Haarlow, W. (2003) *Great Books, Honors Programs, and Hidden Origins: The Virginia Plan and the University of Virginia in the Liberal Arts Movement*, New York and London: Falmer.

Halsey, A. (1961) 'University expansion and the collegiate ideal', *Universities Quarterly*, 16(1), 55–9.

Hill, J. (2012) 'The history man', *AA Files*, 65, 4–19.

Hutchins, R. (1936) *The Higher Learning in America*, New Haven, CT: Yale University Press.

Jackson, A. (1970) *The Politics of Architecture: A History of Modern Architecture in Britain*, London: Architectural Press.

James, E. (1966) 'The start of a new university', delivered 9 February, and printed in M. Ross (ed.) *New Universities in the Modern World*, London and New York: Macmillan and St Martin's Press, pp. 32–52.

James, E. (1975) *Plato's Ideas on Art and Education*, York: Ebor Press.

Jones, L. (2000) *The Hermeneutics of Sacred Architecture: Experience, Interpretation, Comparison*, Cambridge, MA: Harvard University Press.

Kaufmann, V. (2001) *Guy Debord: La révolution au service de la poésie*, Paris: Fayard.

Lasdun, D. (1957a) 'Thoughts in progress: detail', *Architectural Design*, 27(9), 300–1.

Lasdun, D. (1957b) 'Thoughts in progress: summing up II', *Architectural Design*, 27(11), 395–6.

Lasdun, D. (1965) 'An architect's approach to architecture', *RIBA Journal*, reprinted in W. Curtis (1994), *Denys Lasdun: Architecture, City, Landscape*, London: Phaidon, pp. 217–19.

Lasdun, D. (1966) 'A sense of place and time', *The Listener*, 17 February, reprinted in W. Curtis (1994) *Denys Lasdun: Architecture, City, Landscape*, London: Phaidon, pp. 220–2.

Lasdun, D. (1984) 'The architecture of urban landscape', in D. Lasdun, *Architecture in an Age of Scepticism*, London: Heinemann, pp. 134–59.

Maclure, S. (1965) 'The University of East Anglia', *The Listener*, 11 November, 747–50.

Mitchell, C. (1965) 'Building study: University of York', *The Architects' Journal*, 15 December.

Mitchell, C. (1972) 'York University: building revisited', *The Architects' Journal*, 2 February.

Moberly, W. (1948) *The Crisis in the University*, London: SCM Press.

Muthesius, S. (2000) *The Postwar University: Utopianist Campus and College*, New Haven, CT: Yale University Press.

Newman, J. (1859) *The Scope and Nature of University Education*, 2nd edition, London: Longman.

Norberg-Schulz, C. (1963) *Intentions in Architecture*, Oslo: Universitetsforlaget.

Perkin, H. (1991) 'Dream, myth and reality: new universities in England, 1960–1990', *Higher Education Quarterly*, 45, 294–310.

Pevsner, N. (1974) *Yorkshire, The West Riding*, Harmondsworth: Penguin.

Saint, A. (1984a) Recorded interview with Andrew Derbyshire, 18 January 1984, British Library collection, classmark C447/26/01-02.

Saint, A. (1984b) Recorded interview with Andrew Derbyshire, 29 November 1984, British Library collection, classmark C447/09/01.

Saint, A. (1987) *Towards a Social Architecture: The Role of School-Building in Post-War England*, New Haven, CT, and London: Yale University Press.

Saint, A. (2010) *Richard Norman Shaw*, New Haven, CT: Yale University Press.

Sanderson, M. (2002) *The History of the University of East Anglia, Norwich*, London and New York: Hambledon and London.

Segerstad, U. (1968) 'Neo-Brutalist architecture in present day England', a translation of 'Nybrutal arkitektur i dagens England', at LaD/146/3.

Silver, H. (2003) *Higher Education and Opinion Making in Twentieth-Century England*, London: Woburn Press.

Sloman, A. (1963a) 'Reith lectures III: "the training of minds"', *The Listener*, 28 November, 875–8.

Sloman, A. (1963b) 'Reith lectures V: "a university town"', *The Listener*, 12 December, 980–3.

Smith, D. (2008) 'Eric James and the "utopianist" campus: biography, police and the building of a new university during the 1960s', *History of Education*, 37(10), 23–42.

Snow, C. P. (1959) *The Two Cultures and the Scientific Revolution*, Cambridge: Cambridge University Press.

Spence, B. (1960) 'Influences of Greek and Roman architecture in the proposed Sussex University', *Architect and Building News*, 13 April, 469–74.

Spence, B. (1964) 'Building a new university: the first phase', in D. Daiches (ed.), *The Idea of a New University: An Experiment in Sussex*, 2nd edition, London: André Deutsch, pp. 201–15.

Spence, B. (1966) 'The planning and building of the University of Sussex', talk given on 4 November, printed in *Proceedings of the Royal Institution of Great Britain*, 41(2), 198–211.

Stalder, L. (2008) '"New Brutalism", "topology" and "image": some remarks on the architectural debates in England around 1950', *The Journal of Architecture*, 13, 263–81.

Storm-Clark, C. (1981) '"Newman, Palladio and Mrs. Beeton": the foundation of the University of York', in C. H. Feinstein (ed.), *York 1831–1981: 150 Years of Scientific Endeavour and Social Change*, York: Ebor Press.

Taylor, N. (1967) 'East Anglia's flexible grandeur', *Sunday Times*, 1 October.

Thompson, P. (1963) *Architecture: Art or Social Service?*, London: Fabian Society.

Thompson, P. (1965) 'The architecture of the new universities', *Country Life*, 28 October 115–19.

Vereker, C. and Wilson, C. (1962) 'The integration of knowledge', *Universities Quarterly*, 16, 274–82.

Wright, F. L. (1958) *The Living City*, New York: New American Library.

YDP (1962) *University of York Development Plan: 1962–1972*, York: University of York.

9

Science-Driven University Development in the United States

EUGENE P. TRANI

The last two decades have seen an explosion in building construction – new buildings, additions, and retrofits – at America's colleges and universities. In fact, from 1995 to 2010, the annual completed construction amount grew from $6.1 billion to $11.1 billion, with a high of $15 billion in 2006. There are about $12.4 billion in projects that started in 2011. New construction is approximately 70 per cent of the total, with the balance being additions and retrofits. This construction has changed the face of American higher education, and a major part of that construction has been in the fields of science and clinical facilities, which are among the most expensive per square foot to build. The median cost per square foot for new science buildings was $503 in 2011, up from $175 in 1997, and one quarter of these projects cost $626 per square foot or more.[1] As we will see, included in the construction of science and clinical buildings are several very different kinds of structures.

New Science and University-Related Healthcare Facility Design

Institutional aspirations for research pre-eminence encompass basic research, increased undergraduate research, and more cross-disciplinary research, a trend encouraged by the National Institutes of Health and other sources of funding. This multi-disciplinary approach is causing a fusion of laboratory requirements where even engineering and biomedical laboratory components may be combined. A case in point is the construction of Virginia Common-wealth University's (VCU) Health and Life Sciences Engineering addition on to the School of Engineering where that combination has taken place. In planning the facility, designers visited similar laboratories at Rensselaer Polytechnic Institute[2] and Boston University,[3] where there were examples of open, flexible lab design. In those labs, all utility services were delivered through umbilical feeds from the ceiling, leaving the floor unencumbered, allowing for rearrangement of the space to meet the specific requirements of individual researchers. The open concept also allows for 'chance meetings' among re-searchers that can contribute to the multidisciplinary approach to research.

Those principles also have been applied in other research spaces at VCU, including the Molecular Medicine Research Building, renovations to laboratory spaces in Sanger Hall, and the newly opened Engineering East Hall and McGlothlin Medical Education Center. Other principles used include 'chilled beam' cooling systems because of their efficiency and lower operating costs.

The definition of research seems to be expanding to include more 'manipulation of information' than conducting experiments, a feature of many of the new science buildings being constructed at colleges and universities in the United States.[4] Along with the expanded definition, the volume of data collection in research also is increasing. An example of this can be found at VCU in Harris Hall in support of bioinformatics, where significant new infrastructure has been installed to support increased computer requirements. Other universities are building super computers to support their research.

Over the last 25 years, university-affiliated healthcare facility design has made a number of major advances. Driven by the need for ever-safer facilities, design has been positively impacted by human factors engineering, technology, the 'science of safety' and building high-reliability organizations, the demand for efficiency, and the requirement that facilities have the ability to assimilate new technologies easily and less expensively.

With respect to human factors engineering, the Institute of Medicine report, 'To err is human', states that past hospital designs and processes were not always created to prevent human error and resulting patient injury. Today, architects are required to look at work processes in order to design spaces and systems that would interrupt the potential for error. An example is the separation of medication preparation areas from nursing units. While it would appear a small thing, nursing units are, by nature, a hub of activity, conversation, and interruptions. Such an environment conflicts with the highly complex tasks of dose calculation and drug preparation. Hence, designing separate, quiet drug preparation areas away from the bustle of a nursing unit can reduce medication errors. Similarly, new standards in infection control are forcing the abandonment of semi-private/multi-occupancy spaces in favor of private rooms, which promote adherence to best practices in preventing exposure to hospital-acquired infections.

Information and communications technologies also have had a huge impact on healthcare facility design. The integration of clinical information systems and digital communications into almost every aspect of care delivery has yielded significant advances in safety and quality. At the same time, these technologies have necessitated the development of different design standards and code requirements in order to accommodate their infrastructure. Communication rooms, larger interstitial spaces between floors, enhanced air conditioning/air exchange requirements, electrical load, fire suppression, power delivery and emergency power requirements are all examples of design features impacted by the incorporation of technology into clinical processes.

Technology also has impacted the buildings themselves. Modern building management systems, elevator management systems, security systems, energy efficiency (LEED Certification – Leadership in Energy and Environmental Design), new and safer construction materials, waste evacuation, and support systems have been incorporated into new building design.

Additionally, the incorporation of 'evidence-based design' concepts into the construction of new health facilities contributes to improving the ability of hospitals and other healthcare providers to eliminate the risk of error and resulting patient injury from their systems. At VCU, the new Critical Care Hospital was designed with the input of pharmacists, nurses, and physicians, who suggested a number of significant architectural innovations. And finally, the work of other industries such as commercial aviation and nuclear power generation in developing the 'science of safety' as it relates to high reliability operations is being systematically 'transferred' into the redesign of hospital processes and the facilities that house them.[5]

Colleges and universities in the United States have greatly expanded their science and clinical facilities – and, in some cases, developed entire new campuses – over the past 30 years. The University of California, San Francisco, Yale University, and Virginia Commonwealth University are good examples, as they present different approaches to the shared commitment to expand facilities on behalf of scientific and clinical excellence.

At various times in the past decade and a half, all three of our case study institutions embarked on research enterprise growth that was aggressive but carefully planned. These initiatives all involved major infrastructure expansion that included some combination of capital construction, facility renovations, or real estate acquisition. Such infrastructure expansion was strategic in nature and aimed at increasing research capacity, especially in the biomedical and life sciences. In actuality, these activities enhanced each institution's ability to operate in the national and international research arena by providing extant faculty optimal resources for their research and for attracting new grants. Similarly, it provided the institutions with a competitive edge as they sought to recruit talented new faculty and trainees to their research enterprises.

Certainly, these three universities, as is the case with many U.S. colleges and universities, have seen the need to expand their existing campuses or establish new ones because of the tremendous development in the sciences – especially, but not exclusively, the life sciences – over the past 30 years. UCSF opened an entirely new campus, the Mission Bay Campus, in 2003, which is the largest biomedical construction project anywhere in the world. In 2007, Yale purchased 136 acres of property with 1.4 million square feet of buildings and substantial room for additional buildings from Bayer HealthCare in order to dramatically increase laboratory and research spaces, especially for the School of Medicine researchers. At the time of this visionary move, Yale's president also stated his commitment to the ongoing renovation of facilities on the historic Yale campus. Over the past 20 years, VCU, a 'landlocked' university in downtown Richmond, Virginia, has vastly enhanced its teaching, research, and clinical facilities, especially in the sciences, on both of its historic campuses. In the 1990s, VCU also was instrumental in the creation of the Virginia Biotechnology Research Park, adjacent to the medical campus. In total, VCU spent more than $2 billion between 1990 and 2009 on capital facilities. And it is not only the sciences inspiring change, as these three universities, and many more, have increased living, dining, recreational, teaching, research, and clinical facilities as they seek to attract faculty and students in the increasingly competitive global marketplace of higher education in the twenty-first century.

Let us take a detailed look at our three case studies, especially as they relate to science and clinical facilities. But first, some general comments about the 'science wars' between American colleges and universities.

The Science Wars

There are three kinds of 'science wars'. In no order of priority, the first refers to exchanges that have occurred between 'scientific realists and postmodernist critics' in which the latter questioned:

> scientific objectivity, and critiqued the scientific method and scientific knowledge in cultural studies, cultural anthropology, feminist studies, comparative literature, media studies, and science and technology studies. The scientific realists countered that objective scientific knowledge is real and that the postmodernist critics had little understanding of the science they were criticizing.[6]

A second 'science war' refers to the role scientists played in World War II and the Cold War. In World War II, German scientists developed advances in rocketry, such as the V1 bomb, later known as a cruise missile, and the V2 bomb, later known as a ballistic missile, both of which inflicted great damage on London in 1944 and 1945. The German scientists who developed these bombs, led by Wernher von Braun, were moved to the United States after the war, and proved the mainstay of the American scientific effort that sent American astronauts to the moon. Both German and American scientists worked on an atomic bomb. The Manhattan Project put American scientists to work with the U.S. Army to eventually design, build, and manufacture the first atomic bombs, which were used to bring an end to the war with Japan in 1945.[7] In the period of the Cold War with the Soviet Union, science played a major role, with the United States becoming very alarmed when the Soviets developed atomic weapons in 1949 and launched Sputnik, the first space satellite, in 1957. As John Aubrey Douglass has written, 'In the immediate post-World War II era, federal support of science and engineering had already become a central means to maintain technological superiority in domestic and international markets, and to support the nation's relatively new military dominance'.[8] American R&D expenditures grew from $20 billion in 1955 to almost $60 billion in 1985. Some of this money went to the construction of new scientific facilities at American universities and the construction of new federal laboratories, such as the laboratories at Livermore, Los Alamos and Berkeley, which were managed by American universities.

With the collapse of the Soviet Union and the end of the Cold War, a third 'science war' has come into play. Utilizing the 1986 Federal Technology Transfer Act, and 'reflecting the evolving nature of technological innovation and the development of university and industry based consortiums and partnerships, American research universities are now engaged in more applied and developmental research than in any other time in their history'.[9] Traditional fields such as engineering and agriculture, and the new fields of informational technology and biotechnology, have emphasized 'that research universities are increasingly relevant to the nation's economy', a fact reflecting 'an increasingly technology dependent private sector that needs both basic and applied research to remain competitive'.[10] Current estimates are that as much as 50 percent of post-World War II economic growth is related to federal and private R&D investment. While private sector R&D investments now surpass federal expenditures, the combination has had a dramatic effect on American higher education, since both the private and federal sectors fund much of the research of colleges and universities.

American colleges and universities have become major players in economic development, which has, in turn, been added to the trilogy of teaching, research, and community service that have been traditional pillars of the value of higher education to American society.[11] Almost every college and university in the United States fosters and promotes its role in economic development, and all of them have become very concerned about their science facilities for both teaching and research. This has led to a science war between colleges and universities in the United States, and indeed around the world. Newer, bigger, and better science facilities are on every institution's wish list, and that, in turn, has led to a capital construction frenzy in science and clinical facilities.

There are now major conferences on science buildings that attract record attendance. One such conference, held October 4–5, 2012 in San Diego, was the '24th Annual Conference of College and University Science Facilities 2012: Planning, Capital Projects, Operations, Program Growth and Modernization', which included sessions on 'Business and Science in One Facility: Equipping a

New Generation for Global Competition'; '100% Self-powered, Zero-emission Research and Teaching Facilities'; 'State-of-the-art Laboratory Renovations put "Wow" Science Facilities in Legacy Buildings'; 'Interactive Classrooms and New Pedagogies that Improve STEM Student Learning Outcomes'; 'New Instructional Technology Packages for Chemistry and Life Sciences at Community Colleges'; 'Phased Growth Models for Biomedical Research Facilities'; and 'The One-facility Model for Co-mingled Departments, Cost Savings, and Program Growth'.[12] There is a growing body of literature in the how-to aspect of these science and clinical facilities. One such article appeared in the *Chronicle of Higher Education*, October 29, 2012, entitled 'Scientific Discovery, Inspired by a Walk to the Restroom: In the Push to Increase Research Collaboration, Studies Try to Identify the Building-design Elements that Really Matter'. There is great pressure to pursue interdisciplinary research collaboration, and such collaboration, according to a University of Michigan study, points to factors such as 'the amount of shared hallway space on the walk to the restroom' that promote interdisciplinary collaboration. The study showed that:

> Scientists with no prior history of collaboration became 33 percent more likely to institute a joint project when they were moved to the same building . . . The scientists became 57 percent more likely to collaborate when they were assigned space on the same floor . . . Their likelihood of working together grew by about 20 percent for every 100-foot increase in the overlap of their usual walking routes.[13]

The science wars are not just limited to capital facilities. A major fallout of these wars is the competition for talent. The recruitment and retention of funded scientists has significantly accelerated the compensation needed for these investigators.

And the science wars are a worldwide phenomenon. There has been long-term rivalry between Oxford and Cambridge, two of the oldest and most highly rated universities in the world. Over the years, science has been stressed more at Cambridge than at Oxford, with historically about 60 percent of Cambridge's students studying science, technology, and engineering, while the corresponding figure at Oxford was 40 percent. Both universities have been major players in the history of science. Nonetheless, as Joseph A. Soares notes in his book[14] on Oxford University, a charge against Oxford before World War II was that it 'was anti-science and unconcerned with contributing to economic growth'. Since World War II, that has changed, with both Oxford and Cambridge at the forefront of the new economics of information sciences and biotechnology. The Oxford Science Park and the Cambridge Science Park and Cambridge's St. John's Innovation Centre are leaders worldwide in the new sciences, with modern, up-to-date facilities. In fact, a new Cambridge University campus, West Cambridge, has become the emerging center for science in Cambridge, with the opening of the Cavendish Laboratory Building (1974) housing physics and magnetic resonance, William Gates and Roger Needham Buildings (2001) housing computer research, Nanoscale Science Laboratory (2003), Electrical Engineering Division Building (2006), Centre for the Physics of Medicine (2008), and the Alan Reece Building for the Institute of Manufacturing (2009). At Oxford, as well, significant new facilities for science teaching and research have been built in the last 20 years.

In one of the newest universities in the world, Education City in Doha, Qatar, an initiative of the Qatar Foundation for Education, Science, and Community Development, world-class science and clinical facilities have been built in the last decade for three of its partner universities, Weill Cornell University Medical College, Texas A&M School of Engineering and Carnegie Mellon University School of Business and Computer Science, and the Sidra Medical and Research Center, the teaching hospital for Cornell's School of Medicine. These facilities have resulted in the recruitment of first-class faculty and students from all over the world, and the additional development of the Qatar Science and Technology Park has made Qatar a center of science in the Middle East. The establishment of the Qatar National Research Fund also has helped in the development of petro-chemical research. All of this development is part of the science war that is being waged all over the globe. So is Ice Cube, the $279 million telescope facility on the South Pole, 'the world's largest observatory ever built to detect the elusive subatomic particles called neutrinos', which stream through the human body. Ice Cube scientists 'designed the telescope to discover neutrinos with energies far exceeding those produced by man-made particles accelerators'.[15] Ice Cube is a collaborative effort of the University of Wisconsin-Madison, Penn State University, and universities in Belgium, Germany, and Sweden.

In the United States, even universities with some of the oldest university buildings in continuous use have built new science complexes. The College of William and Mary, which features the Wren Building, constructed in 1700, has a brand new science quad. Harvard, where Massachusetts Hall was built in 1722, has recently completed the 530,000 square foot Northwest Science Building, where over half the facility is below ground. Yale, the home of Connecticut Hall, constructed in 1752, has a new life science campus, which will be described in the case studies later in this chapter. And Princeton University, which has Nassau Hall (built in 1754) at the center of its university, has built the James Forrestal Campus over the last 50 years to include the Princeton Plasma Physics Laboratory, funded by the U.S. Department of Energy and managed by Princeton.[16]

These are only a few examples. These science wars, with their resulting new, enlarged, or renovated science and clinical facilities, are occurring all over the United States. The contractor, Skanska, which does an enormous amount of construction at American colleges and universities, features on its website[17] many new buildings under development, including a $600 million, 607,969 square foot project for the life sciences at the City University of New York (CUNY), a phase III engineering building moving engineering at North Carolina State University from the North Campus to Centennial Campus, and a University of Michigan solid-state electronics laboratory addition and renovation project, and also a new computer science and engineering building.

The list goes on and on. It is clear there is a major science war between American colleges and universities as they scramble for the best faculty and students and for national and international recognition, and a major part of that includes the building of science and clinical facilities (new, additions, and retrofits). Now, on to our three case studies.

The University of California, San Francisco

UC San Francisco (UCSF), a graduate-level health sciences university, was founded in 1864 to be a 'public university dedicated to saving lives and improving health'. It is one of the 10 campuses of the University of California and has long been recognized as a nationally ranked center for patient care and research. It incorporates Schools of Medicine, Nursing, Pharmacy, and Dentistry, as well as extensive Ph.D. programs in the biological sciences.

Historically, the main campus of UCSF was Parnassus Heights, where the 600-bed UCSF Hospital is located, along with the UCSF Children's Hospital and Porter Psychiatric Institute and the Beckman Vision Center. The Mount Zion campus contains UCSF's Diller Family Comprehensive Cancer Center. UCSF physicians and residents staff the San Francisco General Hospital and the San Francisco Veteran's Administration Medical Center.

A lack of building space to house UCSF's dramatically growing research enterprise resulted in the establishment of a new campus at Mission Bay, which opened in 2003. This marked the beginning of expansive growth for UCSF expected to take up to 20 years to complete and will ultimately include three new specialty hospitals alongside an extensive research campus; by the end of 2012, development costs for initial phases of construction for laboratory and clinical facilities were approaching $3 billion. As the UCSF fact sheet notes:

> The plan to build a new UCSF Medical Center at Mission Bay was prompted by increased demand for inpatient and outpatient services, the need to address old and outdated facilities and to comply with state-mandated earthquake safety standards for hospitals.[18]

Located on 57 acres near the San Francisco Giants baseball park, the campus is the anchor of the Mission Bay redevelopment project, which covers 303 acres and is the city's largest development project since the building of the Golden Gate Bridge. The land, formerly warehouses and rail yards, is located between Interstate Highway 280 and the San Francisco Bay.

UCSF had long looked to build a new campus. Initially considering 150 different locations, it finally decided on three sites, with Mission Bay being the least developed and most expensive. In 1995, Nelson Rising, the new CEO of Catellus Development Corporation, which controlled much of the Mission Bay site, began negotiations with the city and UCSF, which resulted in Catellus and the city donating 43 acres for the new campus. With the election of Willie Brown as mayor, and with his commitment to keep UCSF in San Francisco, Mission Bay became a reality. As Bruce Spaulding, UCSF's former Vice-Chancellor for Advancement and Planning, has noted, 'If not for Nelson [Rising] and Willie [Brown], this deal wouldn't have come together'.[19]

The progress has been amazing – 1.3 million square feet of university construction has resulted in more than 1.5 million square feet of additional private office and laboratory space and more than 3,000 housing units.

The UCSF Mission Bay campus has allowed the university to substantially increase its funded research, with the 'largest ongoing biomedical construction project in the world'.[20] In fiscal year 2000, UCSF's total research budget was $446 million. By 2011, that had risen to $1,064 million, with nearly $762 million in funding from the National Institutes of Health. The first building, Genentech Hall, funded in part by a settlement of a patent infringement lawsuit with Genentech, Inc., houses structural and chemical biology, and molecular, cellular and developmental biology, as well as the Molecular Design Institute, which focuses on drug discovery, design and delivery, and was occupied in 2003. That was followed by Rock Hall (human genetics and the Center for Brain Development, 2004), Byers Hall (the California Institute for Quantitative Biosciences, QB3, a cooperative effort of UCSF, UC Berkeley, and UC Santa Cruz, 2005), Rutter Community Center (2005), Diller Family Cancer Research Building (2009), the Orthopaedic Institute, the first clinical facility at Mission Bay (2009), the Smith Cardiovascular Research Building (2010), and the Sandler Neurosciences Center (2012). With parking, housing, recreational and dining facilities, the campus has more than 2,000 employees. The 289-bed women and children's cancer hospitals are expected to cost $1.5 billion and are scheduled to open at the beginning of 2015. Core laboratories such as imaging and advanced technology and the Institute of Neurodegenerative Diseases and the Keck Foundation Center for Integrative Neuroscience are located in these new buildings at Mission Bay. The campus also has fulfilled the city's goal of creating a new magnet for bioscience; today, it is surrounded by nine established bio-pharma companies, 10 venture capital firms, five life sciences incubators, and more than 50 start-up companies, most of which have spun out of UC research. Among the private research facilities located near UCSF Mission Bay are the J. David Gladstone Institutes for cardiovascular disease, virology and immunology, and neurological disease.

The UCSF buildings, designed by such architects as César Pelli, Ricardo Legorreta, and Rafael Viñoly, are laid out to foster research collaboration. Genentech Hall, as an example, is organized into 'neighborhoods' where researchers from different disciplines can come together. As one researcher, Keith Yamamoto, has noted:

> The pace of development of the Mission Bay campus shows the determination of the leadership and the vision of the community at large to develop something that is not just more square feet for UCSF, but that addresses the future of the way biomedical research will be done and be translated into something that will improve the health of people.[21]

Rafael Viñoly, who designed the Diller Family Cancer Research Building, has said, 'my design philosophy involved the development of architectural ideas that are powerful, distinctive, and relevant to the specifics of both program and content'.[22] The campus also includes a conference center, Koret Quad (a 3.2 acre landscaped open space), and a dynamic public art program.

All of this development is, of course, part of America's science war, as institutions such as UCSF are spending millions of dollars, indeed billions, to stay at the forefront of scientific and clinical advances. A recent economic impact report[23] shows that UCSF, with 22,000 employees, is the city's second largest employer, with a $3.9 billion operating budget. UCSF plays a major leadership role in innovation and technology, creating 'spin-off' firms and ancillary businesses, and fostering the transfer of knowledge. UCSF is the largest public recipient of research funding from the National Institutes of Health and is among the leading university-based research centers in the United States.

Chancellor Susan Desmond-Hellmann's three-year plan through 2015 has five specific goals:

> Goal 1: Provide unparalleled care to our patients; Goal 2: Improve health worldwide through innovative science; Goal 3: Attract and support the most talented and diverse trainees in the health sciences; Goal 4: Be the workplace of choice for diverse, top-tier talent; and Goal 5: Create a financially sustainable enterprise-wide business model.

A major part of all of these goals is 'to create an environment in which faculty and staff can thrive', with 'infrastructure to support new experiential, team-based interdisciplinary learning models'.[24] And, of course, at the center of all of this is the Mission Bay campus, which is only a decade old. As is the case with the Yale expansion to be described next, it is noteworthy that the USCF Mission Bay facilities are dedicated to areas of research that are thematic and focused, with an emphasis on interdisciplinary research that transcends traditional departmental boundaries.

Yale University

Yale University, founded in 1701, is the third oldest institution of higher education in the United States. A premier research university, it typically ranks among the top 10 universities in the world. Located in New Haven, Connecticut on a campus of almost 300 acres, it has 5,300 undergraduate and 6,300 post-graduate students, with an academic staff of more than 3,600. Its endowment exceeds $19 billion. The Yale–New Haven Health System has hospitals in Bridgeport and Greenwich, Connecticut, in addition to the 966 bed acute and tertiary care Yale–New Haven Hospital, which includes a children's hospital, a psychiatric hospital, and a cancer hospital. With nearly 14,000 employees, including a medical staff of more than 5,000, the Health System's budget is $2.1 billion.

A founding member of the prestigious Association of American Universities, Yale University has a library of over 12.5 million volumes, the second largest university library in the United States, and 49 Nobel Laureates have been students, faculty, or staff of Yale. Five American Presidents have graduated from Yale, along with 19 Supreme Court justices. Founded to train religious and political leaders, it expanded to become a general university and, in 1861, became the first U.S. university to award a Ph.D. By any measurement, Yale ranks among the elite of universities in the United States.

Noted for its Collegiate Gothic architecture, Yale's buildings range from the oldest, Connecticut Hall (1752) to the modern buildings, Ingalls Rink and the Ezra Stiles and Morse residential colleges designed by the Finnish-American architect alumnus Eero Saarinen. Other notable buildings include Sterling Memorial Library, Battell Chapel, Peabody Museum of Natural History, Beinecke Rare Book Library, and Harkness Tower.[25]

Science at Yale University has a history of being focused in certain areas, rather than generally across the university. In addition to arts and sciences, Yale established a School of Medicine (1810), the Sheffield Scientific School (1847), which was phased out in 1956 and replaced by the School of Engineering, the School of Forestry and Environmental Studies (1901), and School of Public Health (1915), all important parts of its science focus. In the fields of behavioral studies, biology, forestry and environmental studies, and medicine, Yale has been at the forefront of advances in science. Nonetheless, a recent article in *Yale Scientific* began:

> Science at Yale, in the physical form if not always in the academic, has always existed on the fringe of campus life. In the nineteenth century, Yale consciously denied chemistry laboratories space on Old Campus. The early twentieth century saw the development of Science Hill, even farther away from central campus.[26]

Science Hill was developed over the course of the last century with such landmark buildings as the Osborn Memorial Laboratories, Sterling Chemistry Laboratory, and Sloane Physics Laboratory, and new structures such as Kroon Hall, the home of the School of Forestry and Environmental Studies, a model of sustainable design. The planned Yale Biology Building on Science Hill, a 286,000 square foot facility, will house molecular, cellular and developmental biology, ecology and evolutionary biology, and molecular biology and bio-physics.[27] As a result, there is little space on Science Hill that is left for modern science expansion, and that had become a major topic of discussion at Yale in the early 2000s.

All that discussion ended, for all practical purposes, in June 2007, with the dramatic announcement that Yale had purchased the 136-acre Bayer Health-Care campus, between West Haven and Orange, Connecticut, seven miles from Yale's campus, for a reported price of approximately $100 million. The campus includes 17 buildings, with approximately 1.4 million square feet of laboratories, offices, and warehouses, of which 550,000 square feet is laboratory space. An article in the *New York Times* noted that the field of biology:

> is one of the hottest areas of competition among top universities, which are under pressure to hire big-name scientists and find space for their research. Yale took what it hopes will be a giant step in that race with its announcement.[28]

The *New York Times* article cites the competitors: Harvard's new 530,000 square foot Northwest Science Building (since completed), and the University of Pennsylvania acquisition from the United States Postal Service of 24 acres adjacent to the university. Robert Berdahl, president of the Association of American Universities, was quoted in the *New York Times* article as saying the purchase was 'a real boost' for science at Yale. He went on to note that 'acquiring the right kind of laboratory space to allow people from different disciplines to work together is critical', and that 'virtually all this new space that Yale is acquiring has that character'.

Then Yale President, Richard Levin, called the acquisition 'a once-in-a-century opportunity' and 'an amazing windfall for us' with 'enormous implications for the university in the long run'. A prime goal in this purchase was to accelerate the expansion of Yale's science and medical facilities. The university was clear from the beginning that what is called 'the West Campus' would not be the site for relocating existing academic activity from New Haven, but rather for additional activity, 'expanding some interdisciplinary science and accelerating some other research efforts'. The main attraction was 'fabulous' lab space, which would have cost four to five times the price Yale paid and taken up to 20 years to build, provided enough land was available. The Dean of Medicine applauded the move and quoted President Levin as saying, 'One hundred years from now, if we don't buy it, people will look back on it as one of the stupidest decisions the Levin administration made'.[29]

Yale's West Campus stands as a great contrast to the UCSF Mission Bay Campus. Both have become reality for the same reason, the need for dramatic new and expanded modern science space, part of the science wars among American colleges and universities. But while UCSF chose to completely develop a site, converting a self-contained campus into new facilities, Yale purchased an existing site. UCSF had the vision and developed the space to match; Yale bought the space and is now developing the vision. Because the buildings of Yale's West Campus already existed, architecture is less an issue than it was with UCSF.

More pertinent is how Yale is developing this space, while at the same time revitalizing the existing Science Hill Campus and integrating both the West Campus and Science Hill into the rest of the university. Yale has traditionally been known for its liberal arts and humanities and always emphasized inter-disciplinary study. With that perspective, integrating science faculty and students into the life of the university is very important. In many ways, this development and Yale's mindset is more similar to Cambridge University's development of its West Cambridge Campus than UCSF's Mission Bay, especially with the announcement that the Yale School of Nursing would move to the West Campus, the first educational unit at the university to locate there.

So what is 'the future of science at Yale'? Physically, it will be two sets of integration. One will be the integration of Science Hill and the West Campus, two very different kinds of space, into one coordinated program. Architecture professor Kent Bloomer has said, 'there is something Frankenstein-like about [Yale's] old science buildings, like Sterling Hall of Medicine. They loom dark and heavy, as if some mad scientist was working away inside', while the West Campus 'has nothing to say that science, let alone that Yale, is here'.[30] Nonetheless, they will be put together, academically. Careful consideration is being given to how to keep students involved, so that the 'West Campus doesn't forever remain just Bayer Corporation's old corporate headquarters. Instead, it has the potential to become the twenty-first century chapter of Yale's great architectural tradition.'[31] Interdisciplinary labs are being developed on the West Campus, the first being cancer biology, molecular discovery, nanobiology, energy sciences, chemical biology, biodesign, systems biology, and microbial diversity, each with up to 10 research labs. As an example, the Institute of Microbial Diversity has representatives from 10 different departments from the Medical School and Science Hill. Core laboratories, such as the Center for Genome Analysis, the Center for High Throughput Cell Biology, and the Small Molecule Discovery Center are also being located on the West Campus. Additionally, for the West Campus, Yale has received a $25 million gift to establish an Institute for the Preservation of Cultural Heritage, in which the world-class museums of Yale (the Peabody Museum of Natural History, the Center for British Art, and the University Art Gallery) and the Yale Libraries will combine science and technology with art in collaborative work on object conservation and digitization. And, clinic facilities of the Yale–New Haven Health System will locate on the West Campus.[32] The numbers of employees located on the West Campus are not large – fewer than 500 – but the number will grow.[33]

Juxtaposing interdisciplinary research institutes and core facilities forms a supportive and collaborative environment that creates a competitive edge in seeking research grant funding. It also creates an attractive environment for recruiting new junior and senior faculty, and both kinds of hiring activities are under way in helping grow the research base of the Yale West Campus.

The other integration is Science Hill into the main campus of Yale, with two new residential colleges designed by Robert Stern, Dean of the School of Architecture, being built there. Other new buildings are the recently completed Yale Health building and Rosenkranz Hall for Political Science.

What all of this means is that science will become an increasingly important part of every student's life at Yale, and that is certainly another aspect of the science wars at America's colleges and universities. This also is very important for the economy of Connecticut, which is trumpeting Yale's move and the decision of the Jackson Laboratory's JAX Genomic Medicine to build a $1.1 billion structure that will house a major research center, in a cooperative venture with the University of Connecticut Medical Center in Farmington.[34]

Virginia Commonwealth University

Virginia Commonwealth University, located in Richmond, Virginia, was created in 1968 with the merger of the Medical College of Virginia (1838) and the Richmond Professional Institute (1917).[35] The VCU Health System, first created in 1996, is now made up of the clinical operations of the university hospitals, physicians, and a large health maintenance organization (HMO). The university enrolls more than 31,500 students in 13 schools and one college, employs 18,000 people, has a sponsored research budget of more than $250 million, and a combined university and health system budget of $2.2 billion.

The university has two major campuses in downtown Richmond, separated by two miles – the Monroe Park Campus, and the Medical College of Virginia (MCV) Campus. The College of Humanities and Sciences, with its Schools of Mass Communications, World Studies, and Government and Public Affairs, and the Schools of the Arts, Business, Education, Engineering, and Social Work, are located on the Monroe Park Campus, while the Schools of Allied Health Professions, Dentistry, Medicine, Nursing, and Pharmacy are on the MCV Campus.[36]

While the merger of the Medical College of Virginia and the Richmond Professional Institute officially took place in 1968, it was not until 1990 that the university began to integrate the two entities academically and build the necessary facilities for a modern research university. Between 1990 and 2009, more than $2.2 billion of new and renovated construction was completed by the university, the health system, and its affiliate, the Virginia Biotechnology Research Park.[37] And a number of new academic programs were instituted in the areas of science that facilitated the true creation of a single unit, Virginia Commonwealth University.

During this time, the VCU Medical Center clinical and research facilities were entirely reconfigured. New clinical facilities included the VCU Medical Center at Stony Point, Gateway Medical Building, Ambulatory Care Center, and Critical Care Hospital, which were part of a $427 million construction budget spent for new and renovated clinical facilities at the Medical Center. This construction resulted in a modernized acute and tertiary care health system, with significantly increased patient volumes and dramatic advances in a number of subspecialties such as cardiac surgery, where the VCU Medical Center now ranks second in the country in number of artificial hearts implanted in the United States. At a time when many acute and tertiary urban public hospitals in the United States have lost much of their volumes of patients because of outmoded clinical facilities, the VCU Health System remains prominent in a very competitive health care market that has four Hospital Corporation of America (HCA) Hospitals and four Bon Secours Health System Hospitals.[38]

A second part of the renovation of the VCU Medical Center was in the area of academic buildings, especially the construction of new research facilities.[39] With the opening of the Kontos Medical Science Building, the Goodwin Cancer Research Laboratory, the School of Nursing, the Molecular Medicine Research Building, the Perkinson Dental Building, and the McGlothlin Medical Education Center, the VCU Medical Center has been able to add dramatic new research space to its inventory and recruit teams of leading scientists to VCU. Much of VCU's infrastructure planning for science at the VCU Medical Center depended on creative use of existing space, as well as demolition of dated buildings to create land on which to build. The first laboratory facility in the plan came online in 1996, and by 2009 a total of nine new buildings were in operation. Four of these consisted exclusively of laboratory and research support space. The remaining five buildings contained significant research space, accounting for 20–40 percent of the total square footage. The medical education center building, which opened in early 2013, has three of its 12 levels devoted to research. In aggregate, the addition of these 10 buildings increased the assignable square footage for research from approximately 434,000 to 727,000 – a 67 percent addition to VCU's research infrastructure. The total construction costs amounted to approximately $496 million and came from university, state, and philanthropic sources.

As this building plan moved incrementally through the first decade of the millennium, the institution deployed a strategic research initiative. Its aim was to hire some 100 new research faculty in its School of Medicine during the period 2006–11. The university reached its goal, and as a result its NIH awards portfolio grew significantly causing a jump in the NIH awards rankings of medical schools. The increased research capacity made a positive impact beyond the School of Medicine, allowing additional recruiting of research-focused deans and increases in federal and non-federal grant dollars. By 2011, VCU had positioned itself among the top 100 ranked universities in both federal and total research expenditures; a first for the institution. Also, in 2011, the success of research achievements university-wide resulted in VCU being placed in the Carnegie Foundation category of Research Activity-Very High Research Activity, a classification shared by only 108 research universities. VCU now has five members of the prestigious Institute of Medicine and one member of the National Academy of Engineering whose field is biomedical engineering. The result is that the research budget of the university, largely health science related, grew from $71.3 million in 1990 to $223.8 million in 2008.[40]

While the medical center was being reborn, especially because of the construction of new clinical and science facilities, equally important developments were taking place on the Monroe Park Campus in the area of science. A new School of Engineering was started in 1996, with major focuses on advanced manufacturing and life sciences engineering.[41] The school has departments of biomedical, chemical and life sciences, computer sciences, electrical and computer, and mechanical and nuclear engineering. The school also has brand new facilities, jointly with the School of Business, that have resulted in 330,000 square feet of engineering teaching and research space at a cost of more than $130 million. This school has provided a major scientific bridge to the

VCU Medical Center with joint research and teaching programs. A second scientific development of the Monroe Park Campus was the creation of VCU Life Sciences, whose major focus is the study of biological complexity.[42] VCU Life Sciences uses a highly interdisciplinary, systems-based approach to teaching and research, bringing together several hundred faculty members from both campuses. A major focus of VCU Life Sciences is its relationship to the health sciences, with the Rice Center Campus, on the James River promoting a second focus on environmental studies. VCU Life Sciences also has a new building, the Eugene and Lois Trani Center for the Life Sciences, which houses the Department of Biology in the most advanced teaching and research facilities.

Science, with the development of the Virginia Biotechnology Research Park, adjacent to the MCV Campus, also has contributed to the growth of inter-disciplinary programs between VCU's two campuses.[43] Started in 1992, with current construction approved and under way, the park will have 1.3 million square feet of occupied research and office space on a 30-acre site, employing more than 2,700 people in approximately $600 million of facilities. Major tenants include the Virginia Department of Forensic Science; the Virginia State Medical Examiner; the Virginia Division of Consolidated Laboratory Services; the United Network for Organ Sharing, the nation's only organ procurement and transplant network; Altria's Center for Research and Technology; Health Diagnostic Laboratory, Inc.; and various university labs, such as the VCU Institute for Psychiatric and Behavioral Genetics and the Mid-Atlantic Twin Registry. The park is home to a number of foreign companies from Israel, China, the UK, Germany and France, among other locations, making it a truly international scientific community as well. VCU faculty and students from both campuses work with all the tenants of the park.

Science and new science and clinical buildings, far beyond their scientific output, have been a unifying force at Virginia Commonwealth University. The physical reconfiguration of the sciences at VCU from 1990 to 2009 proved to be very important in focusing the two entities that originally formed the university into one unit. Politically, it is another example of the power of 'big science' in modern universities.

Summary of Case Studies

Infrastructure expansion such as that exemplified in our case study institutions affirms a commitment to contribute a significant investment in the research enterprise, which, in turn, positions the institution to more effectively com-pete for external grant dollars. Expansion allows for enhancement of internal research programs, providing them with space that will allow successful research programs to achieve new growth and development. Equally important, new research space attracts new research-focused faculty. Large amounts of new, contiguous space provide opportunities for faculty to form inter-disciplinary groups that work together under the aegis of a research institute or center. The availability of such space also allows the effective formation or consolidation of shared core services to support research. Competitive recruiting is enhanced by the availability of new or improved facilities especially in terms of attracting senior faculty with mature programs or groups of faculty recruited simultaneously to quickly build expertise in specific areas. These kinds of faculty assets provide the strength needed for the university to successfully compete for multi-programatic, multi-investigator grants (e.g. NIH program project or NIH center grants), which, when funded, result in major infusions of resources.

Over the course of 2004–11, each of the institutions discussed here added double-digit percentage increases to their research budgets as measured in total and federal research expenditures published by the National Science Foundation.[44] UCSF's total research expenditures over this period rose 47 percent, reaching $1.06 billion in 2011. The corresponding increase for Yale was 55 percent ($657 million) and for VCU was 43 percent ($208 million). Growth in federal expenditures over the period 2004–2011 was: UCSF, 43.6 percent, reaching $761.7 million in 2011; Yale, 57 percent, reaching $520 million in 2011; and VCU, 54 percent, reaching $153 million in 2011. Boosting federal research expenditures at each institution during this period was the funding of NIH Clinical and Translational Science Awards (CTSA) made to UCSF and Yale in 2006, and to VCU in 2010. The network formed by CTSA awardee institutions is limited to 60. Thus, members of the CTSA network comprise an elite group of institutions recognized for their accomplishments and promise in clinical and translational research.

Finally, within the past decade, each of these three institutions engaged in a major activity to enhance the research training environment for postdoctoral fellows. Postdoctorals are important contributors to the university research enterprise, typically devoting all or almost all of their effort to active research. They have skills and knowledge obtained in their graduate training that makes them valued members of the laboratory research team. Typically, they are able to quickly achieve and maintain research productivity. However, historically, the treatment of postdoctorals as professionals has been poor, characterized by low salaries, few and inferior benefits, and little recognition within the overall academic environment. All three of our case study institutions have invested significant resources in enhancing the postdoctoral training experience. UCSF's office to support postdoctorals was launched 2001, Yale's in 2002, and VCU's in 2007. Resources have included benefits coordination and subsidies, career counseling and development, and various types of assistance, including tuition payments for courses, travel stipends, and other items. The formation of the National Postdoctoral Association[45] in 2003 continues to promote the enhancement of the training environment for fellows, and many academic institutions are working to develop and refine support for trainees and their training environment. The formation and operation of offices to support postdoctoral activities at UCSF, Yale, and VCU have promoted the continuing need for training that is crucial to the research enterprise and its competitive status. The most recent data published by the Center for Measuring University Performance[46] reports the number of postdoctorals at UCSF and Yale among the highest in the country, 1,132 and 1,195, respectively. Although the number of postdoctorals at VCU is smaller (233), VCU ranks 44th among public research institutions in terms of the size of its postdoctoral fellow population.[47]

Conclusion

Overall, more university leaders have scientific backgrounds, and more decisions at universities are being made with 'big science' in the forefront, rather than in the background. Research funding, national and international awards, such as Nobel prizes and membership in the National Academy of Sciences, and private funding are all areas of competition between and among American colleges and universities, and science plays a major role in this competition. Simply put, science is higher on the priority list in American higher education than it ever has been – a feature that seems to be a worldwide phenomenon – and is certainly illustrated in the construction of new science and clinical facilities at America's colleges and universities.

What are the consequences of these science wars for American colleges and universities? The armed races for facilities and faculty seem unremitting and perhaps have begun to distort the focus of American higher education. Differential support, significantly different compensation schedules, varied tuitions, scholarships and employment possibilities, and more political involvement in setting the missions of the institutions all show the growing importance of science to national security, economic development, and institutional prestige. Only time will tell whether this emphasis is justified by the scientific advances it produces.

Acknowledgements

The author would like to thank Margaret Acquarulo, Donald Cosgrove, John Duval, Frank Macrina, and all of Virginia Commonwealth University, for their assistance in the researching and writing of parts of this essay. In addition, the author thanks Richard Levin, President of Yale University, for reviewing the Yale case study, and Kristen Bole, Assistant News Director at UCSF, for reviewing the UCSF case study.

Notes

1 Figures from Peter Li Education Group (2011) 'College Construction Report', available at: www.peterli.com/cpm/resources/_rptscpm.shtm (accessed July 15, 2012).
2 Center for Biotechnology and Interdisciplinary Studies, available at: www.trade lineinc.com/profiles/03E51DF5-2B3B-B525-862ADDC7CCECC896.
3 Center for Advanced Biomedical Research, available at: www.jenjdanna.com/picture-gallery/boston-university/9181657.
4 Email, Donald Cosgrove, Director of Construction Management, VCU, to Eugene P. Trani, November 28, 2012.
5 Email, John Duval, Chief Executive Officer, MCV Hospitals, VCU Health System, to Eugene P. Trani, December 9, 2012. Resources on these changes can be found in the American Institute of Architecture 2010 Guidelines, National Fire Protection Association 101 (Life Safety Code), as well as the Institute of Medicine and the Picker Institute.
6 'Science Wars', *Wikipedia*, available at: http://en.wikipedia.org/wiki/_Science_wars (accessed November 16, 2012).
7 'Science and Technology of World War II', *The National World War II Museum*, available at: www.ww2sci-tech.org/essays/essay2.html (accessed November 16, 2012).
8 John Aubrey Douglass (1999) 'The Cold War, Technology and The American University', *Research and Occasional Paper Series: CSHE.2.99*, July, p. 2.
9 Douglass, p. 15.
10 Douglass, p. 16.
11 See Eugene P. Trani and Robert D. Holsworth (2010) *The Indispensable University: Higher Education, Economic Development, and the Knowledge Economy*, Lanham, MD: Rowman & Littlefield; and Paul Temple (ed.) (2012) *Universities in the Knowledge Economy: Higher Education Organisation and Global Change*, London: Routledge.
12 Brochure of conference, Tradeline 2012 Conference, available at: www.tradelineinc.com/attachments/BCA69F27-C29C-DD41-ADC7905D17EFAFF7/1205Invite_FINAL.pdf (accessed November 16, 2012).
13 Paul Basken (2012) 'Scientific Discovery: Inspired by a Walk to the Restroom', *Chronicle of Higher Education*, October 29, available at: http://chronicle.com/article/Scientific-Discovery-Inspired/135476/ (accessed November 15, 2012).
14 Joseph A. Soares (1999) *The Decline of Privilege: The Modernization of Oxford University*, Stanford, CA: Stanford University, 1999.
15 'At South Pole, World's Most Extreme Scientific Construction Project', available at: http://science.psu.edu/news-and-events/2011-news/Cowen1-2011 (accessed November 16, 2012).
16 David A. Walsh, 'The Oldest University Buildings in America', *George Mason University's History Name Network*, available at: http://hnn.us/articles/oldest-university-buildings-america (accessed November 15, 2012).
17 www.usa.skanska.com/markets/science-and-technology/ (accessed November 15, 2012).
18 UCSF Fact Sheet, June, 2011, available at: www.ucsf.edu/sites/default/files/documents/kb-mb_facts-june_2011.pdf (accessed September 14, 2012).
19 'Dealmaker of the Year: Bruce Spaulding', *San Francisco Business Times*, March 28, 2010, available at: www.bizjournals.com/sanfrancisco/stories/2010/03/29/focus4.html?page=all (accessed September 14, 2012).

20 'University of California, San Francisco', *Wikipedia*, available at: http://en.wikipedia. org/wiki/University_of_California,_San_Francisco (accessed November 15, 2012).

21 www.ucsf.edu/locations/mission-bay/mission-bay-campus (accessed September 14, 2012).

22 www.rvapc.com/works (accessed September 14, 2012).

23 'The Power and Promise of UCSF', June 2010, prepared by Economic Planning Systems, Berkeley, California.

24 'UCSF Post Final Three-Year Plan with Tactics', available at: www.ucsf.edu/ about/ucsfs-2014-2015-plan (accessed September 14, 2012).

25 'Yale University', *Wikipedia*, available at: http://en.wikipedia.org/wiki/Yale_ University (accessed November 15, 2012).

26 Kevin Adkisson, 'The Future of Science at Yale', *Yale Scientific*, February 14, 2011, available at: www.yalescientific.org/2011/02/the-future-of-science-at-yale/ (accessed October 30, 2012).

27 'Science Hill Plan – Facilities at Yale', available at: www.facilities.yale.edu/SHWS/ SHP2.html (accessed December 5, 2012).

28 Karen Arenson, 'At Yale, a New Campus Just for Research', *New York Times*, July 4, 2007, available at: www.nytimes.com/2007/07/04/education/04yale.html_r=0& pagewanted=print (accessed December 5, 2012).

29 Mark Alden Branch, 'Yale Buys a Second Campus', *Yale Alumni Magazine*, July/August 2007, available at: www.yalealumnimagazine.com/issues/2007_07/ l_v.html (accessed December 4, 2012).

30 Kevin Adkisson, 'The Future of Science at Yale', *Yale Scientific*, February 14, 2011, available at: www.yalescientific.org/2011/02/the-future-of-science-at-yale/ (accessed October 30, 2012).

31 Kevin Adkisson, 'The Future of Science at Yale'.

32 Mark Alden Branch, 'Deal of the Century', *Yale Alumni Magazine*, September/ October 2010, available at: www.yalealumnimagazine.com/issues/2010_09/west campus4250.html (accessed October 30, 2012).

33 See Margot Sanger-Katz, 'The Pioneers: Three innovative West Campus labs', *Yale Alumni Magazine*, September/October 2012, available at: www.yalealumni magazine.com/issues/2010_09/wscience568.html (accessed December 4, 2012).

34 'Biotechnology Investment: Gains and Losses', *Nature*, May 30, 2012, available at: www.nature.com/naturejobs/science/articles/10.1038%2Fnj7400-667a.

35 The best existing history of Virginia Commonwealth University is Virginius Dabney, *Virginia Commonwealth University: A Sesquicentennial History* (Charlottesville, VA: University Press of Virginia, 1987). Eugene Trani and his collaborator, John Kneebone, are currently at work on *A Promise Fulfilled: Virginia Commonwealth University and Richmond, Virginia, 1968–2009*.

36 'Virginia Commonwealth University', *Wikipedia*, available at: http://en.wikipedia. org/wiki/Virginia_Commonwealth_University (accessed November 15, 2012).

37 *Defining the Urban University: The Legacy of VCU President Eugene P. Trani, 1990–2009* (Richmond, VA: Virginia Commonwealth University, 2009), pp. 8–11.

38 *Defining the Urban University*, p. 25.

39 www.vcu.edu/medicalcenter/.

40 www.vcuhealth.org/.

41 www.egr.vcu.edu/.

42 www.vcu.edu/lifesci/.

43 http://vabiotech.com/.

44 www.nsf.gov/statistics/infbrief/nsf13305/.

45 www.nationalpostdoc.org/.

46 http://mup.asu.edu/.
47 Email, Frank Macrina, Vice President for Research, VCU, to Eugene P. Trani, December 10, 2012.

References

Adkisson, K. (2011) 'The Future of Science at Yale', *Yale Scientific*, 14 February, available at: www.yalescientific.org/2011/02/the-future-of-science-at-yale/ (accessed 30 October 2012).

Arenson, K. (2007) 'At Yale, a New Campus Just for Research', *New York Times*, 4 July, available at: www.nytimes.com/2007/07/04/education/04yale.html_r=0&pagewanted=print (accessed 5 December 2012).

'At South Pole, World's Most Extreme Scientific Construction Project', available at: http://science.psu.edu/news-and-events/2011-news/Cowen1-2011 (accessed 16 November 2012).

Basken, P. (2012) 'Scientific Discovery: Inspired by a Walk to the Restroom', *Chronicle of Higher Education*, available at: http://chronicle.com/article/Scientific-Discovery-Inspired/135476/ (accessed 15 November 2012).

Branch, M. (2010) 'Deal of the Century', *Yale Alumni Magazine*, September/October, available at: www.yalealumnimagazine.com/issues/2010_09/westcampus4250.html (accessed 30 October 2012).

Branch, M. (2007) 'Yale Buys a Second Campus', *Yale Alumni Magazine*, July/August, available at: www.yalealumnimagazine.com/issues/2007_07/l_v.html (accessed 4 December 2012).

Center for Biotechnology and Interdisciplinary Studies, www.tradelineinc.com/profiles/03E51DF5-2B3B-B525-862ADDC7CCECC896.

Center for Advanced Biomedical Research, www.jenjdanna.com/picture-gallery/boston-university/9181657.

The Center for Measuring University Performance, http://mup.asu.edu/.

Cosgrove, D. Email to E. Trani (28 November 2012).

'Dealmaker of the Year: Bruce Spaulding', *San Francisco Business Times*, 28 March 2010, available at: www.bizjournals.com/sanfrancisco/stories/2010/03/29/focus4.html?page=all (accessed 14 September 2012).

Douglass, J. (1999) 'The Cold War, Technology and the American University', *Research and Occasional Paper Series*, CSHE.2.99, 2.

Duval, J. Email to E. Trani (9 December 2012).

Economic Planning Systems (2010) 'The Power and Promise of UCSF'.

Kaplan, K. (2012) 'Biotechnology Investment: Gains and Losses', *Nature*, 30 May, available at: www.nature.com/naturejobs/science/articles/10.1038%2Fnj7400-667a.

Macrina, F. Email to E. Trani (10 December 2012).

National Postdoctoral Association, www.nationalpostdoc.org/.

National Science Foundation (2012) www.nsf.gov/statistics/infbrief/nsf13305/.

Peter Li Education Group (2011)www.peterli.com/cpm/resources/_rptscpm.shtm (accessed 15 July 2012).

Rafael Viñoly Architects, www.rvapc.com/works (accessed 14 September 2012).

Sanger-Katz, M. (2012) 'The Pioneers: Three innovative West Campus labs', *Yale Alumni Magazine*, September/October, www.yalealumnimagazine.com/issues/2010_09/wscience568.html (accessed 4 December 2012).

'Science Hill Plan – Facilities at Yale', www.facilities.yale.edu/SHWS/SHP2.html (accessed 5 December 2012).

'Science and Technology of World War II', *The National World War II Museum*, www.ww2sci-tech.org/essays/essay2.html (accessed 16 November 2012).

'Science Wars', *Wikipedia*, http://en.wikipedia.org/wiki/_Science_wars (accessed 16 November 2012).

Skanska (2013) www.usa.skanska.com/markets/science-and-technology/ (accessed 15 November 2012).

Soares, J. (1999) *The Decline of Privilege: The Modernization of Oxford University*, Stanford, CA: Stanford University Press.

Temple, P. (2012) *Universities in the Knowledge Economy: Higher Education Organisation and Global Change*, London: Routledge.

Tradeline (2012)www.tradelineinc.com/attachments/BCA69F27-C29C-DD41-ADC790 5D17EFAFF7/1205Invite_FINAL.pdf (accessed 16 November 2012).

Trani, E. and Holsworth, R. (2010) *The Indispensable University: Higher Education, Economic Development, and the Knowledge Economy*, Lanham, MD: Rowman & Littlefield.

UCSF Fact Sheet (2011) www.ucsf.edu/sites/default/files/documents/kb-mb_facts-june_ 2011.pdf (accessed 14 September 2012).

UCSF: The Mission Bay Campus, www.ucsf.edu/locations/mission-bay-campus (accessed 14 September 2012).

'UCSF Post Final Three-Year Plan with Tactics', www.ucsf.edu/about/ucsfs-2014-2015-plan (accessed 14 September 2012).

'University of California, San Francisco', *Wikipedia*, http://en.wikipedia.org/wiki/ University_of_California,_San_Francisco (accessed 15 November 2012).

'VCU Engineering', www.egr.vcu.edu/.

'VCU Health System', www.vcuhealth.org/.

'VCU Life Sciences', www.vcu.edu/lifesci/.

'VCU Medical Center', www.vcu.edu/medicalcenter/.

'Virginia Bio-Technology Research Park', http://vabiotech.com/.

Virginia Commonwealth University (2009) *Defining the Urban University: The Legacy of VCU President Eugene P. Trani, 1990–2009*, Richmond, VA: Virginia Commonwealth University.

'Virginia Commonwealth University', *Wikipedia*, http://en.wikipedia.org/wiki/Virginia_ Commonwealth_University (accessed 15 November 2012).

Walsh, D. 'The Oldest University Buildings in America', *George Mason University's History Name Network*, available at: http://hnn.us/articles/oldest-university-buildings-america (accessed 15 November 2012).

'Yale University', *Wikipedia*, http://en.wikipedia.org/wiki/Yale_University (accessed 15 November 2012).

10

'Let's Go for the Chicken-Drum'

The Everyday Production of Social Space in a Chinese University

ZHONGYUAN ZHANG

Introduction

The physical aspects of universities have always been an important part of higher education, but only quite recently has a body of work emerged to highlight the relevance of space in educational research (Temple and Barnett 2007). Many studies focus on how the physical forms of universities play central parts in promoting universities' functions of offering education, conducting research, and providing services. For instance, the design and location of educational facilities have important impacts on students' learning experiences (McLaughlin and Faulkner 2012). The distribution of information centres (Tikhomirov *et al.* 2009) and the layout of research labs (Toker and Gray 2008) are said to be related to the outcomes of innovation activities in universities. To accommodate the fast growth of e-learning, universities are advised to create new flexible spaces inside old buildings (Ghasson 2004). Timetabling lecture rooms also helps to increase effective uses of teaching space (Beyrouthy *et al.* 2009). And natural landscaping on campus may reduce students' stress levels as university lives become increasingly busy (Lau and Feng 2009). In short, space is an important means for achieving universities' ends.

But universities are not just organizations with certain functional ends to achieve. 'All organizations are relations of power – even the most egalitarian' (Brown *et al.* 2010: 525), and universities are certainly no exception. Studies on organizational space (Dale and Burrell 2008; Taylor and Spicer 2007), inspired by foundational works in social geography (Lefebvre 1991), highlight that space has a social dimension beyond its apparent functionality, and already, evidence accumulates to suggest that campus space materializes power relations in universities. For instance, campus buildings are often embedded in the clashing interests of designers, student and faculty bodies, and other stakeholders (Gieryn 2002). Culturally sanctioned forms of civility are designed into lecture rooms, for instance by making students face their professors (Muetzelfeldt 2006). Hierarchy is spatially defined on campus: for instance, faculty staff work in relatively private offices while students share noisy corridors (Hurdley 2010). University space is also potentially gendered. What appears to be standardized office space calls on women staff to act out their gendered roles through bodily comportments (Tyler and Cohen 2010). In line with this development, Beyes and Michels (2011) advocate a 'socio-spatial' perspective on higher education; their call concerts with some researchers' efforts in bringing Lefebvre's spatial thinking to the study of university space (Anderson 2006; Peltonen 2011). This body of literature, which approaches university space as 'social materiality' (Dale 2005), is so far only at its emergent stage. However, it is a welcome addition to the mainstream functional focus on university space.

This chapter intends to contribute to our understanding of the social/political nature of university space. It studies how power relations are constructed by the ways students experience and use university space in their everyday lives. The choice is justified by recent developments in studies on organizational space, which I will briefly review in the next section. Here, I argue that although researchers engage with Lefebvre's spatial thinking to pinpoint social space as emerging from everyday lives, little is known about the specific processes involved in such emergence. Thus, this chapter is inspired by, and may potentially benefit, existing studies on organizational space. Following this review, I draw on documentary, observational and interview data from a Chinese university where I work as a faculty member. I present a descriptive account of the ways this university's campus is designed, and of how it is routinely experienced and used by students. The chapter proceeds to outline three processes through which power relations are materialized in campus space in everyday lives. These processes bring us back to existing studies on higher education, organizational space and Lefebvre's thinking.

Key Literature in Organizational Spatial Studies

The French thinker Henri Lefebvre's book *The Production of Space* (1991), 'arguably the most important book ever written about the social and historical significance of human spatiality' (Soja 1996: 6), is a major source of inspiration for studies on organizational space (Beyes and Steyeart 2012; Dale and Burrell 2008; Taylor and Spicer 2007). Lefebvre (1991: 26) argued that '(social) space is a (social) product'. Space is similar to other human products in that it is produced by human labour before it offers itself for social consumption. Yet, unlike other products, space is uniquely social: 'Social relations . . . have no real existence save in and through space. *Their underpinning is spatial*' (Lefebvre 1991: 404, original emphasis). This social ontology of space underpins researchers' efforts to 'bring space back' into organization study (Kornberger and Clegg 2004). As organizations are increasingly seen as relations of power, space provides a crucial lens on organizational realities.

According to Lefebvre (1991: 33–9), the fact that space is a social product can be appreciated and analyzed with three interwoven moments. Space is at once *conceived* by planners who order space in mathematical ways and by so doing dominate societies with the ideology of scientific thinking; it is *lived* by space users who seek to appropriate the imposed conceived space with 'clandestine or underground' experiences, often through artistic imaginations; it is also *practiced* by both planners and users in their respective daily routines, which maintain and consolidate space's social 'competence and performance'. Social space is thus a contested terrain constantly formed and reformed as social actors negotiate for power, and its primary mode of existence is that of processual becoming. A proper enquiry of social space as Lefebvre envisaged accounts for the 'interrelations' and 'links' among the moments of the conceived-lived-practiced triad (Lefebvre 1991: 116), moving 'from *things in space to the actual production of space*' (Lefebvre 1991: 37, original emphasis).

In organizational studies, researchers engage with Lefebvre's spatial thinking in two slightly different ways. The first, macro-level approach, represented by Dale and Burrell's (2008) seminal book, examines how organizational space is constructed by larger sociocultural forces and how, once constructed, bears power effects to which organizational members are exposed daily. The authors draw our attention to the ways in which corporate architectures are designed to fix people into places, to impart symbolic and aesthetic experiences, and to engender patterns of mobility in organizations. For them, such processes are deeply political. For instance, in offices (a notable example being the now-demolished Larkin Building in New York state), managers may be placed above employees' open-plan work areas to facilitate surveillance (Baldry 1999). Buildings and their interiors express symbolic messages; for instance, bureaucratic hierarchy is defined by the luxury of office decoration (Rosen *et al.* 1990). Where such direct expressions seem absent, colour patterns, construction materials and the shape of office furniture are carefully combined to generate managerially sanctioned feelings; for instance, vigorousness (Hancock 2006), calmness (Carter and Jackson 2000) and emotional detachment (Witkin 1990). Space also regulates people's movements. By installing large open halls, the management intends to force employees into highly mobile ways of social encountering (Edenius and Yakhlef 2007).

The macro-level approach allows us to see that the conceived space in organizations is far from power-neutral. This is an important insight, but it does not engage closely with the ways organizational members live and practice space daily. Addressing this lack, some recent studies argue that social space is not only produced by larger sociocultural forces, but also by everyday lives in organizations. This is the everyday approach to organizational space. Beyes and Steyaert (2012) argue that social space by nature cannot be conceptualized as static. For them, focusing on corporate architectures blinds us to the ways that 'molecular' space – bodily movements, comportments, successions of actions and affects – emerge in everyday lives to contest and reform power relations in organizations. Similarly, Wapshott and Marlett (2012) point out that people experience and use organizational space not in passive ways; rather, they actively engage space outside what they perceive to be intentional designs to establish their political claims and vie for hegemony. Some empirical evidences can be quoted to support the everyday approach. For instance, Halford (2004) finds that employees responded to the managerial initiative of hot-desking by spatially (re)constructing workplace communities: they put passwords on adjacent computer stations to ward off unfamiliar colleagues. In the Israeli Ministry of Foreign Affairs, employees chose to smoke in and break into forbidden areas to contest managerial power (Wasserman and Frenkel 2011). In UK hospitals, employees narrated space in managerially unsanctioned ways to resist imposed organizational changes (Halford and Leonard 2006). According to these studies, the space of everyday lives is socially significant.

The macro-level and everyday approaches supplement each other, for each highlights ways that organizational space is socially produced, and, as such, they put Lefebvre's spatial thinking into fruitful analyses of organizational realities. However, if social space is produced between the 'interrelations' and 'links' of the moments of conceived, lived and practiced spaces, currently we know little of the ways these moments are interrelated. What we need, both to enrich the emergent literature on university space and existing studies on organizational space, is an account of how a university campus is conceived by designers, and lived and practiced in everyday lives. This chapter endeavours to provide such an account. Below, I introduce the design of a Chinese university campus before describing the ways that the campus is engaged daily by a group of space users, its students.

Everyday Lives at KK University

University Campus Design

KK University (a pseudonym) is one of China's top universities, whose traditional forte lies in natural and applied sciences. In the last decade or so, the university has undergone major changes in line with national policies. In 1998, the university merged with three minor universities in the same city. Such mergers took place nationwide as top universities sought to integrate educational resources and vie for international prestige. The university has substantially expanded its enrolment of undergraduate and graduate students since 1999, and today, it has about 45,000 students and employs over 8,000 staff (including 3,000 faculty members).

The university had an old campus (J campus) in the downtown city, and the three merged universities were scattered in different parts of the city. None of these campuses was large enough to accommodate the population of students and staff that the university holds today. Consequently, in 2001, the university started to construct a huge new campus (Z campus) in the city's suburbs, covering an area of 2.13 square kilometres. The construction of new campuses was common for Chinese universities in the early years of the twenty-first century: examples include the Cangping campus of Peking University, and the Jiangwan Campus of Fudan University. With impressive speed, Z campus came into use in 2002. Today, it accommodates the majority of the university's undergraduate teaching and a part of its postgraduate teaching. Parts of the older campuses (including J campus) are still in use for research and teaching, but many old buildings have since been sold for commercial redevelopment.

Z campus is designed with the principles of 'modernization', 'network mobility' and 'botanic landscaping' in mind, according to one study (Zhu and Wei 2007). By 'modernization', one sees that almost all its buildings are styled in a modernistic fashion, with white and grey external walls. This stands in sharp contrast to the university's old campuses, which consist mainly of brown, Russian-style buildings, witnesses to the honeymoon period between China and the USSR in the 1950s. 'Botanic landscaping' means that the campus spreads itself evenly around a large central lake, which is named, after the university's motto, as the 'lake of truth'. The lake is part of a natural waterway; it has, however, undergone substantial landscaping so that it is now listed as one of the city's scenic attractions.

What is perhaps more interesting to observe is the principle of 'network mobility'. According to an official document, the campus is conceptualized as consisting of a series of 'concentrated architectural groups' connected by vehicle roads and walking paths. Each architectural group is assigned to a broad disciplinary unit, such as social studies, natural sciences and so on. This is to facilitate 'inter-disciplinary learning', but also to assist in management. Common functional areas – dorms, restaurants (the central canteen, sometimes dubbed 'the biggest canteen in Asia', is designed to serve 20,000 people), sports grounds and teaching complexes – are also grouped together. For instance, the east teaching complex stretches about half a mile in length (its central corridor alone is 500 metres long and 6 metres wide); on a rainy day, one could walk from one end of the complex to the other without catching a raindrop. The west teaching complex is a little smaller, but no less impressive. These complexes consist of numerous side corridors and hundreds of lecture rooms that are almost identical in design. Newly enrolled students often get lost here. One freshman described her daily walks through these complexes as 'probing in a pyramid' (Hua, freshman). Another said that the central corridor reminded her of an assembly line (Xu, freshman) – a very apt metaphor, for daily life at KK means moving up and down prefabricated routes of functionality. It seems that the geometric grandeur of these complexes strike their users as ugly, even inhuman.

Moving between the campus functional areas is time-consuming. The campus is designed to accelerate movements, and wide vehicle roads reach into every corner of the campus. These roads are used mixedly for bicycles, cars and motorbikes, with no or little physical demarcation to protect cyclists from car drivers. Apparently, the campus does not encourage walking: not only are pedestrian pavements rather narrow, but also cars and bicycles can be parked where their owners find most convenient. The campus has very limited parking space. This was not problematic 10 years ago when the campus was first designed, for relatively few people owned cars then. Today, it is different. It is not uncommon now for students to drive Audis or Mercedes to lectures, and even though many still rely on bicycles, there is an increasing number of electric motorbikes on campus that are dangerously fast and silent. Like elsewhere in the city, at Z campus, cars have squeezed out the space for cyclists (they are parked on bicycle lanes), and bicycles have squeezed out the space for pedestrians (they are parked on pavements). At certain hours of the day, cars, motorbikes, bicycles and pedestrians jostle with one another for space as they meet in some central intersections, so much so that the university employs temporary traffic wardens to maintain order! In 2011, at the main entrance of Z campus, three tariff booths were erected to charge drivers in or outside the university for parking on campus. This practice has limited effects in reducing the number of cars on campus, for it turns out that only the poor care about parking charges. At weekends, the campus is 'like a show of luxurious cars: Porsche, BMW, you name it' (Ding, sophomore). Many of these cars belong to rich people in the city. Their power to consume entitles them to legitimate and prioritized accesses to the space of the intellect.

Having laid out the spatial stage for everyday lives at KK University, it is time to go into the campus and look in more detail at the ways students routinely engage with their spatial environs. Three kinds of experience stand out from our data: students seek lively narratives in campus space; they are frustrated by a lack of personal space; and they also make some places their favourite haunts.

Telling Spatial Tales

Students take delight in giving nicknames to their spatial environs, and such nicknames become common vocabularies of the university's everyday life. For instance, a side street close to the university's back entrance is known as 'the street of degeneration'. This street has been appropriated by street vendors and cheap food stalls that supposedly lure students to overeating, hence a life of 'degeneration'. The west bank of the central lake is nicknamed 'lovers' valley' because student lovers often stroll in its quietude. Similarly, a big pine tree in front of the J campus main entrance is called 'the BG tree'. In student language, 'BG' is an abbreviation for 'giving someone a treat'. The tree is thus known because:

> It is close to restaurants just across the street, so when someone gives a treat people always meet up at the tree. As time goes by, the expression passes on. 'Let's meet up at the BG tree', everyone knows where it is.
>
> (Pou, second-year postgraduate)

But the most popular tales about campus space are ghost stories. Students love these stories, and during interviews many described them in detail. For instance, like most Chinese universities built in the 1950s, J campus has a big statue of Chairman Mao that depicts the leader waving with his right hand. Rumour has it that the Chairman sometimes takes a rest at night and waves with his left hand instead. At Z campus, the bathrooms of the west teaching complex have much smaller mirrors than those in the east complex, and according to students' jokes, this is because certain ghostly creatures creep around in the west complex: the mirrors are made smaller so that these creatures would not appear to scare people away. The top floor of the administrative building – the highest building on Z campus – is used as a viewing platform. This platform has a peculiar round shape. A tale narrates that the floor is designed to be 'god's eye', which, like the Eye of Sauron in *The Lord of the Rings*, surveys things from the underworld that we cannot see.

Students tell me that, several years ago, a graduate of KK wrote a booklet recording Z campus' ghostly spaces, and this booklet is still being circulated online. With their vivid imaginations, students have come to see campus space in entirely different ways to those of its original designers.

Seeking Personal Spaces

When I ask students how they feel about living on Z campus, many complain that they feel a lack of belonging. 'The campus is too big, and we do not have our own classrooms, not like back at high school' (Ding, sophomore). Another student commented, referring to the tariff booths: 'I was ashamed when I introduced my friends to [Z campus], they said "Ah, so your university is a big car park!"' (Liu, freshman). The feeling of not belonging to the campus was vividly demonstrated in a seminar presentation of my class. A group of freshmen delivered a presentation on the topic 'students' self-concepts'. This group acted out the topic in the following way:

Xiao (the hero of the show), a typical KK University science major, got up one morning and found that he had no lectures that day. However, he could not stay in the dorm because his roommates were playing computer games. He wandered out into the library. He found that the library had been appropriated by student lovers who were behaving rather too intimately. Embarrassed, Xiao went to a lecture room but he could not stay long either, for other students were rushing in and out. Xiao's wandering went on, until he finally came back to his bicycle and said: 'My friend, at least you belong to me!'

The wandering Xiao captures the experiences that many KK students have in common. Moving between lecture rooms, students are frustrated by the lack of personal space. To carve out personal space and, consequently, a semblance of a sense of belonging in the university's mobile campus, students resort to a couple of techniques. One is the use of personal items. For instance, a student said that one of her favourite places on campus was a public bookshelf in the library: 'I keep some of my own books there' (Zuo, sophomore). This student put big signatures on her books so that others would not move them away. Senior students sometimes construct personal territories in more aggressive manners. In some self-study rooms at the west teaching complex, I see back-row seats demarcated by books, stationeries, mugs and dinnerware. Students tell me that these seats belong to 'study tycoons' who read, nap and even eat there. The second way to carve out personal space is, literally, to 'carve' it out. Wooden tables and benches in common areas are inscribed with interesting monologues ('K sat on this bench for many a year') and dialogues ('I am getting old, and must find love now', and somewhere below, apparently by another person, 'I am coming!').

Han, a freshman, found herself a lucky exception to her peers, for she was given a personal space that others had to claim with personal items and signatures. Having lately joined a large student society that had a lounge to its own, one of the first things she did was to put her coffee mug in the lounge. She led me around the lounge and pointed out to me where her coffee mug was kept, and she described how affectionately she felt about the place:

> If I am somewhere around and feel like using the bathroom, I'd take the trouble to come up here to pee. I could take a look around and see how everybody is doing . . . I guess I just like the place.

Frequenting Favourite Places

Although most students do not have Han's luck to use personalized lounges, they have nevertheless created their favourite haunts on campus. Below, we will look at two of these, a cafe called 'KK Memories' and a night stall nicknamed 'Chicken-Drum'. They were brought to my attention by chance. The cafe was demolished a year before I entered the university, but when a senior undergraduate (Tu) learnt that I knew nothing about it, he volunteered to sit for a two-hour interview to tell me what he knew about it. The demolishing of KK Memories was a very big thing for him and his friends. Similarly, I learnt about the night stall only recently when it was threatened with removal by local authorities. Students started to talk about it in classes and seminars. Luckily, the night stall seems to have survived to this day.

KK Memories was a small cafe located on J campus. The cafe was sponsored by a group of KK graduates and it employed some undergraduates as waiters and waitresses. For a period of four years or so, the cafe was the favourite haunt of many KK students and was even listed as a tourist attraction by some websites. During interviews, many postgraduate students cherished fond memories of the cafe:

> There is no place like it. If we want a gathering, or if my friend wants to interview someone, or if we want to celebrate a birthday, the first place we'd think of is KK Memories. In the entire university, you cannot locate a more suitable place for casual gatherings.
>
> (Jun, second-year PhD)

The cafe appealed to KK students for a number of reasons. It was cheap, almost non-profitable. It was conveniently located at the central square of J campus. Also, the fact that drinks were served by KK students seemed to lessen the kind of commercial aura that prevails at Z campus. Importantly, KK Memories was what its name suggested: a memory of the university:

> On the walls, there were pictures of previous cohorts and student groups, a lot of posters and newspapers cuttings [about KK University], and some old T-shirts. It was very disorderly, things heaped on one another. But I could see that the place was full of memories, so I left my own memories. I took a picture with the cafe and stuck it on the wall.
>
> (Cui, KK graduate)

What was attractive about KK Memories, then, was the kind of bonds that students felt through the cafe's (perhaps intentionally managed) messy space, between themselves and a collective that had lived before and would continue into the future. This collective is none other than generations of KK students who pride themselves as being KK students. Cui went on to explain:

> Outside people also came to KK Memories, but I sense our feelings would not be the same. This is like . . . when I was a graduate student I studied

at this building. It was a very commonplace building, a rather run-down place. You may call it shabby really. But my supervisor, and the supervisor of my supervisor, they all taught and lived in the building. So the building means something to me.

KK Memories did not just contain items of memories. The place itself became a piece of memory unique to KK students. The 'run-down' building meant 'something' to Cui because people she admired lived and worked there. Similarly, the cafe was given a particular significance because it brought together certain people. It rendered a period of students' lives as a meaningful part of a larger collectivity of which they proudly claimed membership.

This is perhaps why the forced closure of KK Memories stirred a wave of heated debate. The cafe's space was seized by the university and reconstructed as a psychotherapy centre in 2009. Tu recalled that the closure of the cafe became 'the hottest issue' on the university intranet. 'There was an avalanche of posted articles, and many more responses'. Browsing through some articles that exist to this day, we find that students sought different accounts for the cafe's closure. Some blamed the cafe's management ('If the owner really loved this university as he said he did, then why didn't he negotiate with the university in a better way?'); others blamed the university authorities ('How can the university be so practical ... doesn't it want more history?' 'I heard ... a lot of politics was involved. The water was deep. But this is typical of the university. They want to do it, and they just do it!').

Although the real cause of the closure is hard to uncover, one thing is certain: for a period of time at least, 'the intranets were full of articles that guess the unspeakable and even malicious intentions of the university' (Tu, senior undergraduate). Many posted articles have since been deleted by intranet managers, including Tu's. Fortunately, Tu retained a copy of his writing and made it available to me. In these articles, Tu interpreted the closure of KK Memories as an infringement of students' rights. He also related the incident to other aspects of campus lives, such as strict controls on intranet posting. In the interview, Tu proudly acknowledged that his articles made him a 'thorn' in the eyes of the university authorities but at the same time won him friendship from some like-minded fellow students. A quote from his article suggests why intranet managers did not like him much:

> It is useless to feel angry, alone in your dorm. You need to make your voice heard, by fellow students and the university. You can make use of various means to do this: the intranet, the micro-blog, even by sticking posters on campus. You must go on doing so until things get improved.

Having reviewed the story of KK Memories, we now move on to a second favourite haunt of students. Ask any KK student based on Z campus, and you will learn what Chicken-Drum is. Initially, it referred to a roadside food stall located close to the campus. The stall started business about 10 years ago; its main menu is roasted chicken drumsticks. The stall's business was good, and other local vendors joined in. Today, Chicken-Drum refers to a group of similar stalls that sprawl along about 50 metres of public roadside space. Like many other night stalls in China, they operate in the evening and under rather dubious hygienic conditions. Many stall owners do not hold permanent licenses and thus find themselves constantly in trouble with the local police. Despite this, these stalls are favourite haunts of KK students, and expressions such as 'Let's go for the Chicken-Drum' carry commonly accepted meanings.

The majority of KK students come from middle or lower income families. In a self-mocking way, these students refer to themselves as SPUs (short-poor-and-ugly). The widening income gaps in Chinese society have left visible traces on university campuses. 'Sometimes you could tell that someone is a TRH [tall-rich-and-handsome, the opposite of SPU]; the way she looks at you says very clearly that she does not want to know you' (Wu, sophomore). Hostility between SPU and TRH is often imaginary, but there were instances when tensions surfaced. On Christmas Day 2012, I noticed that a campus restaurant restricted its menu to only two expensive set courses. I posted an article on the intranet to criticize the restaurant, thinking that it was overcharging students. Some responding comments, as far as I could see, showed a bitter sarcasm to the widening of income gaps on campus ('Some people are rich, so why is *that* any of your business?'). Chicken-Drum is particularly favoured by students who perceive themselves as SPUs, as one student said:

> I usually come out of the library around eleven [at night]. Tired and hungry, with no girlfriend but only a creaking bicycle, what can cheer you up better than an oily chicken drum?
>
> (Tian, junior undergraduate)

Students portray a typical SPU as poor, with an unhealthy diet and unattractive to girls. This description is self-mocking more than it is faithful. In my observations, most KK girls would gladly go for an SPU life, even if they come from rich families. For instance, at a New Year party, a group of PhD students staged a fascinating show. On the stage, an SPU was asking a girl to be his girlfriend. 'Would you . . .', he stammered, 'go for a Chicken-Drum with me?' 'How lovely!', the girl exclaimed. She gave him a hug, and the two went off the stage to the wild applause of the audience. More hilariously, shortly after the show, a group of first-year female PhD students sent a micro-blog message that was projected on to the party screen: 'We wait to be taken to the Chicken-Drum!'.

SPU, in fact, stands for a set of values that most KK students take pride (rather than shame) in sharing – poor but honest, hard-working from ordinary families, unaffected – and they use those values, represented by a love for Chicken-Drum, to seek lifetime partners. In intranet articles, students articulate their Chicken-Drum experiences. One article writes that 'What you really get from Chicken-Drum is a feeling. Here you don't have to live up to table manners'. Another article describes the stall as 'the manifesto of the road-side gang'. Thus, the Chicken-Drum, like KK Memories, embodies students' collective identities and values. Students told me that in Chinese university online bulletin board systems, the stall became synonymous with KK University. It is not surprising, then, that to be a (poor, honest, hard-working and unaffected) KK student *is* to be a Chicken-Drum consumer. One student put it this way:

> The first time I went to the Chicken-Drum, I felt fulfilled ... [I asked: *Fulfilled?*] Yes, it is like you have done one of those things that you must do as a KK student. You must have a pet, contribute to a hotly discussed article on the intranet, and of course, eat at the Chicken-Drum.
>
> (Wu, freshman)

Not surprisingly, too, groups of Chicken-Drum goers use the stall for social initiations. One student society holds a tradition in which senior members treat new recruits with meals, and 'the first meal has to be at the Chicken-Drum' (intranet article). Eating at the Chicken-Drum not only binds the society together, it also passes on seniors' values to younger generations of students who might, in their turn, do the same. Similarly, Cui recalled her first experience at the stall:

> I knew this girl for quite a long time and I thought we were friends. But one evening, several months after we first met, she led me to the Chicken-Drum. Her friends were there. I suddenly realized that it was then she received me finally as a friend.
>
> (Cui, KK graduate)

Through Chicken-Drum, students are able to reach out to other com-munities and generations of KK students, because the stall captures meaningful experiences that are unique to KK students, and because it embodies and indeed glorifies students' values that, elsewhere, seem ill at ease with a material-istic society. The stall is essential in the construction of 'we' as particular groups of KK students: students who mock themselves as short, poor and ugly, but also take secret pride in being so. Perhaps it is for this reason that the genealogy of the stall matters. KK Memories had a pure bloodline, so to speak, as it was sponsored and managed by KK graduates. In the following excerpt from an intranet article, students create a pure bloodline, too, for Chicken-Drum. In this narrative, details such as 'bus 89' and 'the bridge', which are familiar geographic features of Z campus, give the stall a sense of permanency:

> That was in 2003. When Li hurried from J campus to Z campus, by bus 89, to meet his girl, he got a rejection, and the sad boy wanted to throw himself off the bridge. Just then, a meteor flew across the sky ... in the form of a big chicken drum. Li was inspired, so he settled down and opened the first stall. Ten years later, Student Li became Cooker Li, but people can always taste the kind of sweet sorrow in his chicken drums.

Reflections on Space at KK University

Like all organizations, KK University planned its space to bear certain 'power effects' that may not seem obvious at the first glance (Dale and Burrell 2008). The design of Z campus was underpinned by at least three spatial discourses that were 'apparently, and only apparently, extra-ideological' (Lefebvre 1991: 6). The first discourse was scientific rationality. Gridded, linear and standardized, campus architectures were saturated with a 'Taylorized beauty' (Guillén 1999), and nature (for example, the 'lake of truth') became presentable only when it was processed through rational landscaping. The second discourse was consumptionism (Jameson 1992). With the installation of tariff boxes at the main gate and the spreading of vehicle roads – whose width was in sharp contrast to narrow pedestrian pavements – into every corner of the campus, the university space offered itself for the prioritized use of students (and faculty) groups with consumption power, namely those that owned motorbikes or cars. The third discourse was fast and aggressive change. The construction of Z campus within a little more than a year, the way that it is constantly remoulded to meet arising needs, and the destruction of older campuses were testimonies to high modernity: all that is solid melts into the air (Berman 2010).

Undoubtedly, these spatial discourses were reflective of the larger social milieu in which the university found itself: a stage in China's modernization that emphasizes, among other things, bureaucratization, domestic demand and accelerated urban development (Zhu 2006). KK University's campus, like so many corporate buildings around the world, is socially produced. And if we move from this macro-level analysis to a micro, everyday perspective, we could see that the university's space was also reproduced in three processes that I call 'reinterpreting space', 'reclaiming space' and 'redefining space'. These processes, as we shall see below, articulate the interrelations between the conceived, perceived and lived moments of Lefebvre's spatial triad.

Reinterpreting Space

The rational, consumptionist and mobile campus was potentially alienating. In many respects, it resembled what Augé (1995) calls a 'non-place': spaces that are devoid of personal relations, histories or identities. Thus, students got 'lost' in the maze of architectural complexes. Such non-places are common-place in today's corporate world as offices are designed to embody principles of efficiency (Martin 2003). They pose a threat to basic human existence because, and sociologists have long pondered on this, a primary imperative for space dwellers is to carve out local places in space (Tuan 1977). Space, seen by its dwellers as abstract, dangerous and potentially alienating, becomes inhabitable only when it is anchored by local places that afford safety, personal meanings, feelings of belonging, and above all, a sense of normality: to have a place is to be in place (Casey 1993).

Research on organizational space reveals that organizational members resort to certain tactics to construct places in everyday lives. They construct place by using personal items to indicate territories (Brown *et al.* 2005), and attach personally meaningful stories to space (Ford and Harding 2004; Halford and Leonard 2006). The everyday campus lives at KK University echo these findings. Sometimes, students' daily navigations of campus consisted of a series of moves whose meaningfulness hinged precariously on the existence of personal items. These items (bicycles, books, and so on) constituted, literally speaking, students' places on campus. And students also invested their spatial environs with vivid and interesting narratives. These narratives sprang from aspects of daily lives (to love, to eat, to treat friends) with which students were intimately associated, and, as such, they transformed what were otherwise meaning-less non-places into familiar, inhabitable places. Narrating campus space in personally meaningful ways, students made the campus their home (Bell 1997).

More importantly, through these narratives, students also reinterpreted designed-in spatial discourses. The spatial home that students built for them-selves was far from rational, consumptionist or transient; rather, it was animated with an affection for the irrational (underground creatures in bathrooms), a disavowal of high consuming power (the 'street of degeneration') and a sense of genealogy (the 'BG tree'). At times, reinterpretations became so dramatic that they rendered official spatial discourses ridiculous (the administrative building, a symbol of bureaucratic hierarchy, was compared to the Eye of Sauron). These interpretations were revealing of students' self-identifies, for to feel psychological ownership of a place is to project our very selves on to that place (Pierce *et al.* 2001).

The spatial narratives that students circulated were driven by the all-too-human desire to carve out inhabitable places; nevertheless, they carry important social implications. Insofar as they are animated with the 'poetics' of personal imaginations and fantasies (Bachelard 1957), they come to embody experiences that are potentially in conflict with dominant spatial discourses. Though perhaps inadvertently, students' place-building managed to suspend some otherwise taken-for-granted social relations such as rationality, consumptionism and aggressive change. In this sense, the process of reinterpreting space articulates a way in which Lefebvre's conceived and lived spaces are contentiously engaged.

Reclaiming Space

The meaningful places that students had carved out on campus were prerequisites for their navigations of everyday campus lives, not only because place rendered space inhabitable, but also in the sense that place gave (otherwise unintelligible) space phenomenological orders (Merrifield 1993; Tuan 1977). This becomes obvious when we look closer at students' moving bodies – indeed, place is necessarily embodied (Merleau-Ponty 1964). When Han chose to 'save' her calls of nature for a remoter but more endearing office bathroom, a whole new structure of spatiality was unfolded before her in which proximity, direction and distance were reorganized to formulate her spatial lifeworld. Similarly, when students occupied public lecture rooms as their study but also eating and sleeping areas, they had disrupted the kind of spatial demarcations between functional areas as laid out by the campus map. The kind of orders designed into the university's space remained unrealized until they were confirmed, suspended or reformulated by students' embodied places. In this sense, everyday uses of space are also generative of new space (Beyes and Steyaert 2012), and the body that is acted upon by space is, at the same time, acting space (Prichard 2000).

An important moment in the university's everyday lives came when students, due to their more or less similar penchant for the irrational, the cheap and the permanent, colluded with one another to construct a number of collective places: the cafe and the night stall. What were hitherto scattered individual places took on settled spatial forms with definitive locations and boundaries. The construction of community areas centred on a dialectical logic. On the one hand, places such as the night stall came to embody students' values. An object that avails itself for use also realizes and defines itself through use; it becomes an expression of users' identities and espoused values (Sartre 2003). Thus, while KK Memories might have started as a convenient spot for cheap drinks, it was made increasingly sacred, through students' patronage, as a symbol of KK student-ness. Looming large in the cafe was the student spirit that valued humanistic traditions over worldly wealth (the cafe reminded Cui of her days in 'run-down' lecture halls). On the other hand, community areas also socially defined KK students' identities and values. When students chose to frequent certain places rather than others, they were not simply maximizing utility, for the choice proclaimed them *as someone* in the eyes of their companions and friends (Goffman 1990). It was a 'manifesto' of personal values and an initiation ritual that differentiated 'us' from 'them'. For younger generations of KK students, to internalize seniors' values was to internalize seniors' space (Berger and Luckmann 1966), and eating at the night stall became necessary in fulfilling students' collective identity.

The result of this mutual construction of student communities and their space was the materialization of alternative ideologies in space. While the campus was designed to highlight rationality, consumerism and ephemeral changes, students had reclaimed, or re-appropriated (Wapshott and Marlett 2012) at least a part of the campus to discourse of the unhealthy, the cheap, and the memorial. Often, students' community areas remained hidden; they were either small in scale or beyond the university's physical boundary. Nevertheless, with the construction of such space, potential conflicts between ideologies became conditioned in the potential conflicts between ideology-laden spaces. For Lefebvre (1991: 33), the practiced space 'implies a guaranteed level of [social] competence'. The process of reclaiming space therefore illustrates a way in which the lived space transformed itself into the practiced space in everyday lives.

Redefining Space

The space of community areas was double-edged. While it materialized ideologies that bound student communities together, it also exposed these ideologies to frontal clashes with dominant ones when community areas were reshaped and reused by the university and local authorities. This is what happened at KK University. Students were suddenly brought to the awareness that their values were threatened as the cafe and the night stall were demolished or relocated ('an avalanche' of protests on the campus intranet).

A breakthrough point in everyday politics comes with the destruction of space. Submerged within the normal course of everyday lives, people are likely to take their routines for granted, and it is only when a different perspective presents itself that everyday normality is cast in a problematic light (Schutz 1976). Space, with all its matter-of-fact functionalities, blinds us to the fact that it is socially significant; that is, up to the moments of its radical changes or destructions. In organizations, it dawned on employees that their habitual ways of occupying office desks carried the power of a workplace community when the management tried to introduce hot-desking arrangements (Halford 2004). The destruction of space reveals spatialized power.

Thus, the removal of students' communal areas can be understood as Lyotardian 'events' (Lyotard 1993): something had happened on campus, and since this happening could not be ignored or willed away, it called upon students to re-examine and re-explain their everyday campus lives. Students were made to realize that certain social groups (for instance, the university authorities) outside themselves have a claim on campus space that students have, up to this point, largely overlooked ('How can the university be so practical?'). This realization pushes students, in turn, to ponder on what they have always assumed about campus space ('Doesn't the university want more history?'). According to Arendt (1998), these reflections and ponderings signified a truly political turn in students' everyday lives. Students had come out of their individual concerns for biological needs to agree or disagree on issues that concerned them as a social collectivity.

For Lefebvre, a political citizen is reflexive of their rights to urban space and their responsibilities for upholding such rights. In this sense, the destruction of community areas had pushed students to become political students. Many students were shocked and bruised by the ways that their right of participating in decision-making about space was not even considered by the university authorities ('They just do it!'). Some, such as Tu, made admirable efforts to voice their concerns on whatever channels they found appropriate. Although full-fledged confrontations with the university authorities were not observed at KK University, Lyotard (1993) tells us that 'voicing' is a potent strategy for marginalized collectivities such as student bodies to come back at dominant social groups with political claims.

Through the destruction of community areas, students redefined campus space not as a container of their routine activities, or a resource for fulfilling biological needs, but a contentious arena where their espoused values and cherished identities were enmeshed in power conflicts with those of other social groups. Insofar as space is practiced by all social groups in everyday negotiations of power (Taylor and Spicer 2007), the process of redefining space illustrates a way in which the practiced space comes back to challenge the conceived space in everyday lives.

Conclusion

This chapter looks at the ways that social space is produced in a Chinese university. It shows that the new campus of the university is designed to reflect power relations embedded in China's social and cultural contexts, notably those of rationality, consumptionism and fast change. Importantly, we also see that power relations are spatially constructed in everyday lives as students reinterpret campus space through imaginative narratives, reclaim campus space to embody collective identities and values, and redefine campus space as a contentious social arena. I have argued that these processes illustrate how the conceived, lived and practiced moments of social space are interrelated in a chain of ongoing dynamics through which students' power conflicts with the university are first rendered possible, then given material basis, and finally released into more open forms of confrontation. In other words, the processes of reinterpreting, reclaiming and redefining space articulate the production of social space in the university's everyday lives.

This chapter makes three general contributions. The first is made to studies on university space. Recently, the physical aspect of universities has received increasing attention (Temple and Barnett 2007). Echoing some researchers' concerns (Beyes and Michels 2011), this chapter highlights that campus space is intrinsically social at the same time that it is functional. Functional thinking of space is in itself a veiled form of ideology. This insight, brought forward by Lefebvre and put into fruitful analyses of organizational space, applies also to university space precisely because alternative power relations emerges in everyday lives in the kind of space that is marginalized by the functional view of space: the uncanny, cheap and (annoyingly) persistent space. What this chapter tries to highlight is not that these apparently 'ugly' spaces need to be sanctified – university space serves its functions for the well-being of the majority and there is nothing despicable about this utilitarian doctrine – rather, it is a call for the functional space to be self-reflective.

Next, the chapter contributes to existing studies on organizational space. Researchers have pointed out that social space in organizations is produced by macro-level sociocultural forces (Dale and Burrell 2008) and everyday experiences and uses of space (Beyes and Steyaert 2012). In both respects, this chapter provides further evidence. Currently, we know little of the specific processes of everyday spatial production that, according to Lefebvre, reside in the interrelations between the conceived, lived and practiced moments of social space. The processes that this chapter outlines help to fill this gap. Of course, limited by the idiosyncratic setting of this study, I suspect whether alternative processes can be found in other national cultures and in different types of organizations. However, in the sense that these processes reveal the inter-relations among the spatial moments of Lefebvre's triad, I think it is likely that they will also surface in other contexts. This chapter also presents some interesting themes that, although insufficiently engaged here, point out the ways for future studies on organizational social space. For instance, is the uncanny space that students constructed at KK University reflective of an aspect of modern organizations that is dark and unnamable (Gabriel 2012)? And if the body that eats, naps and pees seems to occupy such a central stage at KK University, perhaps more effort is needed to unfold the embodied production of social space in organizations?

Lastly, I hope that this chapter contributes to a future reception of Lefebvre's thinking in organizational spatial studies. Lefebvre has inspired admirable efforts in bringing space into organization study (Dale 2005; Hernes 2004;

Taylor and Spicer 2007). This study focuses only on a point that I feel is overlooked by existing research, namely the interrelations between the moments of Lefebvre's spatial triad. There are other ways that this great thinker might benefit our understandings of organizations; for instance, his emphasis on everyday rhythms (Lefebvre 2004), the body (Lefebvre 1991) and everyday lives (Lefebvre 2008), which point towards a holistic acceptance of space as social. Currently, these rhythmic, embodied and everyday aspects of social space wait to be fully expounded. I hope that this study evokes interest in using Lefebvre's work for examinations of the spatiality of human lifeworlds.

Acknowledgement

The study reported in this chapter is supported by the Department of Education of Zhejiang Province (grant number Y201016415) and the Fundamental Research Funds for the Central Universities (grant number 502000*172220135).

References

Anderson, G. (2006) 'Carving out time and space in the managerial university', *Journal of Organizational Change Management*, 19(5), 578–92.

Arendt, H. (1998) *The Human Condition*, Chicago, IL: University of Chicago Press.

Augé, M. (1995) *Non Places: An Introduction to Supermodernity*, London: Verso.

Bachelard, G. (1957) *The Poetics of Space*, Boston, MA: Beacon.

Baldry, C. (1999) 'Space: the final frontier', *Sociology*, 33(3), 535–53.

Bell, M. (1997) 'The ghosts of place', *Theory and Society*, 26, 813–36.

Berger, P. and Luckmann, T. (1966) *The Social Construction of Reality*, Harmondsworth: Penguin.

Berman, M. (2010) *All That is Solid Melts into Air: The Experience of Modernity*, London: Verso.

Beyes, T. and Michels, C. (2011) 'The production of educational space: heterotopia and the business university', *Management Learning*, 42(5), 521–36.

Beyes, T. and Steyaert, C. (2012) 'Spacing organization: non-representational theory and performing organizational', *Organization*, 19(1), 45–61.

Beyrouthy, C., Burke, E., Landa-Silva, D., McCollum, B., McMullan, P. and Parkes, A. (2009) 'Towards improving the utilization of university teaching space', *Journal of the Operational Research Society*, 60(1), 130–43.

Brown, A., Kornberger, M., Clegg, S. and Carter, C. (2010) '"Invisible walls" and "silent hierarchies": a case study of power relations in an architecture firm', *Human Relations*, 63(4), 525–49.

Brown, G., Lawrence, T. and Robinson, S. (2005) 'Territoriality in organizations', *Academy of Management Review*, 30(3), 577–94.

Carter, P. and Jackson, N. (2000) 'An-aesthetics', in S. Linstead and H. Höpfl (eds), *The Aesthetics of Organization*, London: Sage, pp. 180–96.

Casey, E. (1993) *Getting Back into Place: Toward a Renewed Understanding of the Place-World*, Bloomington, IN: Indiana University Press.

Dale, K. (2005) 'Building a social materiality: spatial and embodied politics in organizational control', *Organization*, 12(5), 649–78.

Dale, K. and Burrell, G. (2008) *The Spaces of Organisation and the Organisation of Space: Power, Identity and Materiality at Work*, Basingstoke: Palgrave Macmillan.

Edenius, M. and Yakhlef, A. (2007) 'Space, vision and organizational learning: the interplay of incorporating and inscribing practices', *Management Learning*, 38(2), 193–210.

Ford, J. and Harding, N. (2004) 'We went looking for an organization but could find only the metaphysics of its presence', *Sociology*, 38(4), 815–30.

Gabriel, Y. (2012) 'Organizations in a state of darkness: towards a theory of organizational miasma', *Organization Studies*, 33(9), 1137–52.

Ghasson, S. (2004) 'An assessment of the effectiveness of e-learning on university space planning and design', *Facilities*, 22(3/4), 79–86.

Gieryn, T. (2002) 'What buildings do?', *Theory and Society*, 31, 35–74.

Goffman, E. (1990) *The Presentation of Self in Everyday Life*, London: Penguin.

Guillén, M. (1999) 'Scientific management's lost aesthetic: architecture, organization, and the Taylorized beauty of the mechanical', *Administrative Science Quarterly*, 42, 682–715.

Halford, S. (2004) 'Towards a sociology of organizational space', *Sociological Research Online*, 9(1), available at: www.socresonline.org.uk/9/1/halford.html.

Halford, S. and Leonard, P. (2006) 'Place, space and time: contextualizing workplace subjectivities', *Organization Studies*, 27(5), 657–76.

Hancock, P. (2006) 'The spatial and temporal mediations of social change', *Organizational Change Management*, 19(5), 619–39.

Hernes, T. (2004) *The Spatial Construction of Organization*, Amsterdam: John Benjamins.

Hurdley, R. (2010) 'The power of corridors: connecting doors, mobilising materials, plotting openness', *The Sociological Review*, 58(1), 45–64.

Jameson, F. (1992) *Postmodernism, or Cultural Logic of Late Capitalism*, London: Verso.

Kornberger, M. and Clegg, S. (2004) 'Bringing space back in: organizing the generative building', *Organization Studies*, 25(7), 1095–114.

Lau, S. and Feng, Y. (2009) 'Introducing healing gardens into a compact university campus: design natural space to create healthy and sustainable campuses', *Landscape Research*, 34(1), 55–81.

Lefebvre, H. (1991) *The Production of Space*, Oxford: Blackwell.

Lefebvre, H. (2004) *Rhythmanalysis*, London: Continuum.

Lefebvre, H. (2008) *Critique of Everyday Life, Vol. I*, London: Verso.

Lyotard, J.-F. (1993) *Libidinal Economy*, London: Athlone.

Martin, R. (2003) *The Organizational Complex: Architecture, Media and Corporate Space*, Cambridge, MA: MIT Press.

McLaughlin, P. and Faulkner, J. (2012) 'Flexible spaces: what students expect from university facilities', *Journal of Facility Management*, 10(2), 140–9.

Merleau-Ponty, M. (1964) *Phenomenology of Perception*, London: Routledge.

Merrifield, A. (1993) 'Place and space: a Lefebvrian reconciliation', *Transactions of the Institute of British Geographers*, 18(4), 516–31.

Muetzelfeldt, M. (2006) 'Organizational space, place and civility', in S. Clegg and M. Kornberger (eds), *Space, Organization and Management Theory*, Koege: Liber, pp. 113–28.

Peltonen, T. (2011) 'Multiple architectures and the production of organizational space in a Finnish university', *Journal of Organizational Change Management*, 24(6), 806–21.

Pierce, J., Kostova, T. and Dirks, K. (2001) 'Toward a theory of psychological ownership in organizations', *Academy of Management Review*, 26(2), 298–310.

Prichard, C. (2000) 'The body topographies of education management', in J. Hassard, R. Holiday and H. Willmott (eds), *Body and Organization*, London: Sage, pp. 147–65.

Rosen, M., Orlikowski, W. and Schmahmann, K. (1990) 'Building buildings and living lives: a critique of bureaucracy, ideology and concrete artifacts', in P. Gagliardi (ed.), *Symbols and Artifacts: Views of the Corporate Landscape*, Berlin: de Gruyter, pp. 69–84.

Sartre, J.-P. (2003) *Being and Nothingness*, London: Routledge.

Schutz, A. (1976) *The Phenomenology of the Social World*, London: Heinemann.

Soja, E. (1996) *Thirdspace*, Oxford: Blackwell.

Taylor, S. and Spicer, A. (2007) 'Time for space: an interpretive review of research on organizational spaces', *International Journal of Management Reviews*, 9(4), 325–46.

Temple, P. and Barnett, R. (2007) 'Higher education space: future directions', *Planning for Higher Education*, 36(1), 5–15.

Tikhomirov, V., Tikhomirov, N., Maksimova, V. and Telnov, Y. (2009) 'The integrated knowledge space: the foundation for enhancing the effectiveness of the university', *Informatica Economica*, 13(4), 5–10.

Toker, U. and Gray, D. (2008) 'Innovation spaces: workspace planning and innovation in U.S. university research center', *Research Policy*, 37(2), 309–29.

Tuan, Y.-F. (1977) *Space and Place: The Perspective of Experience*, London: Edward Arnold.

Tyler, M. and Cohen, L. (2010) 'Spaces that matter: gender performativity and organizational space', *Organization Studies*, 31(2), 175–98.

Wapshott, R. and Mallett, O. (2012) 'The spatial implications of homeworking: a Lefebvrian approach to the rewards and challenges of home-based work', *Organization*, 19(1), 63–79.

Wasserman, V. and Frenkel, M. (2011) 'Organizational aesthetics: caught between identity regulation and culture jamming', *Organization Science*, 22(2), 503–21.

Witkin, R. (1990) 'The aesthetic imperative of a rational-technical machinery: a study in organizational control through the design of artifacts', in P. Gagliardi (ed.), *Symbols and Artifacts: Views of the Corporate Landscape*, Berlin: de Gruyter, pp. 325–38

Zhu, W. (2006) 'Domestic demand orientation: the new imperative of China's economic development', *Journal of the Party School of CPC Central Committee*, 10(1), 60–5.

Zhu, Y. and Wei, G. (2007) 'The plan of Zijingang campus' east and west areas in Zhejiang University', *Architecture and Culture*, 39, 56–9.

11

The University and the City

Social Science Centre, Lincoln – Forming the Urban Revolution

MIKE NEARY

> The Urban Revolution is a paen to the space of the city and to the
> possibilities of revolutionary social change that comes from the street.
>
> (N. Smith – Preface to Lefebvre 2003: xiv)

Protest

The continuing assault on universities by governments of capitalist nation
states around the world has led to the emergence of radical alternative models
of higher education created by academic and student activists (Bailey and
Freedman 2011). The main thrust of these alternatives are against increasing
political and economic state violence, the former characterised by the
militarisation of policing (Graham 2011), exemplified by aggressive control of
student marches and punitive prosecutions against students. At the same time,
the marketisation of higher education, exemplified by the intensification of
academic labour and the poverty of student life, continues (De Angelis and
Harvie 2006; Neary and Hagyard 2010). These radical academic and student
alternatives are not a new phenomena, but are the latest manifestation of
subversive academic activist and student action for whom the student-worker
protests of 1968 were a defining moment (Solomon and Palmieri 2011). What
differentiates the current wave of protests from 1968 includes the fact that,
unlike in 1968, the most advanced capitalist societies are currently struggling
to avoid complete economic meltdown, the resurgence of interest in Marxist
social theory (Dean 2012), and the confidence gained from popular uprisings
against despotic governments around the world. All of this has allowed groups
of writers such as the 'Invisible Committee' (2009) to argue, 'Everyone agrees.
It's about to explode', if it has not already.

A key feature of these new radical alternatives for higher education, although
not much discussed in the academic literature, is their strong spatial sensibility.
This is evident from their recognition of the importance of place, the way in

which they problematise the relationship between the local and the global, as well as the physical organisation of teaching and learning within the projects themselves (Toscano 2011). This significance of spatiality is reflected in the fact that one of the defining concepts of the protest movement is itself a concept of space: 'Occupy' – which has become the slogan for a new pedagogy of space and time (Neary and Amsler 2012).

This chapter looks at one such alternative, the Social Science Centre (SSC), Lincoln, a no-fee worker–student cooperative for higher education, based in a city in England, UK. This chapter conjures up the Centre through the practical application of one of the revolutionary theories of urban space that informs its activities, exploring, in particular, the relationship between the university and the city. The theory is based on the work of Henri Lefebvre and his notion of 'the right to the city', reinterpreted by myself as a member of the SSC, Lincoln, as the 'right to the university'. Following Lefebvre, the argument in the chapter is that the SSC might be seen to constitute a new form of 'urban revolution'.

The University and the City

The relationship between the city and the university has become an increasingly important area of academic enquiry (Goddard and Vallance 2013). A key text is Bender's (1991) *The University and the City: From Medieval Origins to the Present*. The book includes a selection of contributions that look at the historical development of universities in specific geographical contexts (e.g. Paris in the twelfth century, Florence in the fourteenth century, and Berlin, London and New York in the nineteenth century). Bender concludes that while the city and the university appear homologous, their relationship is by no means assured. Despite their apparent 'formal sociological similarities, cities and universities are very different constructs' (Bender 1991: 290); the university is cloistered while the city is un-cloistered, neither are unified wholes, but each with a distinct specificity that goes unrecognised by urban sociology. Bender argues that achieving a fuller understanding of the relation between the city and the university requires 'a more precise analysis of the city as a place within a larger geographical system and of the internal relations of the elements of the city itself' (Bender 1991: 291). But, ultimately, he suggests there is a fundamental disconnection: 'The university has always claimed the world, not its host city, as its domain' and that the university has sought to transcend its roots by striving 'for learning that reaches towards universal significance' (Bender 1991: 294). He argues that the university can go some way to reconciling these dichotomies by attempting to connect the enlargement of public spaces and inclusive cultures with the development of the general social intellect (Bender 1991: 295).

In a more recent series of writings, Goddard (2012) and Goddard and Vallance (2013) have attempted to deal with the problematic identified by Bender. They recognise that universities are 'quintessentially urban institutions', and that there is a tension between their global competitiveness and their local mission. Goddard (2011, 2012) and Goddard and Vallance (2013) have attempted to reconcile the university and the city through the reinvention of the university as a 'civic' institution, suggesting contemporary universities need to recover the idealism that inspired the creators of the institutions for higher education that emerged in the great English industrial cities in the nineteenth century as symbols of civic pride. Goddard and Vallance (2013) argue that contemporary universities need to repackage their mission for the twenty-first century based on the notion of civility: as 'civic universities'. A key issue for the notion of civility is to refocus the mission of the university away from the economy and the market, about which much has been done and written, but rather to break down the barriers between the university and the city. Universities should do this by developing the local physical, social and economic infrastructure through forging creative and sustainable partnerships with the local population and institutions based on social innovation and social sustainability. These activities should be grounded in supporting the arts and culture, as well as encouraging democratic participation for the public good and in the public interest. This work can be expanded to the global scale, utilising the local context within which the university is operating to provide a sense of identity and branding. And so, they argue, the university comes to play a key role in the 'leadership of place' (Goddard 2011).

These authors provide rich empirical accounts of the historical and contemporary university, but their desire for spatial coherence between the university and the city fails to provide a framework from which to consider the current crisis of higher education (Collini 2012; Holmwood 2011; Readings 1997). Goddard and Vallance's attempt to refocus away from economics and the market towards the principles of social justice and civility fails to appreciate the extent to which the increasing marketisation of higher education undermines the principles that they espouse, nor the extent to which the ongoing economic crisis has led the capitalist state to abandon social democracy in favour of increasing authoritarian and punitive measures, in which conditions for social cohesion and civility are attacked. Universities are becoming a key weapon for governments across Europe to impose 'austerity for ever' (Neary 2012) by inculcating students with the idea of the omniscient power of the market through the notion of student as consumer and the pedagogy of debt (Neary 2013).

The current revolutionary situation demands a more revolutionary theory and practice to underpin Goddard and Vallance's notion of the 'reinvention' of higher education.

Lefebvre – The University as a Form of Urban Revolution

This more revolutionary theory can be found in the work of Henri Lefebvre and, in particular, his notion of urban revolution.

Lefebvre was a French heterodox Marxist philosopher and sociologist (1901–91): 'the most self-effacing and least narrow minded Marxist who ever lived' (Merrifield 2006: xxiv), providing 'a provocation to conventional Marxist thinking' (Harvey 2012: xiii). Lefebvre's Marxism promoted the power of human agency: class struggle, against the authoritarian models of state capitalism where workers are subordinate to political leaders and academic Marxist intellectuals. Following Marx, Lefebvre's methodology is historical, materialist and dialectical. *Historical*, in the sense that capitalism is not the 'end of history', but only appears as the perpetual present for whom the future is always chaos and catastrophe; *material*, an awareness that capitalism is based on social relations of production in which use-values (positive values based on enhancing the quality of life) are subordinated to exchange-values (negative values based on the quantitative expansion of capital through human misery); and *dialectical*, the understanding that social institutions are constructed out of the conflicts and contradictions that underpin the social relations of capitalist production. A key issue for Lefebvre was how capitalist spaces are produced, about which he published a seminal text, *The Production of Space* (Lefebvre 1991; original French edition 1974). In this book, and throughout his writing, he goes beyond an economistic reading of Marx to recognise that 'space as a social fact, as a social factor and as an instance of society, is always political and strategic' (Ross 2008: 9); and, as we shall see from a close reading of his early work, the production of space is intrinsically about the production of knowledge.

Lefebvre was in favour of 'an ambitious revolutionary project' as the best chance for human development (Kelly 1991: 62–3). He saw the urban environment as a form of social space where the destructive and non-sustainable capitalist processes of production must be replaced by a new urban revolution based on human imperatives. In his writings, he saw city life as a 'bureaucratic society of controlled consumption' (Lefebvre 2003: 4), and a form of living death: 'cultural cemeteries under the guise of the human: museums, universities, various publications, not to mention new towns and planning procedures' (Lefebvre 1996: 149). Lefebvre wanted to recover the urban as a site built around a new form of human habitation, not 'habitat' (Lefebvre 2003: 81) or 'inhabiting' (Lefebvre 2003: 98), which are limited to functional and instrumental basic needs (Lefebvre 2003: 156), but 'habiting' as a form of subversive life linked to 'the possible and the imaginary' (Lefebvre 2003: 82), or a sort of 'lived utopianism' (Merrifield 2006: 37).

The problem for Lefebvre is that urban society is based on the logic of capitalist production in which all space is rendered homogeneous through the rationality of exchange-value. Lefebvre argues for socialist/differential space based on use-values that support the positive qualities of human life instead of the negative quantitative sameness of capitalist space (Lefebvre 2003: 98–9). This is not an idealist ambition, but is the expansion and intensification of what already exists within cities, as gardens and parks and the life-enhancing activities that emerge from the street:

> as a place to play and learn ... and as a meeting place ... a form of spontaneous theatre ... the street is disorder. All the elements of urban life, which are fixed and redundant elsewhere, are free to fill the streets ... where they meet and interact ... This disorder is alive. It informs. It surprises.
>
> (Lefebvre 2003: 18–19)

For Lefebvre, street life is disruptive, creating the possibility for counter-projects (Lefebvre 1991: 383). This is a very different vision of urban life from that espoused by other heroes of civic renewal; for example, Jane Jacobs, for whom the rejuvenation of the city was to be based on the renewal of already existing social arrangements, such as alienated communities, destroyed by voracious property developers (Jacobs 1961). To be clear, Lefebvre is arguing for nothing less than a new form of human sociability, or 'urban communism' (Lefebvre 2003: 105), a new form of human living based on Marx's definition of communism 'from each according to their ability, to each according to their need' (Marx 1875).

For Lefebvre, the urban revolution is about the politics of space, which, despite its meta-philosophical connotations, is brought down to earth by his notion of 'the right to the city'. This right to the city is not a legal right, making a claim to the city as a form of private property (Lefebvre 1996: 174); rather, 'the right to the city is like a cry and a demand' (Lefebvre 1996: 158). In practical terms, this means that those who live in the city should not be excluded from formal political processes and should have a role in decision-making where the search for solutions to urban life is predominant (Lefebvre 2003: 5).

New Science

For Lefebvre, the urban revolution is a political strategy but it is also a knowledge strategy, without any gap between them. Here, the 'right to the city' presents itself as a relation between science and political power, as a dialogue that actualises the relations between theory and practice (Lefebvre 1996: 156). At the centre of urban revolution and 'the right to the city' lies the idea for a new kind of knowledge institution based on a new science of urban society: 'a critique of everyday life' (Lefebvre 1996: 139).

This new form of knowledge institution (subversive knowledge) is very different from the already existing mainstream institutions of higher education. Lefebvre argues that the current model of university is characterised by a separation into faculties and disciplines, whereas his new knowledge institution should be based on 'the unity of the sciences'. Lefebvre is fundamentally opposed to the notion of interdisciplinarity, arguing that any results from science based on 'interdisciplinarity . . . remains inconclusive' (Lefebvre 2003: 54). The problem with interdisciplinarity for him is that academics and scientists synthesise arguments from the point of view of their own field (Lefebvre 2003: 54). In that way, interdisciplinarity is intrinsically dogmatic (Lefebvre 2003: 54) and authoritarian (Lefebvre 2003: 57), with the result for science being 'mediocre compromise' (Lefebvre 2003: 54).

He argues that the science of urban revolution could result only from 'a convergence of all of the sciences' (Lefebvre 2003: 56), to move from fragmentary knowledge to complete understanding (Lefebvre 2003: 56). He recognises that the university can no longer make a claim for total understanding based on an appeal to philosophy or some other universal principle such as humanism (Lefebvre 2003: 61). He replaces these philosophical approaches with his own meta-philosophy derived from the defining principle of Marxist social theory: negative dialectics, or 'dialectical anthropology', or the concept of 'immanent critique' (Lefebvre 2003: 65). The main aspect of this methodology is that solutions are not pre-ordained, as is the case with political ideologies, nor are they based on acquired knowledge with a pre-fabricated final goal (Lefebvre 2003: 67); rather, solutions emerge from out of the urban problematic that is under review and the grounded social relations within which the problem is produced. The result is that from out of the conflict and contradictions that underpin these relationships, clear pathways are created to reveal a horizon (Lefebvre 2003: 66), with the possibility of new forms of urban practice: social institutions that are appropriate to the problem of urban society as a new form of urban strategy or urban science (Lefebvre 2003: 72–6).

Lefebvre has a methodology for this new utopian science, which he refers to as 'transduction':

> This is an intellectual operation which can be methodologically carried out and differs from classical induction, deduction, the construction of 'models', simulation as well as the simple statement of hypothesis. Trans-duction elaborates and constructs a theoretical object, a *possible* object from information related to reality and a problematic posed by this reality. Transduction assumes an incessant feedback between the conceptual framework used and empirical observations. Its theory (methodology) gives shape to certain spontaneous mental operations of the planner,

the architect, the sociologist and the philosopher. It introduces rigour in invention and knowledge in utopia.

(Lefebvre 1996: 151)

Transduction is then the substantive methodological programme of experimental research out of which emerges the 'imagination to be deployed' (Lefebvre 1996: 155) or 'the point at which the horizon opens up and calls for actualisation' (Lefebvre 1996: 165), not as fantasy, but as a sort of 'social science fiction' (Neary 2003).

Lefebvre does not provide us with any concrete examples of what the outcomes of transduction/differential society might look like, although he does suggest an organisational principle by which these new forms of social institutions might be achieved in practice, which he refers to as 'self-manage-ment'. He describes self-management not as a panacea or magical solution, but a form of 'social pedagogy' (Lefebvre 1968: 86), implying 'self-criticism and continuous active scrutiny of the relations between the functional and structural limits of a self-managing entity and society as a whole' (Lefebvre 1968: 87). He saw this social pedagogy as the antithesis of university management whose subordination to the logic of the market 'deprive them of critical activity, and drive pedagogy and knowledge into a state of immobility more pronounced than ever' (Lefebvre 1968: 87).

Lefebvre's work is fascinating and attracting increasing interest, but it is not to be followed uncritically. His appeal to the power of negative dialectics can be criticised for not being dialectical or negative enough. For example, the claims he makes on behalf of use-values against the destructive categories of exchange-values fails to appreciate the extent to which use-values are themselves the product of capitalist social relations; so, rather than favouring one set of values over another set of values, the social relations that produce capitalist values must be dissolved (Holloway 2002; Neary and Amsler 2012). Similarly, his positive affirmation of the working class as the radical subject of revolution leaves under-theorised the pernicious tendencies of capitalist work, and excludes the importance of other social protests against capitalism (Postone 1993). Notwithstanding these conceptual difficulties, the best way to critically engage with Lefebvre is by taking up his demand to create a new institutional form of subversive social knowledge. This is the task for the next section, when I discuss the Social Science Centre, Lincoln.

Social Science Centre, Lincoln: A Strategy of Politics and Knowledge

The SSC was not formed with reference to Lefebvre's theory of urban revolution, although, for my own part, the setting up and development of the

SSC was grounded in versions of Marxism with which Lefebvre has much affinity: 'Open Marxism' and the Situationist International (Charnock n.d.), along with a shared sense of Lefebvre's revolutionary ambition and as a self-conscious practical attempt to bring critical social theory to life. As I become more acquainted with Lefebvre's writing, it is apparent that his work can be used to enrich and substantiate the work that is going on in Lincoln: linking revolutionary social practice with revolutionary social theory. There is much connectivity between Lefebvre's urban revolution and the SSC around the relationship between a strategy of politics and knowledge, transduction and the power of imaginary, differential space and self-management, out of which can emerge a new institutional form of higher education based on a 'unity of the sciences'.

Politics and Knowledge

The SSC, Lincoln was established in 2010 as a direct response to the coalition government's decision to defund university teaching in the arts, humanities and social sciences, making up the shortfall through student fees of £6,000–9,000 backed by government loans and the concomitant student debt. Taught programmes in the arts, humanities and social sciences will now endure only to the extent that they are attractive to students who are forced to see themselves as consumers and proto-employees, encouraged 'to consider undergraduate study as a form of "human capital" investment, or the purchase of a financial asset, the returns on which are to be seen after graduation in the form of higher earnings' (McGettigan 2013: 13). This new funding regime, which includes a massive reduction in the university block grant from £5 billion to £2 billion by 2014/15, together with the intention to create a market-based system of higher education – opening the sector to private companies – threatens the quality of the education provision, as well as the academic integrity of what has been an internationally admired system (McGettigan 2013: 1–3).

Members of the Centre see this new funding regime and further market-isation of higher education not only as a barrier for those who are unwilling to take on the burden of debt, but a policy that will undermine academics for whom a critique of capitalist modernity is the substance of their academic discipline (Harney and Moten 2013). In response, members of the SSC have sought to establish the conditions for subversive knowledge by establishing an autonomous institutional form of higher learning that is not connected to any university. In this way, they hope to maintain the conditions for critical academic activity to flourish in an environment where the market-led model of social development is seen as the problem, not the solution.

The SSC responds to this pedagogy of debt by being entirely self-funded and operating on the basis of its members' contributions. All members of SSC are asked to pay a subscription, which is based on the level of their income (usually one hour's wage of a monthly net salary). There is no subscription fee for anyone who is unemployed or who has a low income. The SSC accepts monies and other forms of 'payment in kind' from donors who share the SSC's ethics and values. No one is paid for their work with the Centre. The Centre's members donate their time and expertise freely and do not receive any monetary payment; all monies received are reinvested into the Centre's work. Currently, the Centre has 70 members, although not all are active, with more than 100 names on the emailing list. The Centre is run by a core of 10 people, including a recent school leaver, a PhD student, a recently retired banker, a self-employed education consultant, academics, school and college teachers, as well as those who support teaching and learning in schools.

This no-fees arrangement is an economic response to government higher education policy, but the SSC expands the way in which it problematises higher education beyond economics to consider the issue in terms of the relationship between knowledge and power. The SSC offers opportunities to engage in a cooperative experience of higher education. Run as a not-for-profit cooperative, the SSC is organised on the basis of democratic, non-hierarchical principles, with all members having equal involvement in the life and work of the SSC. The cooperative principles that guide the organisation of the SSC also extend to the ways in which courses are designed and run. All classes are participative and collaborative in order to ground inquiry in the experiences and knowledges of the participants. Members have opportunities to design courses together, and those new to teaching and independent learning are offered generous support from others. All members are able to work with academics and other experienced researchers on research projects, and to publish their own writings and other work through the SSC. One key guiding principle of the Centre is that 'teachers' and 'students' have much to learn from each other. All of this offers a real concrete example of what Lefebvre would call 'self-management' in action. The SSC envisages that this model for self-management could be adapted by other academics, students and activists in the UK and transnationally to establish similar alternative models for higher education based on the organisational form established in Lincoln.

The SSC is not framed around specific disciplines, but studies themes that draw on the core subjects in social science: sociology, politics and philosophy, as well as psychology, economics, journalism and photography. Members of the group are interested in biological science, and increasingly debate issues around the relationship between the natural and social sciences, featuring the works of Darwin and Marx. In that sense, the SSC is a critique of interdisciplinarity and, by implication, in favour of unity of the sciences, around the controversial constructivist theme that all sciences are essentially social.

The Centre organises study and research at all levels including under-graduate, masters and doctoral. The SSC has no formal connection to any university or other provider of higher education. The SSC's awards are not university degrees and are not recognised by any official degree-awarding body in the UK. They are, though, 'validated' through academic review, using colleagues not involved in the core group, in the same ways as external examiners are used in the current mainstream system.

The SSC, as with Lefebvre, recognises the importance of the imaginary. Programmes at SSC include one with 'Imagination' in the title: 'Social Science Imagination' (SSI), after the work of C. Wright Mills. This is an open course run by and for people who want to develop a critical understanding of the social world, and the conditions and possibilities of their own lives, through social scientific inquiry. Scholars on the course have spent time exploring concepts of social analysis; writing on concerns about gender, economy, institutions, culture, knowledge, ethics and power; and reading and discussing one another's work. A wide range of questions emerged from this work; these were documented, compiled, collectively coded and used to form the basis for the coming year's programme of study.

This sense of imagination and the imaginary extends to the way in which the Centre is managed and run, with time set aside to consider the meaning and purpose of the Centre, using the critical concepts established in the SSI sessions, gender, ethics and power, to build our own sense of collective pro-social activity. These critical reflective sessions are vital, but tend to get subsumed within meetings to organise and manage the work of the Centre. Where we do work critically and reflectively, our practice follows a process that is similar to Lefebvre's transductive critical incessant feedback loop, based on the ideas and theories that inform our work and how we can best carry them out in practice. These critical sessions can lead us to challenge our own working practices, including, and in particular, how power is distributed across the collective and whose knowledge within the group is privileged. As members of the cooperative, students are not subordinate to their teachers, but have an equal say in how the Centre is managed. This is a model for student engagement that goes far beyond even the most student-centred universities, where power and decision-making is concentrated in the role of vice-chancellor and senior management teams. These critical, power-sharing sessions help us to plan future work, including finding ways to extend our activities across the city, organising more regular public talks, making links with similar projects in the UK and internationally, as well as deepening our understanding of the SSC's own place in the history of alternative radical forms of education and higher education.

Differential Space

The SSC is profoundly aware of the importance of space and spatiality. The reference to Lincoln is included in the Centre's title not as a form of global branding or to establish a 'leadership of place', but to recognise the importance of grounding our work in the heart of a capitalist city and the everyday lives of its population. Following Lefebvre's inspiration, the SSC does not have to invent new spaces, but rather seeks to expand and intensify the already existing life-enhancing activities within Lincoln. The Centre uses a variety of different sites across the city, including the Revival Centre, a community social enterprise run as a cooperative for general health and well-being; the Croft Street Community Centre, which provides facilities for social, educational and sporting activities for the benefit of local residents and the wider community; the Angel Coffee House, a local cafe that, in the best traditions of eighteenth-century coffee houses, supports discussion and debate; 'The Collection' archaeology museum and the Usher Gallery, both funded by the local council; and other organisations and individuals, including the Arts Council. The SSC makes extensive use of the Pathways Centre, a project for the homeless and vulnerably housed adults in the city, owned and managed by Framework Housing Association and run in partnership with the Nomad Trust, a charitable organisation providing welfare services in Lincoln. The SSC runs a course in social photography: 'Our Place, Our Priorities' in the Pathways Centre for users of this facility. This real presence in the city is supported by a website by which the Centre can present its work and engage more broadly with a wider constituency. The Centre recognises the importance of the virtual environment, but the SSC is not a form of online provision: an essential characteristic of its activities is that it is based on direct and personal engagement.

'The Right to the University': Doing Things Differently

Insofar as I am concerned, the SSC is not a community project or even a form of public engagement, but rather, after Lefebvre's notion of 'the right to the city', it is an attempt to transform the social relations of urban life away from the bureaucratic norms of 'controlled consumption' towards a reconnection of the relationship between power and knowledge based on the 'unity of the sciences'. This urban revolution is to be developed through new forms of social institution, such as the SSC, grounded in an organising principle that insists that human life and nature are the project and not the resource, and where those involved with the Centre and its city life take a central role in decision-making processes. The combination of power-knowledge-urban-science-democracy suggests a re-conceptualisation of the problematic identified at the beginning of this chapter: the relationship between the city and the university.

The SSC seeks to establish the importance of the production of critical, practical knowledge as a substantive basis for human emancipation. And, in this way, to breathe life into Lefebvre's notion of the imaginary by constructing a real project that demands not only 'the right to the city', but also 'the right to the university'.

This is an ambitious revolutionary project, but it has, at the same time, a more modest objective: to show that there are ways of constructing alternatives to the current system of higher education. Writing in *Times Higher Education*, Professor Alastair Bonnett, in an article about the current state of radical academic publishing and its relationship to radical academic practice, put it like this:

> I believe that, over the coming decades, the radical tradition will be reoriented and reimagined in institution-building of another kind. It is towards institutions that deliver housing, jobs, services or even higher education that the radical compass is pointing. The journals will carry on the good fight, questioning and provoking. But we will learn to expect less of them.
>
> So I'll conclude with a different type of dissident institution. Although it has the rather grand title of The Social Science Centre, Lincoln, it is tiny. This not-for-profit co-operative, founded only this year, is attempting to establish 'a new model for higher and co-operative education'. More specifically, the centre is 'designed for students who do not wish to take on the burden of debt currently imposed by the government, but do wish to receive a higher level of education'. Harvard it ain't. But no matter their scale, such ventures do something important. They show us how things can be done differently.
>
> (Bonnett 2011)

References

Bailey, M. and Freedman, D. (2011) *The Assault on Universities: A Manifesto for Resistance*, London: Pluto Press.

Bender, T. (1991) *The University and the City: From Medieval Origins to the Present*, Oxford: Oxford University Press.

Bonnett, A (2011) 'Are radical journals selling out?', *Times Higher Education*, 3 November, pp. 35–9.

Charnock, G. (n.d.) *Challenging New State Spaces: The Open Marxism of Henri Lefebvre*, available at: www.socialsciences.manchester.ac.uk/disciplines/politics/research/hmrg/activities/documents/Charnock.pdf.

Collini, S. (2012) *What are Universities For?*, London: Penguin.

De Angelis, M. and Harvie, D. (2006) *Cognitive Capitalism and the Rat Race: How Capital Measures Ideas and Affects in UK Higher Education*, International Conference on Immaterial Labour, University of Cambridge, available at: http://firgoa.usc. es/drupal/node/34766.

Dean, J. (2012) *The Communist Horizon*, London and New York: Verso.

Goddard, J. (2011) *The Civic University and the Leadership of Place*, available at: www. talloires2011.org/wp-content/uploads/2011/06/Civic-University-and-Leadership-of-Place-John-Goddard.pdf.

Goddard, J. (2012) *The University and the City: New Perspectives on Higher Education and the Grand Challenges of Urban Development*, available at: www.utwente.nl/mb/ cheps/Conference%20New%20Perspectives%2030-10/CHEPS%20Distinguished%20 Lecture%202012.pdf.

Goddard, J. and Vallance, P. (2013) *The University and the City*, London: Routledge.

Graham, S. (2011) *Cities Under Seige: The New Military Urbanism*, London and New York: Verso.

Harney, S. and Moten, F. (2013) *The Undercommons: Fugitive Planning and Black Study, Minor Compositions*, New York and Port Watson: Wivenhoe.

Harvey, D. (2012) *Rebel Cities: From the Right to the City to the Urban Revolution*, London and New York: Verso.

Holmwood, J. (ed.) (2011) *A Manifesto For the Public University*, London: Bloomsbury, available at: www.bloomsburyacademic.com/view/A-Manifesto-for-the-Public-University/book-ba-9781849666459.xml.

Holloway, J. (2002) *Change the World Without Taking Power*, London: Pluto Press, available at: http://libcom.org/library/change-world-without-taking-power-john-holloway.

Invisible Committee (2009) *The Coming Insurrection*, Semiotexte, available at: http:// libcom.org/library/coming-insurrection-invisible-committee.

Jacobs, J. (1961) *The Death and Life of Great American Cities*, New York: Random House.

Kelly, M. (1991) 'Obituary', *Radical Philosophy*, 60(Spring), 62–3.

Lefebvre, H. (1968) *The Explosion: Marxism and the French Upheaval*, New York: Monthly Review Press.

Lefebvre, H. (1991) *The Production of Space*, Oxford: Blackwell.

Lefebvre, H. (1996) *Writings on Cities*, Oxford and Malden, MA: Blackwell.

Lefebvre, H. (2003) *The Urban Revolution*, Minneapolis, MN, and London: University of Minnesota Press.

McGettigan, A. (2013) *The Great University Gamble: Money, Markets and the Future of Higher Education*, London and New York: Pluto Press.

Marx, K. (1875) 'Critique of Gotha Programme', *Marx and Engels Selected Work*, Volume 3, 13–30, Mosco: Progress Publishers.

Merrifield, A. (2006) *Henri Lefebvre: A Critical Introduction*, London and New York: Routledge.

Neary, M. (2003) *All Power to the Power Workers: Emerging from the Darkness – Electricity and Progressive Politics in South Korea, a Social Science Fiction in Korean Transformations: Power Workers, Probation and the Politics of Human Rights*, Resource Centre for Asian NGOs, Sungkonghoe University.

Neary, M. (2012) 'Teaching politically: policy, pedagogy and the new European university', *Journal of Critical Educational Policy Studies*, 10(2), 234–57.

Neary, M. (2013) 'Pedagogy of debt: what higher education teaches us', *Adults Learning NIACE*, available at: http://shop.niace.org.uk/media/catalog/product/a/d/adults-learning-extra-mar2013-part-time-he.pdf.

Neary, M. and Amsler, S. (2012) 'Occupy: a new pedagogy of space and time', *Journal for Critical Education Policy Studies*, 10(2), 106–38.

Neary, M. and Hagyard, A. (2010) *The Pedagogy of Excess: An Alternative Political Economy for Student Life The Marketisation of Higher Education and the Student as Consumer*, London and New York: Routledge.

Postone, M. (1993) *Time Labour and Social Domination*, Cambridge: Cambridge University Press.

Readings, B. (1997) *The University in Ruins*, Harvard, MA: Harvard University Press.

Ross, K. (2008) *The Emergence of Social Space: Rimbaud and the Paris Commune*, London: Verso.

Solomon, C. and Palmieri, T. (2011) *Springtime: The New Student Rebellions*, London and New York: Verso.

Toscano, A. (2011) 'University as a political space', in M. Bailey and D. Freedman (eds), *The Assault on Universities: A Manifesto for Resistance*, London and New York: Pluto Press, pp. 81–90.

12

Decoding University Ideals by Reading Campuses

Exploring Beyond the Democratic Mass University

PAUL BENNEWORTH

Introduction

How is the institution of the university evolving? There is a widespread sense among academics and managers that universities are changing, but there is little consensus about the particular form that this change takes (inter alia Barnett 2003, 2011; Delanty 2002). Although there is agreement that 'modernisation' and the rise of new public management have profoundly influenced the nature of universities, it has proved much harder to interpret what this means in the abstract. This chapter attempts to contribute to this debate by using the physical forms of universities as expressions of their underlying ideas. By exploring the campuses of two universities planned around a very strong ideal of an earlier age (the democratic university), we contribute to these debates about the changing idea of the university.

The physical form of a university is partly determined by the unique nature of the institution of university, reliant on both independence from direct material concerns, but at the same time dependent on sponsors willing to tolerate that independence. Universities have always, in their physical form, reflected the relationship back to the original sponsors. Early medieval universities resembled spiritual communities because of their sponsorship by the church, and their use of church assets to create semi-autonomous communities of scholars able to educate an expanding priesthood (Rüegg 1992). At the same time, universities have evolved in response to societal evolution and the changing nature of societal demands placed upon them. Bender (1988) traces at length the urbanisation of the university as cities became an organising principle of European societies. Each new pressure has both led to the creation of new institutional forms, but at the same time led to changing physical forms of existing universities.

Late capitalist society is immensely complex, and it is hard to discern at this point a 'grand narrative' for the changes currently under way, in contrast to the societal upheavals of the 1960s. Universities are now subject to so many different societal pressures that it is hard to discern a narrative to the changing idea of a university. There have been many attempts – primarily coming from within institutions themselves – to define new kinds of universities in response to their own experienced pressures. But these purposively defined institutional forms – the entrepreneurial university, the virtual university, t he enterprising university, the engaged university – all carry a strongly normative sense of desirability rather than representing a considered analysis of how universities have evolved in response to this complex institutional environment.

This chapter approaches this challenge from the opposite direction, looking at the effects that all these pressures have had on the physical form of the university. The central question this chapter explores is, 'what explains the physical evolution of two 1960s campus universities in the last half-century?'. Studying how these university campuses have evolved provides a more measured understanding of how these new pressures are rebuilding universities, both visibly in their physical form, but also invisibly as a new form of organisation in late capitalism. Unsurprisingly, one can observe the intensification of the university, with a broader and more diverse internal community, growing closer to and interdependent with its host external communities and society and increasingly important wider network linkages: the university can be regarded as evolving into a form of societal 'entrepôt'. While the thrust of literature dealing with modernisation stresses the autonomy of universities as independent atomistic institutions, this chapter argues that universities are evolving into institutions more interwoven with the wider social fabric. This is used to speculate that a new model of university governance beyond new public management is required that takes account of the more collective and socialised uses of knowledge in society.

The Campus and the Idea of a University

This chapter seeks to understand the changing idea behind a university by interpreting its changing spatial form. In this chapter, we refer to this with the term 'campus', the estate belonging to an institution of higher education through which its core functions – teaching, research and engagement – are discharged. Central to our argument is that any kind of configuration of buildings can be understood in terms of two key characteristics, their function and their form. A campus is organised to facilitate particular activities – learning is a socialised process, and so university buildings may provide shared learning spaces. Likewise, their spatial arrangement will also constrain what can be achieved in terms of this function, and they will be managed to ensure that they can discharge this function. But a university campus will also have a particular form, a configuration, an aesthetic or appearance that people experience and relate to in their experience of the university.

Studying form provides insights into function – geographers study scratches on rocks to obtain insights into glacial processes, and the compactness of settlements gives an indication of immediate reliance of residents on one another, for example in response to an external threat. Our argument in this chapter is that the function of the university has become so complex that looking at form provides a way of simplifying this picture. A careful reading of universities' form provides insights into their functions, and a careful reading of the evolution of their form provides insights into their evolving functions. In this chapter, we argue that this also provides an insight into the changing idea of a university.

The Campus as a Spatial Fix Between Universality and Particularity

The first step in our argument is that the campus of the university is sensitive to outside pressures: changing societal demands and expectations on universities result in a changing physical form, from which those changing – and invisible – social demands can be 'read off' and interpreted. Universities have, at their heart, a sponsor dependence that makes them dependent on securing the support of patrons:

> No modern university has ever lived entirely from the sale of its services. Universities have received subsidies from the church, the state, and private philanthropists as individuals and as foundations.
>
> (Shils 1988: 210)

Likewise, Biggar observes:

> Right from their medieval beginnings, [universities] have served private purposes and practical public purposes as well as the sheer *amor scientiae* ['knowledge for knowledge's sake'] . . . popes and bishops needed educated pastors and they and kings needed educated administrators and lawyers capable of developing and embedding national systems.
>
> (Biggar 2010: 77)

Universities have emerged because they are a response to a particular need of those sponsoring them, and that is for a universalist form of knowledge. Biggar's point was that the best way of training pastors, administrators and lawyers was in providing a very generalist form of education, initially derived from a classical knowledge canon. Universities were not established to train lawyers – rather, there was an appreciation that this canonical classical education equipped students with a set of reasoning and judgement-forming skills that equipped them to be most effective in their tasks. Collini (2011) makes the point very eloquently that it would clearly be cheaper to set up vocational educational institutions, but the reason that the institution of university had emerged and then thrived was that the university as an institutional form was a means to partly insulate academics and teachers from patrons' direct pressures to be useful.

From its creation, the university as a social form emerged because it was capable of balancing between these two pressures. First, universities were capable of maintaining a position at a degree removed from society to avoid the pressures of becoming too close to sponsors, and therefore losing the universalism that sponsors actually valued. Second, universities were capable of maintaining sufficient connections into societies to ensure that they did not retreat into mysticism and self-referentiality. Collini (2011) points out that the most successful technical vocational institutions have been those that have evolved towards the universalist knowledge ideals of the university.

And Bender (1988) argues that this is why the campus form evolved what might be considered as a spatial fix that helps to embed this dualistic quality – the campus is a place that is, on the one hand, semi-protected from sponsor pressure but still close enough for social dynamics to be visible and perceptible to those in the university. Thus, our argument is that the spatial form of the campus can be read as emerging between two sets of tensions: on the one hand, providing sufficient connections into host societies, but at the same time, mediating and regulating these tensions.

Social Purposes and Spatial Forms – The Historical Evolution of the University

The campus provided the university with a spatial fix by giving an impermanent and shifting community of learning a physical form and permanent presence in a particular place. The functional demands of sponsors affected the ways that universities were able to organise their activities, their form. But it was the form rather than the functions that had an enduring permanence to them. While graduates and teachers might move, university buildings tended not to change. The result was that the buildings began to embody the idea of a university, and it has become difficult to think about particular kinds of universities without thinking about their spatial form: in the words of Churchill, 'We shape our buildings, and afterwards our buildings shape us'. When one thinks of University College London or the University of California at Berkeley, one immediately thinks of a building or campus, such as the Wilkins Building or the Campanile.

The spatial form of universities reflects the outcome of the struggle between sponsor dependence and autonomy to create universalist knowledge. Therefore, it is possible to see, in time, a co-evolution between the physical form of the university, related to the discharge of its functions towards its sponsors, and the 'idea' of a university. This is related to a historical evolution of the institution of university, with each substantive change in the organisation of society leading to parallel changes in the nature of universities. When the Western European university emerged between the eleventh and thirteenth centuries, there was not a sharp distinction made between spiritual and temporal powers: the university existed at the interstices of that power, using ecclesiastical privileges to support scholarly communities able to educate elites for both these estates. The physical form of the university in this period was indistinguishable from the religious communities within which these universities were first incubated. The idea of a university acquired connotations associated with cloistered communities: removed from society, but with a societal role, delivered largely independently because that is commonly how independent communities outside noble courts were organised.

The next substantial shifts in societal organisation were the emergence of distinct temporal powers and cities, changing universities' sponsors' interests and dependencies. The emergence of 'free cities' (cities whose citizens were not tied through feudal obligations to their lords' lands) created a challenge for feudal lords seeking to capture via taxation the benefits of commerce (Ferruolo 1988). The university evolved in this period as an organisation away from its close ties to the established church, but the spatial form of the cloister continued as a form of organisation. Cities, with concentrations of wealth, potential students and sponsors provided a fertile ground for the establishment and expansion of new universities (Ernste 2007). Locating the university in the city changed the dynamic of university-society spatial relations. The University of Leuven was created as one of the first 'urban universities', supported in its creation by wool merchants who sought a new impulse to develop economic activities as the centre of gravity of their lucrative trade shifted northwards (Tobback 2009).

The next main evolution in society was the university's emergence as a means of creating and reproducing elite cultures. Grafton (1988) charts the emergence of the University of Leiden created as part of the independence campaign against Spanish occupation by the northern Netherlands. This role acquired a distinctly nationalistic connotation after 1648, as universities became an increasingly common part of the repertoire of post-Westphalian nation-builders, creating universities as a means of supporting a strong national culture along with language standardisation (often through Bible Editions), the raising of professional armies and the standardisation of national canonical education (Harvie 1994). The post-Westphalian universities show a subtle evolution in their spatial form from being part of the 'city as a crossroads' to being part of the 'city as an assemblage and demonstration of temporal power'. Universities from this period, such as Lund and Copenhagen, started to resemble a royal court and palaces, rather than the more traditional cloisters.

The next main change in society was what Bauman described as the shift to the modern, progressive society, with the institutionalisation of manufacturing capitalism, and its capacity for generating efficiencies through innovations and improvement in a division of labour. This shift marked one of the great challenges for universities: in the UK, the ancient universities of Scotland and England failed in the late eighteenth century to respond adequately to the demands of industry, and were partly supplanted in Scotland by learned societies (Phillipson 1974, 1988). The saviour of the idea of the university from obsolescence was a series of innovations in Berlin, which institutionalised the idea of universities composed of professorial research groups also teaching students (McClelland 1988). In the UK, the relative lack of organisation of industrial capital slowed the response, but from the 1830s, led by University College London, a new set of technological universities, with innovative chairs in subjects such as engineering, began to respond to these challenges. These new industrially-oriented institutions had, for the first time, the requirement for a radically different form of space, the laboratory, both for the new research mission but also for the education of students, and this increased the space required by a university, and hence its relationship with the city. The rise of new disciplines and research activities led to a differentiation of the university estate and the possibility of universities starting to comprise coherent districts within cities. With the rise of the Land Grant universities in the late nineteenth-century US, separate urban communities with spaces for living, recreation, teaching, research and business engagement emerged: the campus as we know it today.

The final set of societal changes came in Western Europe and America in the course of the twentieth century with an increasing democratisation of capitalist society. Universities became an engine for emancipation, in different ways in different times, initially about creating new kinds of elite, and later a mass democratic system. In the Netherlands, universities were part of the consocial pillar system whereby each of the main cultural groups in society – Socialist, Calvinist, Lutheran, Liberal and Catholic – developed their own social institutions such as schools, political parties, unions and even leisure organisations (Pellings 1997), and the role of the new Catholic universities (Tilburg and Nijmegen) was educating an elite class for the Catholic pillar. In 1960s Europe, in the wake of the May 1968 protests in France, there was a shift towards universities providing increasing individual access to the

Table 12.1 The evolution of the idea of a university and its physical form.

Social change	Sponsor urgent desire	Novel spatial form of university	Exemplar of a university
Agricultural revolution	Reproducing religious administrators	Cloister (eleventh-century Italy)	Bologna (eleventh-century Italy)
Emergence of nobility	Educating loyal administrators	Independent ('free') cloister	Paris (twelfth-century France)
Urbanisation	Educated administrative elite to manage trade	The university as a marketplace at the city crossroads	Catholic University of Leuven (fifteenth century)
Sustaining national communities	Validating the state by imagining the nation	The university as an expression of power	Lund University (seventeenth century)
Creating technical elite	Creating a technical besides admin elite	The university as a factory	Humbold University, Berlin
Promoting progress	Creating economically useful knowledge	The campus as a partner	Land Grant universities (nineteenth- to twentieth-century USA)
Supporting democracy	Creating non-traditional elites	The campus as a microcosm of democracy	Dutch Catholic universities (twentieth-century Netherlands)
Creating mass democratic societies	Educating Habermasian deliberative citizens	The campus as a model of democratic society	UK 'plate glass' universities of Robbin era

Source: Author, after Pinheiro et al. (2012)

opportunities to participate in a democratic society via education (Daalder and Shils 1982). The classic urban form of these institutions was to continue the trend for the campus as an integrated community, and to emphasise through the spatial form the equality of community members (cf. Ossa-Richardson, this volume).

These changes are summarised in Table 12.1, which shows how changing societal demands on universities was reflected in their physical form, which has changed throughout their history. The physical form of universities provides their spatial frame, and a starting point from which they evolve in response to these changing societal demands and contexts. University campuses are located on sites that are not isolated land parcels, but exist within a wider set of relationships to geographical systems, and there is a clear materiality here – those wider geography systems shape what emerges. But at the same time, the act of building a university on a site affects the configuration and connectivity of those geographical systems, both physical and human, much as the development of a city is shaped by its physical landscape, but over time the urban landscape is shaped by human activity. This can be categorised as a landscape dialectic – with human activities being shaped by, but also shaping, those landscapes. It is possible, for example, in the current fabric of the University of Oxford, to see a range of different styles in the different colleges and central buildings reflecting both their creation and their modification over time.

The Evolving University in a Late Modernity of Decentred Metanarratives

It has proven extremely difficult to identify a new ideal type for the university in the later modern period, although many forms have been put forward, in part related to the absence of a clear meta-narrative for understanding the direction of societal development in late modernity. One might relate to a process of individualisation and fragmentation of communities of citizens into individualised consumers as suggested by Beck's Risk Society thesis. But at the same time, the idea of a knowledge society offers the potential for mobilising new online and virtual communities that are capable of innovating, creating new knowledge and offering new societal capacity, creating a post-political citizenry without completely fragmenting them. Benneworth (2011) argues, more generally, that there are three kinds of societal changes that are pulling universities in multiple directions: the decline of party politics has created demands for new kinds of accountability; increasing technological uncertainty is challenging scientists' 'license to practice'; and citizens are demanding more voice in directions of scientific progress. Universities are subject to many demands on their resources, and face many pressures to respond, what Enders and De Boer have referred to as 'mission stretch', and others have referred to as 'mission overload' (Ćulum *et al.* 2013; Damme 2009; Enders and Boer 2009; Jongbloed *et al.* 2008).

Universities are expected to contribute to a much wider domain of societal problems, problems that are themselves becoming more complex, requiring coordination through networks of stakeholders and knowledge producers. Governments are also pushing for increased efficiency in universities through competitive mechanisms, with growing student numbers and falling overall funding, while at the same time encouraging excellence and concentration of research. The very nature of knowledge production has changed as new communications technologies have shifted in nature from bilateral to collective and social, facilitating new kinds of collective learning, but at the same time challenging the privileged positions of universities and academic scholars in these knowledge creation activities (Rutten and Boekema 2012).

Barnett (2011) identifies what he calls, after Wyatt (1990), the four future possibilities of universities: the liquid, authentic, ecological and therapeutic. Benneworth *et al.* (2010: 1615), likewise, note that:

> Various authors suggested archetypal forms, from the entrepreneurial university (Clark 1998), through the virtual university (Cornford and Pollock 2002), the engaged university (Watson 2003), the ethical university (Garlick 2005) and the useful university (Goddard 2007).

It seems risky directly to tie the idea of a new kind of university to an over-arching social change. This suggests that the late modern idea of a university, rather than produced by a wave of change, is being produced by the intersection of these various societal tensions, fault lines and complexities. This suggests that the ideal type of the late modern university will be an emergent property of the way that these tensions play out on existing institutions, and can be seen in new institutions that are created. The heuristic from the preceding section of a dialectic evolution between university and location provides a means for us to continue the table forward beyond the mass democratic university of Daalder and Shils (1982) and Delanty (2002).

Taking our notion that a close reading of spatial form can provide insights into function, and that function evolves partly in response to societal pressures, looking at spatial form can, by implication, provide some insights into changing societal pressures. That is what we do in this chapter: we take two campus universities whose spatial form at the time of building reflected the ideas of the democratic mass university, being campuses built on greenfield sites at a similar time (the early 1960s), and explore how these changing tensions have been reflected in their built environment. This provides the means to ask three sequential and related questions:

- How much remains of the original idealism of the campus?
- Is there an obvious new organising logic visible in the spatial form of the campus?
- What does this suggest regarding the ideal type late modern university?

The Case Studies and Method

To answer these questions, we use case studies taken from two universities created in the early 1960s as part of deliberate government attempts to expand higher education, both in terms of student numbers, but also geographically, socially and in terms of subject coverage. Both the case studies presented were created as single-site campus universities in regions without a tradition of substantial higher education, offering new subjects, novel pedagogic approaches and offering a progressive social mix and experience. The choice of the case studies is, to some degree, serendipitous – during a period as a guest researcher at the University of Twente in the Netherlands, studying spin-off companies, I had a chance conversation with an architectural researcher, Peter Timmerman, concerning the architectural logic of the University of Twente (UT). This led to two co-publications specifically concerned with the architectural ideas behind the UT campus (Benneworth and Timmerman 2005; Timmerman and Benneworth 2006).

It was natural to ask the question whether there were wider lessons that could be drawn, and a set of potential comparator institutions were identified. RCUK Academic Fellowship Funding provided the opportunity to undertake a much smaller case study of one of these comparators, at Lancaster University in the UK, which involved a series of site visits and a limited number of interviews in 2007, and the opportunity to acquire a number of publications concerning the university's history. I continued to develop both case studies during this period, in part as a side effect of the work on university spin-offs and was greatly helped by Timmerman's own *magnum opus* regarding the campus form, *Architecture with a Capital A* (Timmerman 2011). The two case studies are therefore, to some degree, exploratory and stylised, attempting to set out the original intentions and ideals embodied in the plans, exploring how these were implemented in the first instance in practice, and how these have evolved over time.

This has been done through a largely secondary method: luckily, both universities sought to capture various moments in their history and produced substantive and well-researched volumes. The original spatial philosophies of the two campuses are well described in *Een Experiment in het Bos*

('An experiment in the woods', Sorgdrager 1981) and *Quest for Innovation* (McClintock 1974). The current status quo has been described, in UT's case, through a series of publications that appeared in 2011 for the Golden Anniversary, including Timmerman (2011), De Boer and Drukker (2011) and Krijnsen (2011). Likewise, in 2011, Lancaster University published *Shaping the Future* (McClintock 2011), which updated her 1974 volume; this has been augmented with material from the 'History of the university' website, produced as part of the university's 'History in the community' course (Vickers and Edwards 2006). The material from the shift is drawn from a mix of interviews, site visits, master plans produced at the point of change, the Shepheard Epstein Hunter website (Lancaster University's architects) and from the ex-post explanations offered in the Golden Anniversary material outlined above.

The first university studied is the University of Twente (UT), in the eastern Netherlands. UT was created as the Technische Hogeschool Twente (THT) in 1961 after lobbying at the national level by a group of regional industrialists. UT was created to provide technical skills in the growing engineering sector, which the two existing technical universities at Delft and Eindhoven had not been able to provide. The town of Enschede was chosen for the location because the municipality owned a well-suited site, the former country estate of a textile baron that had been expropriated because of his wartime collaboration (Gellekink 2001). The park location provided the ideal setting for what would be the first proper Dutch campus university, including substantial on-site residential accommodation. The university was created around a cluster of technical faculties, and attempted to offer an innovative curriculum, including a common first year for all students, and a short-cycle (three-year) technical degree, against a Dutch norm of five years (Sorgdrager 1981). Its creators were wary of the effects of bringing students to a strongly working-class town, and created the campus in a way that emphasised its isolation from the city, as a self-contained community at the city's edge. The main change in its campus form was that the estate reached the end of its planned 40-year life in 2002, and the university was ordered by the mayor in 1998 to completely rebuild the campus within 10 years for public safety reasons. The university has since used the rebuilding to integrate the campus into the neighbouring Business and Science Park to create a single knowledge space, Kennispark.

The second university studied is Lancaster University, in north-west England. Lancaster University was created at a time of expansion in the UK's higher education system at the behest of the University Grants Committee (McClintock 1974). Although created around the time of the 1963 Robbins report into higher education, and sometimes referred to as a Robbins-era expansion university, the decision to create a university for Lancashire predates the Robbins Committee. Lancaster was preferred over the other potential location, Blackpool, because Blackpool's most obvious land parcel was already earmarked for development with a substantial entertainment complex, and Lancaster had the agreement of the owners of the Bailrigg Mansion to sell their estate for the development of a new campus. Lancaster was created as an experimental institution, with all students initially studying three subjects in their first year, including a science and arts subject, prior to later specialisation. A further innovation was the campus, whose original idea was – given the relief of the Bailrigg site – to have the characteristics of a Mediterranean hill village: compact, closed to the outside (and the prevailing westerly winds), with high functional integration, maximising internal interaction. The campus was developed with the idea of organising students into 'colleges' where they would be accommodated, and could walk within 15 minutes to any point of the campus. The main change to the campus came in the course of the 1990s, when Lancaster sought to expand, and therefore had to find a way to develop beyond the 'village wall' of the internal ring road. The university took the opportunity to create an internal functional differentiation on the new site, creating a new accommodation zone and converting original buildings towards academic functions.

The Spatial Organisation of Drienerlo and Bailrigg

'The Experiment in the Forest': UT as a Cloistered Academic Environment

The University of Twente was commissioned as a university with the power to experiment in a range of areas, from degree structure to organisation, through a 10-year derogation from the relevant clauses of the national Higher Education Law (Sorgdrager 1981). Arguably the most important of the experiments was the fact that the university was to be the Netherlands' first campus university, which created an opportunity to offer a distinctive academic formation process. Student housing at that point in the Netherlands was organised through fraternities ('student corps'), which, while providing an intense and formative experience, were also elitist and exclusive. The campus sought to democratise the benefits of corps life and make it accessible to all students, so that their experience would be both an educational and a socialising one (cf. Grit 2000). At the same time, the university used its experimental powers to make it compulsory for all students to spend their first two years on campus. Sorgdrager notes that university policymakers were aware of the risk that this raised, that isolation would breed insularity, but regarded it as a risk to be dealt with emergently rather than one to be designed-out of the campus. The development of the campus was placed in the hands of two architects, Van Embden and Van Tije, who chose, for a triple concentration, the concentration of activities on a single campus, functional concentration within three zones,

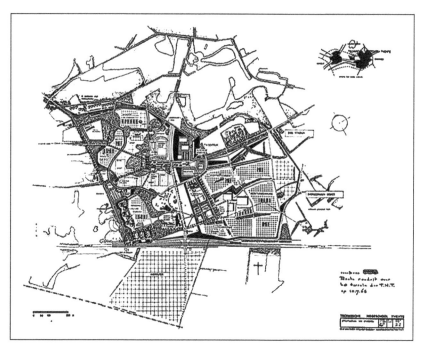

Figure 12.1 The original plans for the development of the Drienerlo site.

and faculty concentration within single tower block buildings (Timmerman 2011). Their plan was to create a campus to be eventually occupied by 4,000 students and 100 professors, with considerable numbers of the university community as campus residents.

The spatial form of the campus reflected the landscape character of the Drienerlo estate, to the east primarily farmlands and to the west the stately home and gardens. The campus was to be planned with a function division reflecting this: the functionality of the eastern side would provide a suitable seat for the professional community functions (the academic faculties), and the landscaped parkland on the western side suitable for residential areas. These would be linked by a central axis providing supporting services such as the library, shops, sports and cultural facilities (Groenendijk and Vollaard 2006; Sorgdrager 1981: 80). Housing in the western area was to be provided both for staff (houses) and students (flats), both out of the abstract desire to create an inward-looking community, as well as for the practical reason that there was very limited housing close to Enschede that would be acceptable to professors migrating from the west of the Netherlands. Academic spaces in the eastern campus were to be developed as separate buildings for each faculty, mixing classroom, lab and office space in one building, and with substantial spacing between the buildings to recreate an element of 'park life'. A campus boulevard was created around a sports centre, canteen area and library in the central zone. A flyover was created along the south side of the campus to separate it from the north-western edge of the city of Enschede, while the northern border was formed by a reservoir network landscaped with forests.

Bailrigg and the Quest for Innovation: Lancaster as a Miniature Democratic Community

Lancaster University was created in the early 1960s as a response to an anticipated expansion in higher education, not only in the number of students, but also the types, their backgrounds, and the physical location of these universities (cf. Ossa-Richardson, this volume). Lancaster University opened in the city centre while the campus at the Bailrigg site was developed in the early 1960s. The site was naturally isolated from Lancaster, at a distance of some 5 kilometres, and bounded to the east by the main west coast motorway, the M6, and on its other sides by farmland. Its development was placed in the hands of the architects Shepheard Epstein (having a single site architect was a Ministry recommendation), who, according to McClintock (1974), proposed the essence of their design at their interview, the single spine plan, which formed the basis for the master plan. Shepheard Epstein's architectural principle for the site was to create a single coherent community; a key decision was to prohibit vehicular traffic from the site within a central ring road. The relief of the site, on a west-facing hill, suggested that the central spine arrangement should run from north to south, maximising the use of natural light while avoiding substantial height differences along the site, which would necessitate terracing, thereby breaking up natural circulation and interaction within the site. The plan also envisaged a cloistered design providing significant shelter from the elements, with the central spine being planned so it was possible to move between any two buildings within 10 minutes without being exposed to rain.

Within this idea of a cloistered, closed and isolated campus, there were two additional levels of integration provided, intended to help develop well-rounded students, comfortable in the social worlds of arts and sciences. The first was the adoption of the college system, which provided a layer between the university and the student, additional to the department. Colleges were halls of residence that mixed students from different departments, but also provided social opportunities and pastoral care via academic tutors. The intention was that these colleges would be the natural locus for student socialising, and preclude the risk that subject-based departments would be that basis, replicating the feared divide between arts and sciences. The second integration was provided in the individual buildings, which would provide 'a fruit salad of functions' (Peter Epstein, quoted in Vickers and Edwards 2006), including

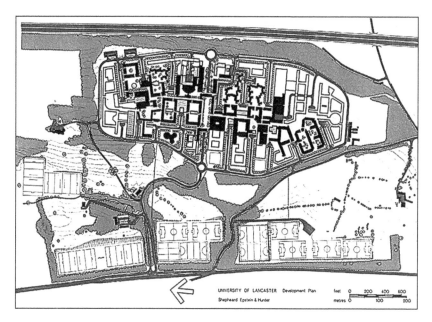

Figure 12.2 The original plans for the development of the Bailrigg site.

student residence, leisure and cultural facilities, teaching rooms, and office space. Sports facilities were to be provided at the western side of the campus, where the land was less even and unsuitable for building, separated from the core community area by general recreation land incorporating shelter belts, parkland gardens and courtyards (SHE website 2007, www.lancaster.ac.uk/unihistory).

Replanning the Democratic Campus in an Entrepreneurial Age

From Country Estate to Knowledge Campus: The Rise of Kennispark at UT

The original Van Embden and Van Tije master plan developed for the first 40 years of its life with a variety of modifications. In 1995, the university began a substantial renovation plan for its campus, the ownership of which had passed to the university from the government without corresponding resources. De Boer and Drukker (2011) document how the university came to a 10-year agreement with the municipality to completely renovate the campus by 2008, with a total estimated cost of around fl. 310 million (€150 million). The first step was the 2001 master plan revision (Hoogstad 2001a, 2001b), which abandoned the strict division lines in the campus, and intensified and integrated the professional buildings into an education and research area. However, these plans were accelerated in 2002 when a fire destroyed half of the Cubicus building, forcing the university to hire space off campus to house the Social Sciences faculty. The question of campus redevelopment became a pressing issue for the university, and to find cost-sharing partners for the exercise, the university proposed to integrate the campus with the adjacent Business and Science Park, which had emerged beyond the viaduct (Benneworth and Hospers 2007; Benneworth *et al.* 2011). The 2001 spatial plan was recalibrated to plan the entire university campus and BSP as a single coherent entity, to be called Kennispark (Knowledge Park), a title that had emerged out of a series of late 1990s policy discussions.

The idea underpinning the first Kennispark master plan (2009) was to create a single functional integrated space stimulating interaction between its various elements. It was conceived of as a single space bringing two worlds together, business and science, to stimulate innovation and economic development, and with the concrete target of creating 10,000 new high-technology jobs by 2020 (cf. Benneworth *et al.* 2011). The focus on campus development shifted to upgrading the teaching buildings, creating a single teaching and research zone (called the O&O area, after the Dutch phrase Onderzoek en Onderwijs

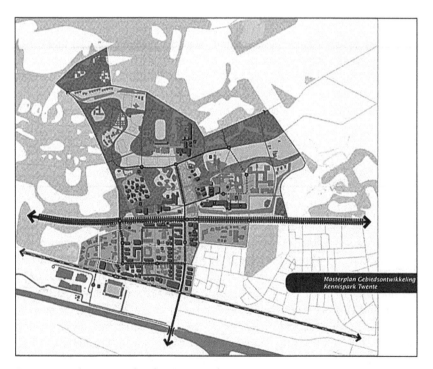

Figure 12.3 The master plan for Kennispark in 2009.

meaning teaching and research), which physically connected a range of formerly separate teaching buildings and research laboratories. This was to be at the heart of a green crossroads, with its axes being the former flyover and the parkland area between the teaching and service campus areas. The southernmost campus building was to be developed as a business location (called the 'Gallery'). The flyover between the university and the business and science park was to be removed and made into a landscaped dual carriageway. Land reclaimed from the flyover was also to be developed with units where 'business could meet science', with the explicit intention of stimulating further innovation. The funds for these developments were to come not only from university capital investments, but also from local and regional government, as well as private real estate investors. Space already made available on campus for starting businesses was to be expanded within the laboratories, removing the strict functional distinction between research and entrepreneurship-building functions. Finally, the campus was to be rezoned as within the built-up area (affecting speed limits and parking in and around the Kennispark area).

From Mediterranean Hill Village to Ivory Tower:
Lancaster's Revised Master Plan

The master plan at Lancaster was revised in 1991 at a turning point in university policy, with a move towards a new massification. The early 1980s had been a difficult period for British universities, with budgets cut between 10 and 40 per cent, with student numbers frozen. Capital spend completely dried up in this period, but in 1986, with a reversal in government policy following the appointment of Kenneth Baker as Secretary of State, there were signs that universities, including Lancaster, could expand. The incoming vice-chancellor (Harry Hanham) decided in 1985 that the university should plan for a huge expansion, to encompass 20,000 students, and this would have impacts on the nature of the estate. Shepheard Epstein were commissioned in 1991 to rework the master plan to allow for this expansion, by concentrating academic functions within the ring road, and creating a new accommodation area at the south side of the campus, which would form the new campus area, 'South West Campus'. This master plan therefore envisaged the introduction of a functional specialisation on campus between accommodation and academic facilities, alongside an expansion of the campus's overall spatial footprint.

Although the university never reached the anticipated target of 20,000 students, student numbers grew in this period relatively rapidly to 12,000, where they have stabilised. From 1991 to 1995, a large number of new building projects were begun inside the ring road, and as these new buildings came on stream, this led to the 'crisis of the spine', which was that, for 10 minutes every hour, the campus faced gridlock as much greater numbers tried to move

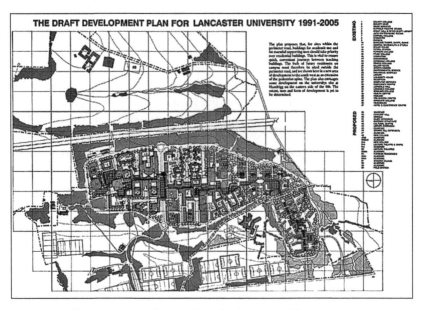

Figure 12.4 The 1991 master plan for the redevelopment of the Bailrigg campus.

between lectures along the single path. The architects proposed a new outer pedestrian road to create a more radial flow within the campus and diffuse this pressure. The expansion projects led to some financial issues for the university in the late 1990s, and therefore additional funding was sought for completion of the expansion project. The expansion of student housing was to come through the creation of new colleges, housing units organised around a single courtyard with shared collegiate leisure and support facilities, which also cohered into a specialised accommodation zone. This was achieved in association with private partners, who developed the accommodation and will receive an income stream for a fixed period, after which the facilities will revert to the university. In the early 2000s, Lancaster looked to its regional partners to help finance further campus developments, including the regional development agency and the Northern Way, a consortium of three northern RDAs working together to strengthen cross-regional linkages. Substantial grants were made from public sources into two facilities providing support for enterprise, the Infolab21 and Lancaster Environment Centre, to host a series of knowledge and business centres to stimulate business innovation. Located at the south and north ends of the old campus, respectively, these centres brought new functions on to the campus and introduced an additional level of functional differentiation into the formerly homogenous 'fruit salad' of the campus estate. The university also planned to develop, in conjunction with the city council, a science park on non-university land immediately to the north of the campus as a potential location for growing companies emerging from their knowledge exchange centres.

The Changing 'Spatial Philosophy' of Drienerlo and Bailrigg

When universities evolve in a particular place, they have a particular spatial dependence – they are framed and constrained by what already exists, and that is evident in the way both Drienerlo and Bailrigg have evolved. Both universities sought to evolve starting from a common 1960s ideal of universities as a site of academic identity formation. These campuses were to be model societies – with students granted space to develop their academic identities by enjoying a degree of remove from outside society. This was implemented in different ways on the two sites, reflecting the nature of the sites, as well as the architects' wishes: UT used a strict functional delineation reflecting the spatial form of the site, while Lancaster created a structure of mini-communities (colleges) mixing scholarly and social activities on the site. In both cases, campus created a separation and isolation of the university from society, both through a physical distance from the local cities, and minimising interactions between the university and city. The net effect was to realise, both physically and practically, isolated campuses as the sites of elite reproduction.

However, universities are, as we have previously noted, always dependent on patron support, and in the post-war era, from governments, who, in turn, are held electorally accountable. In both these cases, the isolation of the campus led to its partial abandonment by the lead sponsor, through estates ownership passing to universities in the Netherlands in 1991, and in the seven-year investment freeze in the UK (1979–86). It became clear at these points that the universities could not, through their own activities, maintain their estates in parallel with this privileged isolation, which drove two processes. The first was of gradual run-down of the physical estate, as the two universities could not afford to fund active maintenance out of their recurrent incomes, the magnitude in the case of the Netherlands signalled in 1998 by the mayor's threat to withdraw the university's public safety certificate (effectively its license to operate). The spatial effects of this degradation process could sometimes be dramatic, as with the Cubicus fire at the UT or the 2000 floods on the Lancaster campus, but at the same time permeated each campus with a feeling of abandonment rather than constructive isolation, which threatened to harm the students' learning experiences, and therefore demanding a constructive response.

The second effect was that the universities sought to address these problems by reconnecting with and replacing the universities within various circulation flows. There has, on the one hand, been an attempt to exploit the university assets on campus more intensively to generate surpluses to fund estate renovation. Lancaster was active in renting out its rooms to tourists and visitors during the summer vacation (I stayed there for three days in the summer of 1986) as a means of generating additional income to fund these developments. Both universities have hotels located on-site, and those hotels have been used by the university to expand their education provision towards (the more lucrative) post-initial education in business and management studies. But at the same time, both universities have, to an extent, invited new investors into the campus, and each of those groups of investors have their own interests in the spatial form and function of the campus. Some are commercial investors situated within wider capital networks, and this has exposed the campuses to these pressures (manifested, for example, in problems of build quality in phase 1 of the South West Campus (McClintock 2011)). Others are public investors seeking to leverage the university's knowledge assets through processes of innovation and entrepreneurship, demanding new kinds of hybrid university space for entrepreneurship, including Lancaster's Infolab21 and UT's Nanolab (cf. Lam 2010). These changes have also reconnected the campus to the wider outside world, and re-imposed external demands on universities, which, it can be argued, managed to shelter themselves from these demands in the early years, partly through their experimental status, but also through the isolated physical frames within which they operated.

The most obvious point about the spatial manifestation of these changes is that the campuses are bigger, and that growth has come in at least three dimensions. The first is in terms of campus spatial footprints. Lancaster has developed an additional campus zone for housing, and two new substantial knowledge exchange centres outside the boundary road. UT has been active in the creation of the Business and Science Park, now incorporated into the Kennispark idea. There has also been an intensification of activity – both campuses now accommodate more than twice the number of students originally planned for, without a doubling in the size of the campus's spatial envelope. This has been dealt with through a much stronger functional differentiation within the campus, including a functional difference of scholarship into teaching and research alongside a reduction of the space made available for individual activities. There has been an expansion in campus functions, and, in particular, the emergence of new kinds of business spaces, which provide a degree of connectivity back to innovative businesses, in part by creating a community of high-technology businesses in close proximity to, but also with strong functional linkages to, university research activities. There has also been an infrastructural reconnection of the university campus back into the city – much more clearly in UT, which has been formally rezoned as urban space, but Lancaster's senate debated in 1999 the possibility of relocating to an inner-city site, and the university has continued to creep back towards the city with its new science park plans.

If the original campuses were a reflection of the idea of the formative university creating elites for a democratic society, how can these evolved campuses be understood, and indeed towards what kind of ideal type do they indicate? While universities have always been, in some sense, 'marketplaces of ideas' (cf. Harding *et al.* 2007), these campus evolutions involved the universities becoming places where non-university elements participated in knowledge exchange. UT has physically rearranged its original three-way division into creating the campus as a topological crossroads based around two physical axes. Lancaster has created new kinds of hybrid spaces at the edge of the campus that physically connect the university back into the economy, as well as bringing external interests, demands and pressures back into the campus. The campus still has some degree of isolation, but at the same time there are important hinges or membrane spaces mediating external pressures back into the university. Returning to the idea of an urban metaphor, this suggests a kind of 'entrepôt' city as a global hub, with a series of special zones and enclaves mediating local access to the privileges of the global space (cf. Budd 2006). Although I am wary of suggesting a new ideal type of university, the idea of an 'entrepôt university' provides a means of reflecting on the changing societal pressure.

Exploring the Idea of the 'Entrepôt' University

In putting forward the idea of the entrepôt university, there are clear resonances with Bathelt *et al.*'s (2004) idea of clusters as having global pipelines with local buzz: universities serve as entry points to wider global knowledge networks. It is important to highlight the negative sides of the entrepôt – they restricted entry to outsiders, and locals often did not benefit from those trading relationships. The entrepôt metaphor highlights the Faustian pact that a university brings – on the one hand, universities can provide access to wider circuits of knowledge that may stimulate local economic development. That knowledge penetrates, through the varieties of universities' local relationships and connections, into the wider region. But, on the other hand, there is a fuzziness in these universities' territorial relationships, and those universities may assume that they have a natural right to those privileges, without properly considering whether local actors are really able to derive benefits from the university presence. Although universities might not restrict local entry as did nineteenth-century colonial entrepôts, they remain exclusive institutions – that exclusivity serves a purpose, but at the same time is not a natural condition of the university. And a city that allows itself to be dominated by entrepôt interests may itself weaken, as demonstrated by the UK's fiscal problems originating in entrepôt behaviour in the City of London.

The key issue facing the entrepôt university is in balancing between these local and global pressures and the apparent asymmetry of the question of who benefits. Local pressures may be 'small' and quotidian while 'global' pressures appear urgent and overwhelming. But if one assumes that the institution of the university will not dissolve into the ether of Web provision, then these campus evolutions sensitise us to the fact that universities retain a very strong local dependency for their spatial framework, and ultimately their capacities and functionalities. Both universities dealt with their spatial problems by building local coalitions of supporters, and these local supporters have, arguably, had a far greater impact on this spatial framework than global stakeholders. Managing these local dependencies as a set of duties deriving from dependencies, rather than as responsibilities deriving from rights, is necessary to avoid privileging the interests of these apparent global actors over those of more local, if less glamorous, actors.

It is this local dependency issue that has been lost in much of the discussions of the modern university. The idea of a world class university (Salmi 2009) has emerged as the apparent ideal type, promoted by a range of transparency tools and ranking instruments that emphasise only a few elements of what universities do, and completely omit any kind of local spatial dependence. Governments, universities and the media seem entranced by the idea of virtual competition between institutions in very different national and local contexts, and this has, in turn, led to real effects, shaping flows of students, research grants, additional national funding programmes, and, ultimately, the shape of national higher education systems. University governance is focused on making singular strategic choices, while managing the entrepôt university requires dealing with the hybridity, fuzziness and discordance of the entrepôt position, rather than chasing advantage in wider global networks. This is encouraged by higher education policy systems that provide simple steering mechanisms through competitive market systems. Indeed, governments have exacerbated this trend, creating neo-markets in chasing the world-class university ideal, through programmes such as Germany's Excellenzitiativ, France's Opération Campus and Finland's creation of Aalto University (Cremonini *et al.* 2013).

But at the same time, laying an accent on the idea of world class universities emphasises only one element important to the entrepôt university, that of the global networking and connectivity, and risks over-privileging the global dimension over the equally important local dimension. There seems to be a need to rethink approaches to higher education's governance to reflect the dissonance of the entrepôt university, locally dependent in a globally competitive world. Only then can it be managed to meet the needs of its societal stakeholders, and continue its sustainable evolution as a stable institutional form.

Acknowledgements

The author would like to thank the copyright holders of the images in the text for their kind permission to reproduce the images. Figure 12.1 is reproduced by permission of the University of Twente Photographic Archive, Figure 12.3 by permission of Kennispark Twente, and Figures 12.2 and 12.4 from Shepheard Epstein Hunter.

Bibliography

Barnett, R. (2003) *Beyond All Reason: Living with Ideology in the University*, Buckingham: Society for Research into Higher Education; Open University Press.

Barnett, R. (2011) *Becoming a University*, London: Routledge.

Bathelt, H., Malmberg, A. and Maskell P. (2004) 'Clusters and knowledge: local buzz, global pipelines and the process of knowledge creation', *Progress in Human Geography*, 28, 31–56.

Bender, T. (1988) 'Introduction', in T. Bender (ed.), *The University and the City: From Medieval Origins to the Present*, New York and Oxford: Oxford University Press, pp. 3–10.

Benneworth, P. (2011) 'Towards a strategic management agenda for knowledge exchange', *MODERN Executive Report*, Brussels: ESMU.

Benneworth, P. S. and Hospers, G.-J. (2007) 'Urban competitiveness in the knowledge economy: universities as new planning animateurs', *Progress in Planning*, 67(2), 99–198.

Benneworth, P. S. and Timmerman, P. (2005) 'Changing urban forms in the knowledge economy', *Town and Country Planning*, 74(12), 376–8.

Benneworth, P. S., Charles, D. R. and Madnipour, A. (2010) 'Universities as agents of urban change in the global knowledge economy', *European Planning Studies*, 18(11), 1611–29.

Benneworth, P., Hospers, G. J., Jongbloed, B., Leiyste, L. and Zomer, A. (2011) 'The "science city" as a system coupler in fragmented strategic urban environments?', *Built Environment*, 37(3), 317–35.

Biggar, N. (2010) 'What are universities for?', *Standpoint*, 24, 76–9.

Budd, L. (2006) 'London: from city-state to city region?', in I. Hardill, P. Benneworth, M. Baker, M. and L. Budd (eds), *The Rise of the English Regions*, London: Routledge, pp. 245–66.

Collini, S. (2011) *What are Universities For?*, London: Penguin.

Cremonini, L., Westerheijden, D., Benneworth, P. and Dauncey, H. (2013) 'In the shadow of celebrity: world-class university policies and public value in higher education', *Higher Education Policy*, advance online publication, 15 October 2013; doi:10.1057/hep.2013.33.

Ćulum, B., Rončević, N. and Ledić, J. (2013) 'Facing new expectations – integrating third mission activities into the university', in U. Teichler and E. A. Hohle (eds), *The Academic Profession in Europe: New Tasks and New Challenges*, Dordrecht: Springer, pp. 163–95.

Daalder, H. and Shils, E. (1982) *Universities, Politicians and Bureaucrats: Europe and the United States*, Cambridge: Cambridge University Press.

Damme, D. V. (2009) 'The search for transparency: convergence and diversity in the Bologna process', *Mapping the Higher Education Landscape*, 39–55.

De Boer, J. and Drukker, J. (2011) *High Technology, Human Touch: A Short History of the University of Twente*, Enschede: University of Twente Press.

Delanty, G. (2002) 'The university and modernity: a history of the present', in K. Robins and F. Webster, *The Virtual University: Knowledge, Markets and Management*, Oxford: OUP, pp. 31–48.

Enders, J. and and Boer, H. (2009) 'The mission impossible of the European university: institutional confusion and institutional diversity', in A. Amaral, G. Neave, C. Musselin and P. Maassen (eds), *European Integration and the Governance of Higher Education and Research*, Dortrecht: Springer, pp. 159–78.

Ernste, H. (2007) 'The international network university of the future and its local and regional impacts', in A. Harding, A. Scott, S. Laske and C. Burtscher (eds), *Bright Satanic Mills: Universities, Regional Development and the Knowledge Economy*, Aldershot: Ashgate, pp. 61–91.

Ferruolo, S. C. (1988) 'Parisius-Paradisus: the city, its schools, and the origins of the University of Paris', in T. Bender (ed.), *The University and the City: From Medieval Origins to the Present*, New York and Oxford: Oxford University Press, pp. 22–43.

Gellekink, A. (2001) 'Drienerlo, van landgoed tot campusuniversiteit', in B. Groenman (ed.), *Van landgoed tot kenniscampus 1961–2001*, Enschede: UT Press, pp. 6–12.

Grafton, A. (1988) 'Civic humanism and scientific scholarship at the University of Leiden', in T. Bender (ed.), *The University and the City: From Medieval Origins to the Present*, New York and Oxford: Oxford University Press, pp. 59–78.

Grit, K. (2000) *Economisering als probleem: een studie naar de bedrijfsmatige stad en de ondermende universiteit*, Assen: Van Gorcum.

Groenendijk, P. and Vollaard, P. (2006) *Architectural Guide to the Netherlands 1900–2000*, Amsterdam: Nai UIngevers.

Harding, A., Scott, A., Laske, S. and Burtscher C. (eds) *Bright Satanic Mills: Universities, Regional Development and the Knowledge Economy*, Aldershot: Ashgate.

Harvie, C. (1994) *The Rise of Regional Europe*, London: Routledge.

Hoogstad architecten (2001a) *Uitwerking masterplan: #1 Uitgangspunten*, Rotterdam: Hoogstad architecten.

Hoogstad architecten (2001b) *Uitwerking masterplan: #2 Structuurplan*, Rotterdam; Hoogstad architecten.

Jongbloed, B., Enders, J. and Salerno, C. (2008) 'Higher education and its communities: interconnections, interdependencies and a research agenda', *Higher Education*, 56(3), 303–24.

Krijnsen, M. (2011) *The New Campus: Learning and Living at the University of Twente in the 21st Century*, Enschede: University of Twente Press.

Lam, A. (2010) 'From "ivory tower traditionalists" to "entrepreneurial scientists": academic scientists in fuzzy university–industry boundaries', *Social Studies of Science*, 40(2), 307–40.

McClelland, C. E. (1988) '"To live for science": ideals and realities at the University of Berlin', in T. Bender (ed.), *The University and the City: From Medieval Origins to the Present*, New York and Oxford: Oxford University Press, pp. 181–97.

McClintock, M. E. (1974) *The University of Lancaster: Quest for Innovation, a History of the First Ten Years 1964–1974*, Lancaster: The University of Lancaster.

McClintock, M. E. (2011) *Shaping the Future: A History of the University of Lancaster 1961–2011*, Lancaster: Lancaster University Press.

Pellings, P. (1997) 'The evolution of Dutch consociationalism, 1917–1997', *The Netherlands' Journal of Social Sciences*, 33, 9–26.

Phillipson, N. T. (1974) 'Culture and society in the 18th century province: the case of Edinburgh and the Scottish Enlightenment', in L. Stone (ed.) *The University in Society: Volume II – Europe, Scotland and the United States from the 16th to the 20th Century*, London: Oxford University Press, pp. 407–48.

Phillipson, N. T. (1988) 'Commerce and culture: Edinburgh, Edinburgh University and the scottish enlightenment', in T. Bender (ed.), *The University and the City: From Medieval Origins to the Present*, New York and Oxford: Oxford University Press, pp. 100–18.

Pinheiro, R., Benneworth, P. and Jones, G. A. (2012) 'Beyond the obvious: tensions and volitions surrounding the contributions of universities to regional development and innovation', paper presented to *7th International Seminar on Regional Innovation Policies*, Porto, Portugal, 7–11 October 2012.

Rüegg, W. (1992) 'Themes', in H. de Ridder-Symoens (ed.) *A History of the University in Europe*, Cambridge: Cambridge University Press, pp. 3–34.

Rutten, R. and Boekema, F. (2012) 'From learning region to learning in a socio-spatial context', *Regional Studies*, 46(8), 981–92.

Salmi, J. (2009) *The Challenge of Establishing World-Class Universities*, Washington, DC: World Bank.

Shils, E. (1988) 'The university, the city and the world: Chicago and the university of Chicago', in T. Bender (ed.), *The University and the City: From Medieval Origins to the Present*, New York and Oxford: Oxford University Press, pp. 210–29.

Sorgdrager, W. (1981) *Een Experiment in het Bos: De Eerste Jaren van de Technische Hogeschool Twente 1961–1972*, Samson: Alphen aan den Rijn.

Timmerman, P. (2011) *Architecture with a Capital A*, Enschede: Faculty Club Foundation Press, University of Twente.

Timmerman, P. and Benneworth, P. S. (2006) 'Campusarchitectuur: Het Twentse kennisavontuur' ('Campus architecture: the Twente knowledge adventure'), *Kunst en Wetenschap*, 15(1), 11–12.

Tobback, L. (2009) 'The relationship between the city and university in Leuven, Belgium', keynote speech to presented to Understanding and Shaping Regions: Spatial, Social and Economic Futures, Regional Studies Association International Conference, Leuven, Flanders, 6–8 April 2009.

Vickers, E. and Edwards, E. (2006) 'History of the university', available at: www.lancs. ac.uk/unihistory/ (accessed 21 May 2013).

Wyatt, J. (1990) *Commitment to Higher Education*, Buckingham: Open University Press.

Index